REMA

GW00750667

3|18

Overdue items may incur charges
as published in the current
Schedule of Charges.

L21

LOUISE TILLIN

Remapping India

New States and their Political Origins

HURST & COMPANY, LONDON

First published in the United Kingdom in paperback in 2013 by
C. Hurst & Co. (Publishers) Ltd.,
41 Great Russell Street, London, WC1B 3PL
© Louise Tillin, 2013
All rights reserved.
Printed in India

The right of Louise Tillin to be identified as the author of
this publication is asserted by her in accordance with the
Copyright, Designs and Patents Act, 1988.

A Cataloguing-in-Publication data record for this book
is available from the British Library.

ISBN: 9781849042291

www.hurstpublishers.com

This book is printed on paper from registered sustainable
and managed sources.

CONTENTS

ACKNOWLEDGEMENTS

This book began life as my DPhil thesis at IDS, Sussex and my first thanks must therefore go to my supervisor, Jim Manor, an inspirational and indefatigable guide to Indian politics. Secondly my thanks to Newnham College, Cambridge for providing the valuable opportunity of a research fellowship during which the book started to take its present shape.

So many of the debts incurred in the course of research were in India. The project would not have been possible without the willingness of many dozens of people to respond to my requests for interviews, discussions and materials. Over four years between 2007 and 2011, the research took me to each of India's newest states Chhattisgarh, Jharkhand and Uttarakhand, as well as their 'parent' state capitals (Bhopal, Lucknow and Patna), and Delhi. I also made additional visits to Telangana in Andhra Pradesh, Vidarbha in Maharashtra and to Uttar Pradesh to investigate ongoing demands for statehood in more—and less—active phases of mobilisation. The book rests on insights garnered in over 150 interviews with a cross section of politicians, activists within social and statehood movements, journalists, academics, civil servants and representatives of other interest groups who have been active participants and onlookers in the process of state creation and regional political life. I also travelled between libraries and archives in many cities to collate regional newspapers, pamphlets, party manifestos and documents, debates from the Indian parliament and state legislative assemblies, and official reports.

Special mention should be made of the staff in libraries and archives in many of these places who went to considerable lengths to assist with my requests for material—especially at *Deshbandhu* newspaper in Raipur, the Nehru Memorial Library in Delhi, and the AN Sinha newspaper

vii

ACKNOWLEDGEMENTS

library in Patna. In Delhi, I am grateful to the Centre for the Study of Developing Societies (CSDS) for affiliation during fieldwork and to Yogendra Yadav and Sanjay Kumar for critical guidance. Colleagues from my former employer, the BBC, offered support and introductions to parts of India that were then new to me. I was also lucky to work with Ajay Kumar and Mayank Tiwari as research assistants in Jharkhand and Chhattisgarh respectively.

The book has developed alongside my journey through a number of institutions: most importantly from the Institute of Development Studies (IDS), University of Sussex to Newnham College, Cambridge to King's College London. At IDS, I would especially like to thank Anu Joshi, who stepped in as my second supervisor at an advanced stage of writing, Andres Mejia Acosta and Mick Moore. Fellow DPhil students in the Governance team, as well as Sally Brooks, Kasia Grabska, Jong-Woon Lee and Donna Simpson have been wonderful companions along the way. The examiners of my DPhil, David Leonard and Andrew Wyatt, offered very useful advice about how to develop my arguments.

I owe particular thanks to a number of friends and colleagues who have been kind enough to read the manuscript at various stages. Emma Mawdsley and Madura Rasaratnam read and commented on the whole text, providing much-needed critical interventions and suggestions. KK Kailash, Peter Kingstone, Heather Plumridge Bedi and Andrew Wyatt also read sections: their reflections have strengthened the book. I am also grateful to two anonymous reviewers for their constructive engagement with the structure and arguments of the book. Any remaining errors and shortcomings in the text are mine alone.

For conversations on themes related to the book and support over time in many locations, I am grateful to Katharine Adeney, Mukulika Banerjee, Stuart Corbridge, Rajeshwari Deshpande, Santhosh Mathew, Emma Mawdsley, John Nemec, Madura Rasaratnam, Alpa Shah, Sara Shneiderman, Carole Spary and Tariq Thachil. At the King's India Institute, my new colleagues Sunil Khilnani, Christophe Jaffrelot, Kriti Kapila, Jahnavi Phalkey, Rudra Chaudhuri among others, as well as our students, have helped to create an exceptionally stimulating setting in which to complete this project and begin new ventures.

I am fortunate to have had the opportunity to present sections of the book at a number of venues including the British Association of South Asian Studies (BASAS) conference; Centre for Research in Arts, Social

ACKNOWLEDGEMENTS

Sciences and Humanities (CRASSH), University of Cambridge; LSE Anthropology of South Asia seminar; Contemporary South Asia seminar, Queen Elizabeth House and the South Asia History seminar, St Anthony's College, Oxford; South Asian Studies colloquium, Yale University; Department of Political Science, University of Hyderabad; Centre for Multi-level Federalism, New Delhi; Giri Institute of Development Studies, Lucknow; Interrogating States Reorganisation conference hosted by Jawaharlal Nehru University and the Nehru Memorial Museum and Library; and the Department of Political Economy, King's College London.

The Economic and Social Research Council (ESRC) funded my doctoral studies. The Senior Members Research Fund at Newnham College, Cambridge provided follow-up travel costs for additional research. I would also like to acknowledge the permission granted by Pacific Affairs to reproduce materials in chapter three that were first published in Pacific Affairs, vol. 84, no. 1 (Spring 2011). Thanks finally to Michael Dwyer at Hurst, and to Sebastian Ballard for producing the maps in the book.

My deepest debts, however, are personal ones to friends and family for life beyond all this. For friendship and unstinting hospitality in India, I thank the Soods, who have been something of a second family in Delhi for over fifteen years. My siblings Jane, Matthew and Alice—their partners, and my nieces and nephew who have arrived in recent years—have provided many happy distractions. Thanks too to Colin and Jo for their encouragement.

Lastly, it is difficult to know how to thank Simon who has lived with this project for as long as I have, and sustained, diverted and kept me going through its many highs and lows. KBO. And my parents—Therese and Clive—who have had constant faith in me and instinctive understanding for what motivated my research in the first place. This book is dedicated to them.

LIST OF MAPS, FIGURES AND TABLES

Maps

Figures

Tables

LIST OF MAPS, FIGURES AND TABLES

LIST OF ACRONYMS

AJSU	All Jharkhand Students Union.
BJP	Bharatiya Janata Party.
BJS	Bharatiya Jana Sangh.
BSP	Bahujan Samaj Party.
CMM	Chhattisgarh Mukti Morcha.
CMSS	Chhattisgarh Mines Shramik Sangh (Chhattisgarh Mine Workers Union).
COJM	Committee on Jharkhand Matters.
CPI (ML)	Communist Part of India (Marxist Leninist).
CPM	Communist Party of India (Marxist).
JAAC	Jharkhand Autonomous Area Council.
JCC	Jharkhand Coordination Committee.
JD	Janata Dal.
JD (U)	Janata Dal (United).
JMM	Jharkhand Mukti Morcha.
KCR	K. Chandrashekhar Rao.
MLA	Member of Legislative Assembly.
MP	Madhya Pradesh.
NDA	National Democratic Alliance.
OBC	Other Backward Classes.
PSP	Praja Socialist Party.
PWG	People's War Group.
RJD	Rashtriya Janata Dal.
RSS	Rashtriya Swayamsevak Sangh (National Volunteer Corps).
SC	Scheduled Caste.
SP	Samajwadi Party.

LIST OF ACRONYMS

SRC   States Reorganisation Commission.
ST   Scheduled Tribe.
TDP   Telugu Desam Party.
TRS   Telangana Rashtri Samiti.
UCSS   Uttarakhand Chhatra Sangarsh Samiti (Uttarakhand Students' Struggle Committee).
UKD   Uttarakhand Kranti Dal.
UP   Uttar Pradesh.
UPCC   Uttar Pradesh Congress Committee.
USSS   Uttarakhand Sanyukt Sangarsh Samiti (Uttarakhand United Struggle Committee).
USV   Uttarakhand Sangarsh Vahini (Uttarakhand Struggle Group).
VHP   Vishwa Hindu Parishad (World Hindu Council).
YSR   Y.S Rajasekhara Reddy.

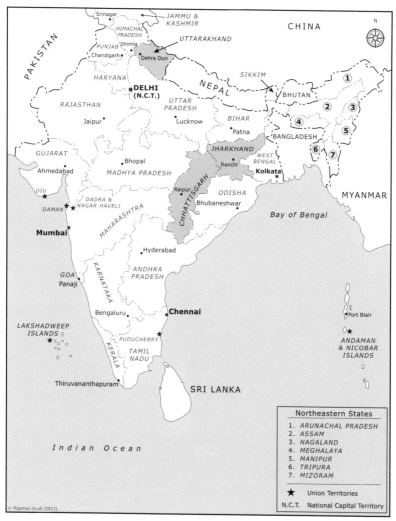

Map 1: Political map of India today showing newest states.

1

INTRODUCTION

THE COMPROMISE POLITICS OF STATEHOOD

The political map of India's internal boundaries has been imagined and re-imagined over time by national political elites, regional movements and ordinary citizens. Alternative ways of thinking about the borders of states within the federal system present competing visions of political communities, markets and economic relations, social life and sacred geographies. Demands for new states have become an everyday feature of the political marketplace in much of India, reflecting the generative and regenerative qualities of Indian democracy, as well as its frustrations. The idea of creating new states rarely occasions concern about the country's unity any longer. Instead the periodic division or reorganisation of states within India's federal system has been celebrated as a realisation of the country's famed 'unity in diversity'. Yet despite such confidence in the resilience of the overarching idea of India, its political geography is not as fluid as might be expected. There is an enduring stickiness to state borders over time, which creates the puzzle of understanding when, where and why new states have been created.

This is a book about the politics of state creation in the era of political and economic decentralisation that has taken shape in India since the 1980s. The advent of multi-party coalition government in New Delhi from 1989 and economic liberalisation in 1991 were defining junctures of the new scenario, although both marked the consolidation of longer term trends. At the heart of *Remapping India* is an explanation for the granting of statehood to Chhattisgarh, Jharkhand and Uttarakhand, formed from Madhya Pradesh, Bihar and Uttar Pradesh in November 2000.[1] This is one of four main revisions to state boundaries that India has undertaken since 1947. Earlier revisions involved the merging of princely states and former British provinces at independence, the creation of 'linguistic' states in the 1950s and 1960s, and the formation of autonomous units for minority communities in the state of Assam in northeast India between the 1960s and 1980s. The latest reorganisation in 2000 was the first time that new states had been created within the predominantly Hindi-speaking region of north and central India, often known as the 'Hindi heartland'. State boundaries in this region had historically been particularly resilient to change, despite substantial challenges to their legitimacy by deep-rooted popular movements for a tribal state in Jharkhand and the hill state of Uttarakhand. Today, political parties, and in some regions, people's movements call for the creation of Telangana from Andhra Pradesh, for the division of the populous state of Uttar Pradesh into four, for the creation of Gorkhaland from West Bengal, and for Bodoland from Assam among other demands at more and less active stages of mobilisation.

India's newest states of Chhattisgarh, Jharkhand and Uttarakhand lie at the centre of landscapes of protest and resistance. They are rich in natural resources including minerals, forests and rivers. Iconic social movements have raised questions since the 1970s about the management of natural resources and land, as well as local livelihoods and labour conditions, in the context of state-directed strategies of industrialisation in these regions. Chhattisgarh and Jharkhand are home to sizeable tribal or *adivasi* communities, comprising a third of their total population. In recent years, they have been central sites for the renewed Maoist insurgency in the forests of central India. Much of Uttarakhand, by contrast, is comprised of the hilly and mountainous terrain of the Himalayas. A demand for a tribal state of Jharkhand was first raised in the early twentieth century, making it one of the longest running regional autonomy demands in the country. Mass agitations—for statehood in Uttarakhand paralysed local administration in the mid-1990s. Chhattisgarh is something of an anomaly by comparison to both Jharkhand and Uttarakhand as it was created in the absence of a mass demand. Together, the new states comprise a substantial part of the

INTRODUCTION

Hindi heartland, a region that is undergoing change today but histori-cally has been poorer with more deeply entrenched caste hierarchies, a faster growing population and overall has fared less well in terms of human development than southern and western India.

The Political Power—and Origins—of State Borders

In this book I argue for an understanding of the borders of states within a federal system as a form of institution, underpinned by patterns of social, political and economic power. State boundaries help to structure political and economic life by determining which groups are in competi-tion with each other over the distribution of resources, as well as deter-mining which resources are at stake in this contest. As institutionalist theories would suggest, the locations of state boundaries help to rein-force and reproduce patterns of power. It is for this reason that the reorganisation of states tends to be infrequent—in spite of the number and shrillness of demands for new states. Demands for new states typi-cally begin as challenges to existing power structures. The formation of a new state, in theory, offers the possibility of creating a new type of regional polity in which different groups might find prominence; dis-tinct, territorially concentrated, cultural or ethnic groups might be accorded greater representation; local communities might acquire more direct control over resources (natural and fiscal); and/or in which differ-ent relationships might be negotiated between the local state and sectors of the economy such as industry, agriculture, forestry or mining. Yet—as I will demonstrate—by the time the creation of the new states of Chhat-tisgarh, Jharkhand and Uttarakhand was agreed to by India's central government, statehood demands had become vehicles for multiple actors with divergent visions of political community and economic life. The impetus to create these states emerged as a compromise between interest groups competing for position rather than reflecting a radical break in the distribution of power.

Existing explanations and popular interpretations of the granting of statehood to Chhattisgarh, Jharkhand and Uttarakhand paint several pictures. The first locates the pressure to create new states within state-hood movements that have articulated a sense of cultural identity and regional deprivation as part of a politics of recognition. Such movements in different regions of India over time have drawn on repertoires of protest including demonstrations, *bandhs* (strikes), hunger strikes, *jail bharo andolans* ('filling' jails by courting arrest), election boycotts, as well—less frequently—as violent struggle to pursue their demands. The creation of states, in this view, is seen as following from the forceful articulation of new regional identities. A second set of explanations emphasise instead the changed federal electoral context since 1989, when coalition government became the norm in New Delhi, bringing together regional and national parties in more—and less—stable alliances. According to this view, statehood was granted because it was perceived to be in the electoral interests of the governing coalition in New Delhi, led by the Hindu nationalist Bharatiya Janata Party (BJP), to 'cash in' on the votes to be won by supporting demands for statehood that had been mobilised by popular movements. Thirdly, and differently again, it has been suggested that territorial reorganisation is driven by capitalist expansion and the desire to intensify the extraction of natural resources in the context of economic liberalisation. A final explanation is concerned less with the political pressures for creating new states, and instead with an administrative rationale for reducing the size of states in order to improve 'governance'.

I will discuss each of these academic, and popular, framings in more detail below. There are undeniably features of each that help us account for aspects of the creation of Chhattisgarh, Jharkhand and Uttarakhand. But, as I argue in *Remapping India*, they do not account for the substantial variation between the three cases or for the timing of their creation—which occurred a substantial period after the most intense mobilisation in favour of statehood in Jharkhand or Uttarakhand, and in the absence of any mass movement at all in the case of Chhattisgarh. Moreover by the time the states were created, demands for statehood themselves had changed shape, attracting support from a range of interest groups with divergent reasons for wanting a new state. As a newspaper editor who had been closely involved in the Jharkhand movement in the 1970s and 1980s told me:

> The political situation had become such that you spend a long time fighting for something and you get it when you're not fighting…If Jharkhand was separated in 1983 or 1984, it would have been a different Jharkhand because at that time people were aggressive and agitating for Jharkhand, but when they stopped we got Jharkhand surprisingly.[2]

Each of the existing explanations, taken on its own, overstates the extent to which the act of state creation served the interests of any one group or set of actors. Most importantly, they miss the multi-centred origins of the institutional change, as well as the way that successful demands for statehood have usually become vehicles for unwieldy coalitions of interest groups that might otherwise have been expected to be in competition with each other. Slow, evolving support for changes to state boundaries reflect longer term changes in local structures of power and the relations between social groups. In order to appreciate these shifts a deeper analysis of longer term processes of social and political change is required. As Paul Pierson urges, it is necessary to place 'politics in time' to capture slower moving, incremental causal processes.[3]

In the chapters that follow, I offer the first detailed account of how the three states came to be formed. My argument is that the reorganisation of states in the Hindi heartland was the outcome of three major social and political changes that took shape from the early 1970s onwards. At first glance, these changes do not seem to be directly related to demands for statehood—indeed some appear quite remote. But together they explain how territorial reorganisation became acceptable among competing interest groups and actors at different levels of the federal system (national, state and sub-state). The first change arose from the way in which the new social movements formed in many parts of India in the early 1970s were gradually accommodated in electoral politics as the Congress—once the predominant party in Indian politics—and newer political parties, adapted to a new scenario in which the Congress Party's electoral ascendancy was no longer assured. In Jharkhand and Uttarakhand, interactions between social movements and political parties helped to produce a more determined focus on statehood within these regions. Statehood demands gradually received support from parts of historic social movements and a newer generation of non-Congress politicians.

The second change relates to the challenges to upper caste political dominance in the Hindi heartland, a process that has been described by Christophe Jaffrelot as a 'silent revolution'.[4] New forms of political mobilisation among lower castes increased the salience of horizontal caste identities—in particular among 'Other Backward Classes' or OBCs—which had weak correspondence to existing state boundaries. These changes helped to undermine earlier strident defences of the large size and composite nature of states in the Hindi heartland, which had been underpinned by upper caste political dominance. These shifts in social and political hierarchies meant that momentum for state sub-division came from within state capitals as well as the regions for which statehood was demanded, as state-level politicians came to terms with changing electoral geographies.

Thirdly and lastly, the BJP (and before 1980, their forerunner, the Bharatiya Jana Sangh) changed their approach to federalism and states reorganisation as they negotiated their emergence as a national party that could convincingly challenge Congress as a claimant to power in New Delhi. The BJP had to strike an accommodation between their ideological commitment to Hindu nationalism and diverse patterns of regional politics and social mobilisation across India. One way in which the party did so was to support demands for statehood within individual regions.

In combination, these three processes, linked to the changing party systems of north and central India, helped to produce a good measure of support for reorganising state boundaries in the Hindi heartland. The exact way in which this took place differed from region to region, and the final act of creating the states owed something to contingency in the short-term. But, taken together, these three changes produced the conditions for territorial reorganisation within Bihar, Madhya Pradesh and Uttar Pradesh—and not elsewhere in the country where demands for statehood have also been raised.

In the remainder of this introduction I will situate India's approach to states reorganisation within a wider context by considering approaches to changing internal borders in other federal systems. I will then discuss in more detail the existing explanations for state creation in India, and end by outlining the argument and structure to be adopted in this book.

Comparative International Perspectives on Federal Restructuring

The constitutions of most federal systems make it difficult to reduce or change the territory of constituent units at all, requiring either special forms of majority in the upper house and/or the consent of the sub-units concerned.[5] This reflects a core tenet of the federal bargain that rests upon a combination of 'self-' and 'shared-rule' in which the respective autonomy of the federal government and the sub-units is preserved, in this case by protecting the sanctity of their respective borders. Just as most federal constitutions make it difficult for a central authority to change the boundaries of sub-units without regional consent, so they do

not mandate a right for constituent sub-units to secede—thus protecting the sovereign boundaries of the whole federation.[6] Indian federalism
stands out in comparative terms for the constitutionally mandated powers of the central government to revise state boundaries even without the
approval of the state government concerned.

In most federations, it is easier to change the status of a subunit—for
instance, from a territory to a fully-fledged state or province—than to
alter their boundaries. Nevertheless, most federal systems have created
new sub-units by reorganising the boundaries of existing states at some
stage. This continues to be an active subject for debate, especially in
newer federations. The most extreme example of federal restructuring is
that of Nigeria, which has created thirty-six states from the three regions
it started out with at independence, all during periods of military rule.[7]
Brazil established the new state of Tocantins, and upgraded Amapá and
Roraima to full statehood in 1988 when a new constitution was
approved after the end of the military regime.[8] All three states are located
in Brazil's more sparsely populated 'north region'. In 1999, Canada created the province of Nunavut from its Northwest Territories as a means
of accommodating Inuit claims for a homeland and for their rights to
manage land and natural resources (Inuits form over 80 per cent of
Nunavut's population). In 1979, Switzerland created the new canton of
Jura after a referendum.

The origins of different federal systems are important in shaping the
number, size and boundaries of states, and the processes by which new
states are created or admitted. Where federal systems have been founded
as a result of what Alfred Stepan describes as the 'coming together' of
constituent units for the purposes of defence, trade or other perceived
benefits, the internal boundaries of the ensuing federation can be prede-
termined. This would include the example of federal systems such as
Australia, the United States or Switzerland. On the other hand, in 'holding together' federations, formed as a result of devolution by previously
unitary polities in order to hold together in multi-cultural settings,[9]
there is likely to be greater debate about the boundaries of sub-units
from the outset. India's States Reorganisation Commission recognised
the distinctiveness of India's federal model on precisely these grounds.
Its 1955 report stated, 'In India, the Union is not a federation of sovereign states…This is an important distinction between the Indian Union
and some other democratic federations where the federating units

existed before the federal unions.'[10] Examples of 'holding together' federations include Belgium, India and Spain. Distinctions between the two types of federation are not watertight however: in the 'coming together' US model, the borders of three of the original federating states that formed the United States were contested and then divided in the late eighteenth century (New York, Virginia and Tennessee) and new states were created as the federation expanded westwards;[11] in the 'holding together' Indian model, the princely states can be seen as a form of federating unit. The Canadian model also contains elements of 'holding together' (with the initial devolution of power to English-speaking Ontario and French-speaking Quebec in 1867) and 'coming together' (with the addition of new provinces) origins.[12]

Particularly for 'holding together' federal systems with multi-ethnic populations, decisions about the borders of sub-units are highly consequential. As Katharine Adeney argues, 'the design of provincial units… is crucial for determining the success of a federal system in a multi-ethnic state.'[13] In the literature on democracy and ethnic conflict management, the borders of states are viewed as a critical part of the institutional architecture of federalism which permit the accommodation of the claims to self-governance of territorially concentrated ethnic or national groups. There is much debate, however, about whether federal systems should be designed around ethnically homogenous or heterogeneous provinces. Some scholars have claimed that 'ethnic' sub-units increase the likelihood of secession and the break-up of federal systems, especially in the cases of the former Yugoslavia, Czechoslovakia and Soviet Union.[14] Similar concerns were expressed at independence by India's first Prime Minister, Jawaharlal Nehru, who resisted the creation of linguistically defined provinces. For good reason, however, India is today seen as an example of a federal system in which the territorial accommodation of ethnic identity has reduced conflict, particularly as a result of the creation of linguistic states in the 1950s and 1960s.[15] Furthermore, India has creatively experimented with other mechanisms such as autonomous councils—distinct from statehood—to accommodate sub-state identities.[16]

Beyond the accommodation of identity groups, the size and number of federal sub-units is also a subject of some debate. The ideal size of a state has been long debated by political theorists, more usually however with reference to sovereign states rather than states within a federal system. While continental political philosophers such as Rousseau or Montesquieu argued that republican government was possible only in small states, Madison in the *Federalist Papers* worried that smaller republics were more susceptible to domination by single factions.[17] As will be seen, discussions about state size within India's federal system have raised similar questions.

When judged by the total number of it states, India looks similar to other federations such as Brazil, Nigeria and Switzerland—as can be seen in the tables below. Equally, in terms of geographical area, the size of its sub-units places it in the middle of the federal league-table. But as table 1.2 below shows it is an extreme outlier with regard to the population per federal sub-unit. Even with the creation of Chhattisgarh, Jharkhand and Uttarakhand, India has the smallest number of constituent units in per capita terms of any federal system in the world: twenty-eight plus seven 'union territories'.[18] There is enormous variation in the size of India's states too. The largest, Uttar Pradesh, is home to almost 200 million people which would make it the fifth most populous country in the world, whilst the smallest, Sikkim, has just over 600,000 inhabitants, which would rank it 165th.

Table 1.1: Geographical area of federal sub-units in comparative perspective.

Country	No. of federal sub-units	Size of average unit (sq km)
Switzerland	26	1588
Belgium	3	10176
Germany	16	22314
Nigeria	36	25660
Spain	17	29728
India	30	109575
USA	50	196534
Brazil	26	327495
Canada	10	998467
Australia	6	1290203

Source: Figures on geographical area taken from the *CIA World Factbook*.
Note: The total number of federal sub-units shown excludes smaller territories and autonomous cities (two autonomous cities in Spain; three additional territories in Canada, and two in Australia; Federal Capital Territory in Nigeria; one federal district in Brazil). The total for India includes the twenty-eight states plus NCT Delhi and Puducherry, the two largest UTs. There are another five small UTs.

Table 1.2: Number of federal sub-units relative to population in federal countries.

Country	*No. of federal sub-units*	*Population (million) per unit*
Switzerland	26	0.3
Spain	17	2.5
Canada	10	3.2
Australia	6	3.4
Belgium	3	3.5
Nigeria	36	3.9
Germany	16	5.15
USA	50	6.05
Brazil	26	7.15
India	30	37.7

Source: Population statistics from UN Population Division (all population estimates refer to the year 2005).

Existing Explanations for Territorial (Re)organisation in India

As I have suggested four main types of explanation are commonly offered for territorial (re)organisation in India. These draw respectively on factors relating to sociology, federal electoral politics, political economy and administrative efficiency. They are summarised in the box below. The next section explores how each of these explanations has been used to account for the creation of Chhattisgarh, Jharkhand and Uttarakhand in particular.

Sociological Arguments

According to arguments which foreground sociological dimensions, the states' creation is part of a continuing narrative of federal reorganisation in which borders are remapped in order to better recognise subnational diversity—as part of a 'politics of recognition'—or to respond to the political mobilisation of identities. In this case, the new states are often referred to by the shorthand of tribal or *adivasi* states in the cases of Chhattisgarh and Jharkhand, and a 'hill' state of Uttarakhand. As Alfred Stepan, Juan Linz and Yogendra Yadav write:

> In India the multicultural characteristics are the result of a long history [as opposed to immigration from other societies] and have a distinctive territorial

basis, to which Indian federalism has been a response. Witness the creation of the new linguistic states in the 1950s and the process of creating new states that continues to this day. It should be noted that although the creation of three states (Uttarakhand, Jharkhand and Chhattisgarh) in 2000 was not based on language, it did reflect the logic of political representation of diversities, for these states gave better representation to tribal populations (Jharkhand, Chhattisgarh) or otherwise socioculturally different groups (Uttarakhand).[19]

Figure 1.1: Existing explanations for states reorganisation in 2000.

Category of Argument	Causal Factors	Resulting Interpretations of State Creation
Sociological	Regional social movements or political parties representing or seeking to mobilise particular 'ethnic' or identity groups.	Recognition of distinct territorial identity groups (sometimes portrayed as historically oppressed 'nationalities'); affirmation of India's 'unity in diversity'.
Federal Electoral Politics	Political opportunity structure at federal level created by coalition politics.	States are created according to the electoral interests of national political parties.
Political Economy	Relationship between political and industrial elites; rent-seeking interests of local elites.	Borders more closely aligned with resource rich regions; reorganisation reflects expansion of capitalism and its need for natural resources; more states improve competition within Indian market.
Administrative	New states are created in order to improve administrative efficiency/ achieve efficiencies of scale or allow better targeting of resources.	States are created by the central government to improve the quality of administration.

Ramachandra Guha in his major study of post-independence Indian history writes:

Official acknowledgement of the history of *adivasi* suffering … came through the creation … of two states of the Union named Jharkhand and Chhattisgarh, carved out of the tribal districts of Bihar and Madhya Pradesh respectively. Also formed was the state of Uttaranchal, from the hill districts of Uttar Pradesh, likewise rich in natural resources and likewise subject to exploitation by powerful external interests.[20]

These studies draw attention to the discourses of indigeneity that have been used to link communities of *adivasis* or Scheduled Tribes (to use the 'official' nomenclature) to particular lands and thereby protect them from exploitation by settler populations or 'outsiders'. In Jharkhand, as in parts of northeast India, such a discourse has been linked to calls for political autonomy in the form of statehood. Other demands for statehood in which tribal rights have not been a central theme—such as the ongoing demand for Telangana in Andhra Pradesh—have also embodied assertions of the rights of 'local' populations or 'sons of the soil' to employment, education, land ownership, political representation and social respect or inclusion.[21] Pradeep Kumar argued that demands for statehood made since the 1970s have fused a sense of economic marginalisation with a distinctive cultural identity.[22] Akhtar Majeed has argued that the success of statehood demands has depended on this fusing of economic and cultural identities, and the existence of a popular movement with strong leadership.[23]

Authors such as Kumar and Majeed recognise that the assertion of regional identities is a dynamic rather than static process, responding to the changing conditions of economic, political and social life rather than mobilising 'primordial' identities. Recognising the changing articulation of identities over time, some have therefore called for a more 'cosmopolitan' vision of networked governance for South Asia as a whole in which boundaries become more fluid and trans-national connections between neighbouring countries are facilitated.[24] M.P. Singh points out that 'no reorganization of states can produce an internally homogenous and administratively and financially viable set of states in all cases. Hence endless fragmentation of the Indian nation-state is not a solution but a part of the problem of ungovernability and international instability.'[25] Rasheeduddin Khan, on the other hand, has called for further territorial reorganisation to divide 'sprawling huge states' that perpetuate inequalities. He argues for the creation of units that are socio-culturally homogenous, and administratively and politically manageable.[26] Guha agrees that the Indian republic is still young enough to create more states: 'Regions that have a cultural, ecological or historical coherence, and are adversely affected by their current status as part of a larger unit, could be granted statehood.'[27]

Yet decisions to create new states are not simply responses to the articulation of regional sentiment by statehood movements. Nor can the latest exercise of federal remapping in India be seen primarily as an example of territorialised ethnic accommodation. While there had been a sustained campaign for an *adivasi* state in Jharkhand, initiated by Jaipal Singh, the social base of the movement and parties supporting the statehood demand changed over time as statehood was repeatedly denied. The changing social base also reflected the shifting demography of the region and its growing non-tribal population (almost three-quarters by 2000). In Chhattisgarh, there was no historical demand for a 'tribal state' and the demand for statehood was extremely muted more generally. As I will argue in chapters three and four, far from the new states representing the interests of a particular group(s), the relationship between territorial claims and the assurance that a new state would pro-tect or promote the self-governing rights of any single ethnic or local community, to the exclusion of others, was unsettled before the states were created. The analysis of the historical development of statehood demands, and political convergence in favour of statehood, illustrates that statehood emerged as a demand around which parts of social move-ments and political parties coalesced despite their divergent interests and the diverse socioeconomic groups they represented.

Federal Electoral Politics

The second type of existing explanation points to electoral politics at the federal level to explain when and why the new states were created. Two shifts in the federal political context are particularly relevant for under-standing the creation of new states in 2000: first, the beginning of an era of multi-party coalition government in New Delhi from 1989; and con-nected to that first change, a new landscape of state politics in which the states have become the primary arena of political life.[28] In this new context, two types of actor came to prominence. The Hindu nationalist

Bharatiya Janata Party (BJP) emerged as the only new political party with a claim to a national spread and, as such, the capacity to lead an anti-Congress alliance across India. It was the BJP-led National Democratic Alliance (NDA) government which created the new states in 2000. The second type of party that became a forceful presence in the political life of the Hindi heartland from the 1980s onwards were those that mobilised around caste identities. In north India, the Janata Dal (and later offshoots) and the Bahujan Samaj Party (BSP) appealed to varying coalitions of lower and middle castes and Dalits; in Bihar and Uttar Pradesh these new regional parties succeeded in forming state governments from 1989 onwards. Regional parties from across India became important players within federal coalition governments.

A number of studies have emphasised the role of national political elites within this new federal political context as the decisive factor in placing the creation of new states back on the policy agenda in the 1990s. Most agree that the creation of Chhattisgarh, Jharkhand and Uttarakhand in 2000 marked a significant shift, in that discussion of state creation became a normal political activity in the 1990s, less likely to provoke existential questioning about whether India's federal union would hold.[29] The presence of state creation on the federal government's political agenda reflected a broader confidence in the cohesiveness of the Union more generally. Beyond this, however, some scholars argue that central political elites had their own interests in converting these regions into fully fledged states. Emma Mawdsley highlights the role of short term political expediency in a situation of considerable instability in the formation of national coalition governments. Three general elections were held in the late 1990s—in 1996, 1998 and 1999—because federal governments could not hold together. In a context in which small numbers of seats could be decisive in winning or losing power, Mawdsley argues that different political parties, especially the BJP, became more receptive to the idea of creating new states because of the 'clear potential political pay-offs (in terms of MPs and state governments)' they offered.[30] Yet it should be noted that the BJP had already received most of this 'pay-off' before 2000: they could only hope that creating the new states would consolidate their electoral position in the new states and leave them in a position to form more state governments.

A somewhat different argument is made by Gurharpal Singh who also suggests that it is the attitudes of central political elites that decide where new states are likely to be created.[31] He argues that the Indian state is more responsive to demands for the reorganisation of state boundaries in the 'core' of the country rather than its periphery because such demands accord with the interests of mainstream Hindu elites in the 'core' and do not challenge what Singh describes as India's 'ethnic [Hindu] democracy'. Following from this, Singh (writing before the creation of Chhattisgarh, Jharkhand and Uttarakhand) suggests that calls for reorganisation within the 'core' are likely to be conceded, whereas demands for greater autonomy or the moving of borders in peripheral regions such as Gorkhaland or Bodoland are likely to be resisted because they are seen as separatist in intent. Singh is probably correct to point to a difference between the response of the central government to movements on India's international borders and elsewhere in the country, although not necessarily in deploying the label 'ethnic democracy'. But his argument does not tell us why such calls for reorganisation in the 'core' are likely to gain momentum at particular points in time or where they gain traction: the central government has not been equally responsive to all statehood demands in the 'core'.

Crucially, the BJP's ability to consolidate a position as a national party depended on the way in which it negotiated between a Hindu nationalist ideological agenda and the variety of identities and political patterns in evidence at the regional level. The party's evolving support for federal reorganisation—in the abstract, as well as in the case of particular demands for statehood—was one way in which the party sought to lay regional roots. As the next chapter will document, the BJP—and its predecessor, the Bharatiya Jana Sangh—changed their ideas about federalism in quite fundamental ways as they developed their platform in opposition to Indira Gandhi's increasingly centralised leadership from the 1970s onwards. The party shifted from an outright opposition to federalism and the linguistic reorganisation of states in the 1950s, to a position which embraced the idea of creating more states—albeit as part of a critique of the presentation of India as a 'multinational' federation. Offering support for statehood demands within individual regions that had hitherto been made by regional movements or other political parties helped the BJP to compete with other local actors and forge sub-state regional electoral bases before they were ready to challenge for power across a state. Their support for state creation—part of the political convergence around statehood mentioned above—should be seen as a coun-

terpart to the party's strategy of negotiating alliances with regional
parties in parts of the country where they had a weak base.[32]

Political Economy

The third category of explanation for territorial reorganisation fore-
grounds political economic factors. Some commentators view the creation of these states—in regions rich in minerals, forests and rivers—as
arising from the expansion of capitalism, and the interests of political
and economic elites in resource exploitation. For instance, Ranabir
Samaddar states that:

Probably the interaction of capital and the extra-capital spaces had always been
the main factor in the colonial time in the search for the right size and shape of
units. But if this were so [then], this is now most evident with growth of capital
once again provoking the reorganisation of space.'[33]

Such analyses are intertwined with deeper critiques of the political
economies of Chhattisgarh, Jharkhand and Uttarakhand since their
creation, especially with regard to the industrial policies and patterns of
natural resource exploitation pursued by their new governing elites. A
somewhat different argument suggests that the creation of more new
states is a means of strengthening the market-preserving qualities of
Indian federalism:[34] some proponents of federal restructuring see more,
smaller states as spaces for innovation that will be able to compete more
effectively against each other for investment, thereby reducing regional
inequality.[35]

The new states—both their history and trajectories since statehood—
capture some of the essential dilemmas at the heart of India's recent path
of economic growth: its regionally uneven effects; the increasing mobility it provides for some citizens and forces upon others who move or are
moved from their land or migrate in search of economic opportunities;
and the socially or ethnically mediated nature of access to opportunities
in the market economy and the public sector. Historically, the statehood
demands raised by some social movement activists in Chhattisgarh,
Jharkhand and Uttarakhand evolved in the 1970s to embody critiques
of ethnically uneven divisions of labour or the sense that 'local' communities were being excluded from economic activity and often political
power.[36] The Marxist intellectual A.K. Roy, co-founder of the Jharkhand

Mukti Morcha (JMM) in 1972, argued that Jharkhand was experiencing a form of internal colonialism within Bihar:

In India, the under-developed area is exploited by the developed areas as colonies, as are the underdeveloped by the developed people…The natives of the internal colonies are not only the victims of underdevelopment…but of development as well in Central India, as this development does not mean the development of the people there but their displacement and replacement by the colonies of developed people, the clever people, the politically connected people coming from the developed areas.[37]

Similar arguments were raised by the Chhattisgarh Mukti Morcha (CMM) in the 1970s, led by Shankar Guha Niyogi, which organised *adivasis* who were numerically dominant among the contract labour force employed in insecure and low paid manual work in mines feeding the Bhilai Steel Plant. It should be noted, however, that, unlike the JMM, the CMM did not seriously pursue the idea of statehood as a means of advancing their causes. In Uttarakhand, a central justification of the demand for statehood was that policies formulated in the plains of Uttar Pradesh were often inappropriate for the distinct topography of the hills and their natural resource base—especially the forests and rivers. The Chipko movement and subsequent social movements in the hills asserted the rights of local communities to a forestry policy that was designed with their needs at its heart.

But the assertions that territorial reorganisation reflects the expansion of capitalism, especially in the context of economic liberalisation and globalisation, do not usually assume that states were created in response to such critiques of internal colonialism made by social movements. Instead they imply that the creation of the new states responded to the very logic of capitalism that these movements had critiqued. As will be seen, many politicians interviewed in the course of this research—particularly those associated with the BJP—indeed argued that they had felt the creation of new states would allow for better 'economic development', blaming the neglect of previous state governments for poverty, discontent, as well as distress-induced migration. They argued that the high levels of poverty in Chhattisgarh and Jharkhand especially were inconsistent with their rich natural resources—recognising a 'resource curse' in all but name. Some politicians and numerous other observers—frequently critics of the process of state creation—went further to suggest that the new states had been created in order to make the exploitation of natural resources easier. Developments in Chhattisgarh and Jharkhand since state formation have reinforced an image of the aggressive state-led pursuit of resource intensive industrialisation and land acquisition for mining industries. Samaddar therefore suggests—in a Foucauldian formation—that the reorganisation of states in contemporary India can be seen as a mechanism by which the body politic is disciplined within the federal system in the interests of business and security.[38]

Certainly, as Stuart Corbridge points out, large areas of central and eastern India offer alternative geographies to the 'abstract space' that may be thought desirable by capital.[39] Nevertheless, the argument made in this book challenges the idea that federal reorganisation can be explained through the notion of a state or central government that consistently acts in the interests of capitalists. There is a considerable diversity of interests among business and industry. Furthermore, private economic actors are frequently as likely to be ambivalent about calls for new states as they are to support them. An argument which privileges the interests of capital as the explanation for federal reorganisation runs the risk of reading history backwards by extrapolating from observations of the present situation in the new states, the reasons for their formation. It also fails to locate the political agency involved in the story of state creation.

The ambivalence of some industrialists towards the idea of creating new states can be clearly seen in the case of Jharkhand. Tata Steel has been shaping the industrial landscape of Jharkhand since the early twentieth century, sculpting the company town of Jamshedpur as a modern industrial space. In the 1950s, the period when Jaipal Singh, leader of the Jharkhand Party, was raising a call for the creation of a tribally dominated Greater Jharkhand state drawing territory from Bihar, Orissa, Madhya Pradesh and West Bengal, ideas circulated of this as an 'industrial state'. Yet over sixty years later, asked whether Tata Steel had supported the creation of Jharkhand from south Bihar in 2000, a spokesperson for the company commented to me that 'it was better when Jharkhand was part of Bihar because politicians were further away: that kind of neglect was better for us.' The issue for the Tatas, he went on to say, was that of being an 'island of prosperity in a sea of poverty. Managing that situation is very important. Seven years after 2000, the hopes and dreams of statehood have not been fulfilled.'[40] Another group of industrialists in Jharkhand, interviewed during fieldwork, admitted to supporting the creation of a new state because Bihar had become 'very disturbed' under the Chief Ministership of Lalu Prasad Yadav in the 1990s, with businesses, for example, facing problems of 'dacoity [banditry]' and abductions. And despite a promotional tour to Singapore, Bangkok and elsewhere to attract inward investment, Lalu Prasad Yadav had been inconsistent in his support for industry.[41] Nevertheless, it is not clear that the creation of a new state necessarily holds out the prospect of a state that is able to provide the kind of public goods of value to the business sector including infrastructure, power, security and property rights. After the creation of Jharkhand, the same group of industrialists pointed out that corruption has become 'very bad' with the new state's vast number of independent MLAs (without party affiliation) 'out to make money', and 'no improvement in electricity, no commitment to infrastructure'.[42] Prominent figures in Jharkhand's political elite have been accused of large scale corruption or making illicit profits from the region's extractive industries.

The fixed geographical location of natural resources such as iron ore and coal provide regional specificity to the operation of companies involved in their extraction, but it is useful to distinguish between regional small- and medium-sized businesses, and large-scale industry operating on a pan-Indian basis which can be more footloose. The latter operations, as M.P. Singh suggests, tend to be inclined more towards 'supra-regional nationalism' and involve themselves less directly in debates about federal reorganisation.[43] Regional industrialists are often more directly engaged in debates about statehood, as they rely on close relationships with regional political parties and state boundaries sometimes provide the natural limits for their economic activities. But as the ongoing tussle over the demand for the separation of Telangana from Andhra Pradesh illustrates, local businesses are to be found both supporting and opposing calls for new states, the latter position driven by investments or connections across existing states that would be threatened by bifurcation. In public, within regions for which there is a demand for statehood, businesses often do not take a clear stand and local personnel may be keen not to find themselves on the wrong side of a demand for statehood. In other words, they would rather not be targeted as 'outsiders' as opposed to 'sons of the soil' during a statehood movement, or if a state is created.

Furthermore, an emphasis on the role of capital in shaping federal reorganisation risks losing sight of the cultural elements of many demands for statehood which express resistance to dominant trajectories of capitalist development. The latest phase of pro-Telangana agitation—as in Jharkhand—draws on precisely such cultural forms. As K. Srinivasulu writes: 'what is being celebrated [through folk songs and fiction] as worth remembering about Telangana is its sense of community that is counter-posed to the unbridled individualism of coastal Andhra.'[44] When consensus in favour of statehood emerges in particular regions, it must be seen—at least in part—as a response to such alternative imagineries of state, society and markets. The creation of new states is not merely driven by capital.

A simple attribution of interest, and thereby causal significance, to business and capital in reorganising territory within the federation then both overstates the homogeneity of interests within the business sector and masks the political process by which new states have come into being. The path of economic growth pursued by India since the 1980s has been pro-business in nature, as Atul Kohli has demonstrated, often more than pro-market.[45] Regional and national capital has developed in a close relationship with the state. But the empirical material that will be presented in this book demonstrates that in the act of state creation—as in other areas of political and economic life—it is hard to detect a state that always can or does act in the interests of capital. Nor is it true to say that 'capital' has a singular set of interests. The granting of statehood is better seen as a compromise between different interest groups, in which the notion of the state (in the bureaucratic as well as geographical sense) as a preserve either of capital or of particular ethnic or 'local' communities is challenged.

Administrative Efficiency

The final category of explanation for territorial reorganisation highlights administrative concerns. This was reflected in the 'official' rationale offered by the BJP leadership who oversaw state creation in 2000. As the states reorganisation bills were debated by parliament, Home Minister L.K. Advani explained that the states were being created on the grounds of 'administrative and economic viability', as well as the 'overwhelming aspirations of the people of the region'.[46] Arguments in favour of the creation of new states on administrative grounds are commonly made in light of regional inequality as well as population growth, which has been more rapid in some states of India than others.[47] These arguments sit alongside the creation of new districts by many state governments, as well as decentralisation to the third tier of local government at village level, *panchayati raj* institutions.[48] A vision of more decentralised administration builds in part on Gandhian ideals of government grounded in autonomous village republics, a strong alternative strand of argument in constitutional debates which the Jana Sangh had also drawn on in their earliest thinking about territorial organisation. While it is true that administrative concerns featured in the political discourses around states reorganisation, even BJP politicians freely admit that when in government their decisions about where to push ahead with the creation of new states, and which demands to drop, reflected political conditions more than abstract administrative concerns.

A Historical Institutionalist Framework for Understanding Federal Reorganisation

In the body of this book, I contend that we must look to the constellations of power that underpin state borders to understand when, where and why federal restructuring takes place. I deploy a metaphor that sees state borders as a form of institution, and a historical institutionalist framework to explain why state borders have become less stable—and thus subject to change—in some parts of the federation and not others. That borders should be seen as a form of institution rests on the notion that they are a critical element in determining which groups are in competition with each other over the distribution of which resources. Borders help to set the terms of political competition. Ian Lustick develops the following institutionalist understanding of external borders, which I extend to understand the changes to internal borders within a federal system:

State borders are politically important because they serve as a constraint which advantage certain groups and rival elites within the state at the expense of others. Substantial changes in the territorial shape of a state represent institution transforming episodes. Struggles over the size and shape of the state must accordingly be understood as struggles over the 'rules of the game'... The territorial shape of a state thus helps determine what interests are legitimate, what resources are mobilisable, what questions are open for debate, what ideological formulas will be relevant, what cleavages could become significant, and what political allies might be available.[49]

In the case of the reorganisation of internal federal boundaries, resources include social esteem or recognition, as well as the distribution of and access to economic resources and political power. Boundaries are contested, while also being sticky, institutional features which help to crystallise certain constellations of interests. As Sven Steinmo and Kathleen Thelen point out, in relation to battles over the boundaries of electoral constituencies, new boundaries once agreed 'can save political actors the trouble of fighting the same battle over and over again'.[50] The political significance of new state borders is such that any changes to them will be deeply contested.

Over time, the internal borders of a federal system develop a degree of 'stability' or inviolability such that they are not routinely challenged in the course of ordinary political debate across a given subunit. This definition of the institutional 'stability' of borders does not preclude the idea that there will be some groups within the regions themselves who demand statehood. What it implies is that these attempts to question existing state boundaries are not shared, or entertained, by other actors within the sub-state region, the state- and/or national-level. As Lustick writes:

Operationally, the territorial expanse, or shape, of a state has been institutionalised on a hegemonic basis when its boundaries are not treated by competing political elites within it as if those boundaries might be subject to change. If typical political discussions imply that such change might be advisable or possible…the state-building process with respect to that boundary and territory is plainly incomplete.[51]

In India, parliament in New Delhi has the ultimate responsibility for decisions about reorganising state boundaries. There is no constitutional requirement to hold public referenda in regions for which statehood is demanded (the 'sub-state' level) or to take heed of any opposition raised by the 'parent state' government (the 'state' level). Yet in practice, central governments have always been exceedingly cautious about the creation of new states in most of India. On the whole, they have acted only where there is no significant opposition to the reorganisation at the regional level.[52] With regard to the Hindi heartland, central governments have been more responsive to arguments made within state capitals in favour of state unity than to the demands for separate statehood of regional movements. These practices have reinforced the 'stickiness', as opposed to fluidity, of state boundaries.

INTRODUCTION

Nevertheless such stability can be undermined by processes of economic, social or political change and/or by the agency of key individuals (neither is sufficient on its own). In tracing the processes by which this took place in the states of north and central India this book therefore contributes to work on the origins of institutions or institutional change, as distinct from the role of institutions in structuring political, social and economic life. Much research on federalism has focused on its institutional effects on the stability of Indian democracy.[53] This study poses a distinctive question by seeking to explain the origins of those institutional structures. The analysis takes seriously the conjunction of multiple causes in producing a single outcome, in this case the creation of new states. It pays attention, in particular, to processes that occur according to the semi-autonomous timetables of sub-state, state and national politics and within discrete spaces of the federation.

* * *

Remapping India is structured around levels of the federal system, moving from the sub-state, to the state, to the federal level to consider how political dynamics within each of these spaces—but also their interactions—contribute to the dynamics of federal restructuring. It starts in chapter two by examining the overall approach by successive Indian governments to states reorganisation since independence. This chapter considers the decision to reorganise the states of southern and western India along linguistic lines in the 1950s and 1960s, and looks at why non-linguistic arguments for territorial organisation within the Hindi heartland were given short shrift in this period. I show how the apparent unimpeachability of the borders of Bihar, Madhya Pradesh and Uttar Pradesh—even where confronted by regional movements, as in Jharkhand—was deeply entwined with the dominance of politics in these regions by upper castes and the Congress Party, and an image of Uttar Pradesh in particular as a Hindi-Hindu heartland whose sacred geography necessitated its continued unity. Throughout this chapter runs a concern with the development of the political thinking towards federalism of the Hindu right—the BJP (and Jana Sangh)—especially as it responded to new regional movements and the increasing centralisation of power under Indira Gandhi.

Chapters three and four document the emergence of widespread agreement to the idea of statehood in the then sub-state regions of

Jharkhand and Uttarakhand, and to a somewhat lesser extent in Chhattisgarh. Chapter three examines the evolution of statehood movements in Jharkhand and Uttarakhand. In the course of interactions between political parties and social movements, a call for statehood became a clear focus for multiple actors. Chapter four analyses the history of the statehood idea in Chhattisgarh where it was discussed by regional politicians but there was no popular statehood 'movement' or serious pressure from below for a new state. In each region, statehood emerged as something of a lowest common denominator among competing interest groups: an institutional form that was widely agreed to yet held divergent meanings for the different actors involved in regional political life. In studying the same moment across three different regions, the study provides new insights into the accommodation of social movements and the emergence of new political parties from the 1970s onwards. Those who are interested in the political history of these regions in their own right should find these chapters of particular note.

Local representatives of the BJP were particularly important players in each of the putative new states in offering support to demands for statehood, and their role is considered in these chapters, too. An important consequence of the BJP's support for statehood, and that of other local politicians, was that the association of demands for statehood with any particular local community—particularly *adivasi* communities in Jharkhand and 'sons of the soil' in Chhattisgarh—was weakened. This is a process that has made the representational consequences of statehood once granted very ambiguous. It is not clear who the new states are 'for', if anyone, and this demonstrates the 'compromise politics' of statehood. As James Mahoney and Kathleen Thelen note: 'institutional outcomes need not reflect the goals of any particular group; they may be the unintended outcome of conflict among groups or the result of "ambiguous compromises" among actors who can coordinate on institutional means even if they differ on substantive goals.'[54] The precise processes by which such compromises were forged at the local level differed in each region, but they lend a common logic to the episode of state creation which is explored in chapters three and four.

Chapter five turns to consider the state level. A critical reason why the state boundaries of Bihar, Madhya Pradesh and Uttar Pradesh became more open to question—and therefore somewhat less 'sticky'—from the 1980s onwards was the gradual challenge to the upper caste dominance of politics in these Hindi heartland states.[55] These challenges came into sharper relief during, and after, the election of the Janata Party government in 1977 and with the emergence of the Janata Dal and new regional parties in Bihar and Uttar Pradesh committed to the political mobilisation of lower castes. The politicisation of caste and the emergence of caste-based regional parties in Bihar and Uttar Pradesh began to make the borders of north Indian states appear somewhat less natural or 'given' in a context in which newly politicised lower caste identities did not correspond neatly to state boundaries. This was also a context in which new sacred landscapes could be promoted. This chapter considers the role of three political entrepreneurs—Chief Ministers Arjun Singh of Madhya Pradesh, Mulayam Singh Yadav of Uttar Pradesh, and Lalu Prasad Yadav of Bihar—who played critical roles in bringing the borders of the states they governed into contention across the states. They helped to ensure that by 1997—before the BJP came to power at the centre— all three state assemblies had passed resolutions supporting the division of their states. Changes within state level party systems help to explain why in 2000 it was more feasible to reduce the size of Bihar, Madhya Pradesh or Uttar Pradesh than in the 1950s at the time of the linguistic reorganisation of states when division of states in the Hindi heartland was also proposed but vetoed.

Chapter six turns to consider the shorter-term backdrop within federal government when the states were created. As well as looking at the legislative process at the federal level, the chapter also considers why Telangana and Vidarbha, other statehood demands that had also been on the BJP's agenda at different points in time, were not granted statehood in 2000. I show that in linguistic states in the south and west of India, borders remained more resilient. Although there have been some challenges to the linguistic principle as the basis for statehood (especially in Telangana), these are not yet sufficiently strong to have led to a more general destabilising of the logic of state borders based on language in other linguistic states or in areas outside Telangana in Andhra Pradesh. The stickiness of borders in the south and west is supported not only by language, but the correspondence between linguistic communities and patterns of caste dominance, as well as the emergence of regional parties from the 1960s to 1980s that mobilised around linguistic nationalism with a pan-state reach. It is also supported by the integration of linguistic communities and markets and the centrality of mega-cities such as

Hyderabad and Mumbai to the economies of both Andhra Pradesh and Maharashtra. Demands for new states continue however as chapter seven examines with a discussion of ongoing debates about the potential reorganisation of Uttar Pradesh, as well as Andhra Pradesh.

Finally, in the concluding chapter, I look at the post-statehood scenarios in Chhattisgarh, Jharkhand and Uttarakhand in order to assess some of the consequences of state creation. It remains too soon to examine long-term trajectories but an initial assessment reminds us that these remain contested spaces within India's political and economic landscape.

2

HISTORY OF TERRITORIAL DESIGN
AND FEDERAL THOUGHT IN INDIA

At India's independence from British rule in 1947, the future internal boundaries of its political map remained uncertain. Partition, as well as emerging conflict in Kashmir, accorded a degree of primacy to the question of settling external borders. The integration of former princely states with previously British-ruled provinces was the most immediate challenge in relation to India's internal borders. Religion had been set to one side as a basis for territorial claims in the aftermath of partition, but language remained an alternative source of political community that was only partially reflected by existing administrative boundaries.

This chapter examines the territorial architecture of India's federal system since independence. It explains how the federal system and the history of political thought with regard to the territorial organisation of federalism in India evolved in the context of developments in India's political economy and party system. It begins by looking at constitutional provisions and debate about the design of Indian federalism. It then considers the decision to reorganise states along linguistic lines in the 1950s and 1960s after initial reluctance to do so. It asks why large states were maintained in Hindi-speaking north and central India as the counterpoint to linguistic reorganisation. Maintenance of the boundaries of Bihar and Uttar Pradesh was envisioned as a bulwark against the possible mobilisation of further destabilising claims for statehood on a non-linguistic basis. The resilience of these larger states in Hindi speaking areas, to the consternation of the Dalit leader and constitutional architect B.R. Ambedkar, was also linked to the political dominance of upper castes in north India. The second half of the chapter then introduces the political dynamics that helped to open up discussions about territorial reorganisation, including within the Hindi heartland from the late 1960s onwards. It charts the development of the political philosophy of the Hindu right throughout this period and its changing approach to the federal organisation of power as it negotiated its rise to political power.

Designing the Postcolonial State

In terms of its institutional shape, the constitution bears the imprint of the forms of limited provincial self-government introduced by the British from the late nineteenth century and especially the Government of India Act of 1935. The Constitution of India published in 1950 followed these earlier reforms by distributing powers between the union and state governments, thereby creating separate spheres of authority— a defining principle of federalism. The constitution avoided the word 'federal' altogether however. In some ways it marked a temporary aberration in the story of Indian state formation, establishing a strong centre and an administrative structure that did not provide institutional recognition to identities that might rival an outward looking Indian national identity.

It was India's first Prime Minister Jawaharlal Nehru who exerted the deepest influence on the principles shaping the territorial organisation of the new post-independence administration. Nehru was committed to building a new government machinery to pursue the twin goals of economic and social progress for the new nation. For Nehru, this vision implied that Congress should set aside language as an organising principle of political community in a bid to avoid strengthening regional identities that might impede the consolidation of the new nation. This meant asserting a break with Congress' own principles of internal party organisation. In 1921, Congress had reorganised its own party structure to correspond with language boundaries as the nationalist movement developed a mass base. In seeking to build a mass, pan-Indian nationalist movement, Gandhi had attempted to co-opt the proto-nationalist sentiments of regional linguistic communities such as Oriya, Tamil,

HISTORY OF TERRITORIAL DESIGN

Telugu and Marathi speakers by reorganising the Congress along linguistic lines rather than around British administrative boundaries.[1] From 1903, demands for separate linguistic provinces had been made by Biharis and Oriyas who were then part of Bengal, and by Telugu speakers in Madras province. In 1936, the British created new provinces of Orissa and Sindh. Linguistic regionalism, as Judith Brown suggests, 'bonded speakers of the same vernacular, and generated hostility towards other Indian groups who appeared to "colonise" areas outside their own linguistic regions because of their education and consequent access to administrative employment.'[2] The embrace of regional languages was critical in the deepening of Congress' social base.[3] Congress had repeatedly called on the British to reorganise its provinces along similar lines. But after independence Nehru attempted to sideline the idea of creating linguistically homogenous provinces in order to concentrate on what he regarded as the prior task of nation building.

The immediate challenge for the new government was to incorporate the diverse patterns of administrative and political development of the princely states, which numbered about 560 at independence, with the former British provinces. The provinces had been granted some measure of provincial self-governance before independence with elections held on a very limited franchise, but the princely states represented a collection of more and less authoritarian governments. The reconciliation between the two types of administrative unit was achieved within two years by amalgamating the princely states with the provinces or in small clusters, and creating three categories of states with varying degrees of autonomy from the central government: Part A, B and C states. Separate settlements were reached with the princely states of Hyderabad and Jammu and Kashmir whose accession to India—rather than Pakistan— was contested. In the immediate years following independence, then, India's federal system retained much of the territorial administrative structure put in place by the British, which reflected patterns of the expansion of colonial authority and the arrangements negotiated with a variety of local rulers. The first map of India after independence left the contours of the provinces of British India mainly untouched, except for their merger with territories of the princely states.[4]

But the language question did not subside. A Linguistic Provinces Commission was set up by the Constituent Assembly in 1948 under the chairmanship of S.K. Dar to consider the demands for states by speakers

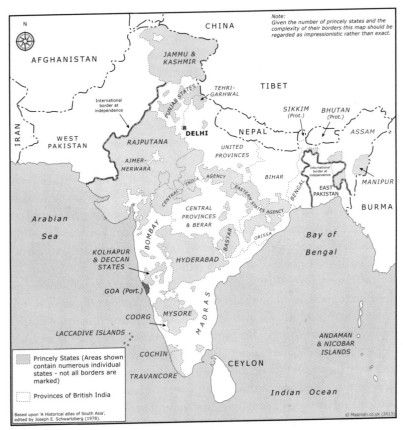

Map 2: India on the eve of independence in 1947.

of Telugu, Malayalam, Kannada and Marathi. The commission argued against creating any more provinces at that moment on the grounds of a paramount concern with national unity and the likelihood of creating a 'fresh minority problem'. In a report that reflected Nehru's concern that the formation of linguistic states would encourage provincialism at a juncture when national unity was the primary concern, the Commission said that language should not be the sole criterion for reorganising boundaries. It recommended setting aside the question of linguistic states for ten years.[5] A Congress committee consisting of Nehru, Sardar Vallabhai Patel and Pattabhi Sitaramayya (the JVP committee) made a similar recommendation. As Sunil Khilnani delineates, Nehru's was a modernist nation-building project which sought to build a new nation on the foundations of economic development achieved through a programme of industrialisation led by a strong central government, and symbolised in the construction of steel plants, large dams and new cities.[6] Through economic development he wished to cement a composite nationalism that would be outward looking, accommodative of difference but moving beyond what he saw as potentially divisive and narrow loyalties to religious community, caste or region. He therefore pushed the Constituent Assembly to respond cautiously to the question of linguistic units.

The Constituent Assembly also designed a centralised federal system. Before independence, the preference of the Congress leadership had been for a strong central government; it had been suspicious of alternative models of looser federation or confederation. With partition an established fact, the Constituent Assembly was concerned above all with providing a strong central government that would protect national unity, as well as supporting social and economic reform.[7] This stood in contrast to pre-partition models such as that envisaged by the Cabinet Mission Plan in which the rights of provinces (Muslim and non-Muslim) were to the fore. The new constitution established a parliamentary system of government with a directly elected lower house, the *Lok Sabha* (Council of the People) and an upper house, the *Rajya Sabha* (Council of the States) comprised of members elected by state assemblies. States were to be represented in the *Rajya Sabha* according to their population size rather than on the basis of parity between states (as in the US or Brazilian Senates, for example). Political powers were divided between the central government and the states according to three lists: the central, state and concurrent (powers shared by centre and states), with residual powers lying with the centre. The collection and distribution of tax revenues was heavily centralised, and the constitution contained a further—and later frequently abused—provision to allow the central government to take over the administration of a state government in the event of a breakdown of law and order by declaring 'President's Rule'. After independence, the new government was labelled the 'Union' (not federal) government.[8] As Mohit Bhattacharya states:

It was basically a unitary mind working on a federal-like issue. The concept of state in the architect's minds was predominantly centre-oriented. Assertive and aggressive spokesmen of the rights of the Constituent units were few and far between.[9]

Yet despite the centralised characteristics of the constitution, the operation of political authority in India has always involved a delicate balance between central and regional power.

India's flexible provisions for territorial reorganisation

Consonant with the centralised federal structure and recognising the likelihood of an eventual need to change the internal borders of the federation, the right of the central government to admit or establish new states is provided for at the very beginning of the constitution in Articles 2 and 3. The creation of new states was therefore made the firm prerogative of the central government. Under Article 3 of India's constitution parliament has the right by law, and on the basis of a simple majority, to:

a. form a new State by separation of territory from any State or by uniting two or more States or parts of States or by uniting any territory to a part of any State;
b. increase the area of any State;
c. diminish the area of any State;
d. alter the boundaries of any State;
e. alter the name of any State

Those who qualify the description of India's system of government as 'federal' often point to this constitutional provision because it appears to heavily circumscribe the rights and integrity of India's states.[10] Fali Nariman, a senior constitutional lawyer has stated that Article 3 undermines India's federal credentials and underscores the fact that India's states 'are so hedged in by restrictions that [they] have no independent "political Sovereignty"'.[11] It is for this reason that India is sometimes called an 'indestructible union of destructible states' in contrast to the US which was described in the nineteenth century as an 'indestructible Union, composed of indestructible States'.[12] In practice, however, these concerns may be over-stated. India's central government has over time paid deep attention to the views of states when confronted with demands for statehood by groups in particular regions.

By the mid-1950s, with a decision in 1953 to create the state of Andhra followed by the appointment of a States Reorganisation Commission to consider other demands, Article 3 had already been called into action to reorganise states in south India along the lines of dominant regional linguistic communities. This resulted in the separation of Tamil-speaking areas of Madras (later renamed Tamil Nadu) from Telugu-speaking regions to create Andhra Pradesh (also incorporating, in 1956, the Telugu-speaking region of Telangana, part of the former Nizam of Hyderabad's domains); the creation of a separate Malayalam-speaking state of Kerala, and a Kannada-speaking Mysore (renamed Karnataka in

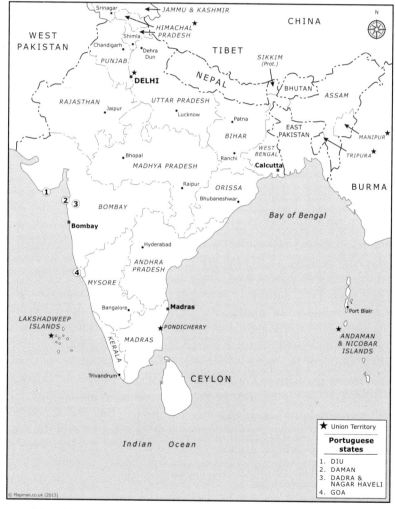

Map 3: Political map of India in 1956 after reorganisation of states.

1973). Ouside south India, the Central Provinces lost Marathi-speaking Vidarbha to Bombay but were merged with the former Part B and C states of Madhya Bharat, Vindhya Pradesh and Bhopal to create the Hindi-speaking megalith of Madhya Pradesh. The former princely states of PEPSU (Patiala and East Punjab States Union) and Punjab were merged to form a single state of Punjab with a mixed Hindu and Sikh population, and Punjabi and Hindi as official languages.

Language as a Basis for Statehood

Most explanations for the reorganisation of states in the 1950s highlight language as a distinctly powerful form of political identity. Nehru had resisted the creation of states along linguistic lines after independence, fearing that they would encourage parochialism, and threaten national unity. His capitulation to the creation of linguistic states within a few years of independence is commonly presented as almost inevitable; the correction of a misguided assumption about the malleability of linguistic identity.

In comparative terms, language is one of the most important facets of territorial—and national—identity and a critical feature in the design of federal regimes: witness the design of Belgian, Canadian, Spanish and Swiss federations.[13] As Sumathi Ramaswamy and Lisa Mitchell have argued, in south Indian contexts, language is an emotive subject about which people have felt so passionately that they were willing to die for its cause.[14] This is what Potti Sriramulu did in Madras Province in December 1952, fasting to death in pursuit of a Telugu-speaking Andhra state. After his death, Nehru was pushed to concede India's first linguistic state, creating the state of Andhra. The States Reorganisation Commission (SRC), which reported in 1955 on demands for other states, was itself guarded about the idea that language was the sole criterion for reorganisation. Encouraged by Nehru, it declared a 'balanced approach' in which linguistic homogeneity was an important principle but not an exclusive one to override administrative, financial, or political considerations. It was a principle that must be balanced with the need to give 'deeper content' to Indian nationalism.[15] But the main logic of borders drawn in the ensuing 1956 States Reorganisation Act was provided largely by language.[16]

Yet we should not see language as a force of nature in propelling territorial reorganisation. Paul Brass, for instance, urges that we must explain why language becomes a subject for political mobilisation in some places but not others.[17] For him the answer lies in the cleavages that become politicised in the pursuit of elite interests: 'Language movements are everywhere vehicles for the pursuit of economic advancement, social status and political power by specific elites.'[18] In south India rising middle castes challenged the dominance of small Brahmin elites through regional language movements, whereas elsewhere in parts of north India such as Punjab and Uttar Pradesh religion became a more important source of tension than language.[19] The political assertion of dominant owner-cultivator castes such as the Kammas and Reddys in Andhra, and the Lingayats and Vokkaligas in Karnataka, propelled the demands for linguistic states. Linguistic boundaries were aligned with the frontiers of these locally dominant landowning castes who sought corresponding political power.[20]

Moreover, the central government has, over time, only responded to those regional demands which have demonstrated widespread support from both the main linguistic group demanding statehood and the other communities within the state concerned. Brass described four rules that have governed the state's response to regional autonomy movements. These are that regional demands must stop short of secession; regional demands based on language and culture will be accommodated, but not those based explicitly on religion; regional demands will not be conceded capriciously—'that is a regional movement must not only have a legitimate case, but it must have broad popular support in the region'; and division of multilingual states must have some support from the different linguistic groups concerned.[21]

As Robert King argues, Nehru was aware that demands for linguistic states concealed more fundamental political conflicts about the distribution of political and economic power. In a speech to the Lok Sabha on 7 July 1952, Nehru said:

I feel that behind the demand for linguistic provinces there lies something more difficult to deal with than the problem of languages. That something is a feeling on the part of the people who make the demand that they have not had a square deal, that if they were left alone to manage their affairs they would see they got it. I cannot say whether there is much justification for the existence of such a feeling but the fact that it exists is not good for us. If we still function in a narrow, provincial way, reserving one group for our favours to the exclusion of another, it is unfortunate.[22]

K. Mukerji, a contemporary observer, said:

Let us be frank and accept the Dal-Roti basis of this enthusiasm. It is the middle class job hunter and place hunter and the mostly middle class politician who are benefited by the establishment of a linguistic state, which creates for them an exclusive preserve of jobs, offices and places by shutting out, in the name of promotion of culture, all outside competitors.[23]

King suggests that by delaying the creation of linguistic states and the battles accompanying their creation, Nehru achieved more than he realised in laying the groundwork for an accommodation between the centre and states that would help preserve Indian unity.[24]

A final factor influencing linguistic reorganisation in the 1950s, and the subsequent mobilisation of regional demands, is the link between territorial structures of government and the development of the Indian party system. The demands for linguistic states in the 1950s were made largely by non-Congress parties, especially the Communist Party and various regional parties.[25] As Adeney argues, linguistic reorganisation was in part a pragmatic move by Nehru to preserve the Congress's electoral hegemony. Reorganisation helped with this for a time: there was a clear reduction in the number of parties contesting elections between the first general elections in 1952 and the second in 1957 from fifty-three to fifteen.[26] Cultural nationalist parties such as the Dravida Munnetra Kazhagam (DMK) in Madras were overshadowed by Congress in the 1957 elections that followed linguistic reorganisation.[27]

Linguistic reorganisation was not 'complete' after the passage of the 1956 States Reorganisation Act in parliament. The SRC had opposed the bifurcation of the then state of Bombay into Marathi- and Gujarati-speaking regions because of the composite character of Bombay City. Gujarati speakers in Bombay had led a 'Save Bombay' movement, fearing they would be sidelined in a Marathi-speaking state.[28] But following the publication of the SRC's recommendations, widespread protests also began in the Marathi-speaking districts demanding a separate state. The Congress leadership hesitated, proposed a compromise that would have left Bombay city a separate state, and protests then spread to the Gujarati districts. In the 1957 elections, the Congress majority in the state was seriously challenged by the Maharashtra Samyukta Samiti (MSS) and Maha Gujarat Parishad. In 1960, on the basis of support from both language communities, the separate states of Gujarat and Maharashtra were formed. Following the division of Bombay, the Akali Dal then began to agitate for the creation of a Punjabi Suba which had been denied by the SRC on the grounds of a lack of popular support. The Congress leadership saw the demand as a challenge to the secular basis of the constitution, with Nehru describing it in parliament in 1961 as 'a communal [Sikh] demand, even though it is given a linguistic base'.[29] The demand was conceded in 1966 once Indira Gandhi had become Prime Minister, and with a change of leadership in the Akali Dal, the statehood demand had been expressed more clearly in linguistic rather than religious terms.[30]

Hindi Language Movement, Hindu Nationalism and Linguistic Reorganisation

The main opposition to the reorganisation of state boundaries in the 1950s came from the Hindu right, in particular the Bharatiya Jana Sangh formed in 1951 as the political wing of the Rashtriya Swayamsevak Sangh (RSS). Hindu traditionalists within Congress who were to be found in the largest numbers within the Hindi-speaking states of the north and were associated with the campaign to establish Hindi as the national language after independence (against opposition from southern non-Hindi speaking states), also sought to protect the existing borders of Uttar Pradesh in north India from the threat of reorganisation. The Hindi language debate struck at the heart of defining the new nation, and occurred alongside discussions about the territorial structure of its federal system. Nehru was wary about linguistic dogmatism in any form and, as his biographer Judith Brown writes, 'disliked the trend towards a presumed purification and Sanskritisation of Hindi, which was linked, in his view, to a bigoted and narrow Hindu vision of India'.[31]

In the 1950s, the Jana Sangh criticised the 'Western concept of distorted multi-nationalism' that lay behind the reorganisation of states along linguistic lines which demonstrated only that 'the hold of our culture is loose'.[32] The party strongly emphasised the theme of national unity, and went as far as to call for the replacement of federalism with a unitary system of government.[33] It proposed that power be decentralised to villages and that the new linguistic states be divided into *janapadas* (administrative divisions delineated in Sanskrit Hindu texts) which would be closer to the people than the present state governments.[34] The Jana Sangh was particularly exercised about the movement for a separate

Sikh state in Punjab, and separatism in predominantly Christian Nagaland (formerly part of Assam in the northeast). In 1960, the Government of India had agreed to grant full statehood to Nagaland and this eventually took place in 1963.

Hindu nationalists in the Jana Sangh and from its establishment in 1964, the Vishwa Hindu Parishad (VHP), described the process of conversion to Christianity as one of 'denationalisation' and used the example of the separatist movement for Nagaland by largely Christian tribals in the northeast (and the statehood movement in Jharkhand) as evidence of the goal of Christian missionaries 'to establish Christian majority states in different parts of the country'.[35] In making this argument, they drew on the Niyogi Report commissioned in 1952 by Congress Chief Minister of Madhya Pradesh R.S. Shukla to investigate missionary activity in India, especially in response to conversions in the tribal belt of Surguja in present-day Chhattisgarh. There was therefore some overlap between Hindu traditionalists within Congress who were particularly associated with the campaign to establish Hindi as a national language after independence, and the thinking of the Jana Sangh. The Niyogi report had found that:

Evangelisation in India appears to be part of the uniform world policy to revive Christendom for re-establishing Western supremacy...The objective is apparently to create Christian minority pockets with a view to disrupt the solidarity of the non-Christian societies, and the mass conversions of a considerable section of Adivasis with this ulterior motive is fraught with danger to the security of the State.[36]

In 1952, the RSS established the Vanvasi Kalyan Ashram with its headquarters in Jashpur, in Surguja district. It was set up to work with tribal communities with the aim of countering the activities of Christian missionaries through social work (especially schools and hospitals), as well as the active propagation of Hinduism. It gradually extended its presence in Surguja and neighbouring districts in Chotanagpur (Jharkhand), as well as other states with tribal populations.

For a time in the late 1960s, the Jana Sangh changed the focus of its attack from Christians to Communists and Muslims, accusing them of promoting the idea that India was a multi-national state. 'The most sinister of an "unholy combine of disruptionists",' the party resolved in April 1969, 'are the Communists who unabashedly propagate that India is a multi-national State.' They singled out the Communist state governments of West Bengal and Kerala for criticism. In Kerala, the Communists were in alliance with the Muslim League, and in West Bengal the Jana Sangh accused them of being 'aligned with pro-League elements' that sought to encourage 'tendencies of disintegration' by offering support to regional movements (in Kerala the idea of creating a Muslim majority district of Malapuram and, in West Bengal, the movement for an autonomous Darjeeling district).[37] 'Unfortunately,' they wrote, 'region-based groups and parties tend to build up their appeal on narrow regional chauvinism so that an invariable outcome of their activities is the generation of regional tensions and the weakening of national unity.'[38] Hardliners in the Jana Sangh began to talk about the need for the 'Indianisation' of Muslims and Christians.[39] Yet, while Hindu nationalists continued to critique language as a basis for statehood after the 1950s, they subsequently moved away from their principled opposition to any reorganisation of borders.

In retrospect, linguistic reorganisation is generally held to have been a successful reform. It helped to accommodate cultural nationalism and to deepen democracy by making regional languages, rather than English, the language of state politics. Less recognised, but also significant, is that it was the creation of linguistic states that most effectively sidelined the former rulers of the princely states who had been given important roles equivalent to governors within the amalgamated states created after independence but who were removed from power in 1956.[40] On the whole, linguistic reorganisation helped to weaken not strengthen separatist sentiments. India's decentralised and cross-cutting social cleavages helped to ensure that once language was recognised as a basis for statehood, different types of identity were politicised within the new states drawing on caste, class, religion, and sub-state regions. As James Manor argues, these multiple sources of identity have undermined the development of secessionist sentiment in most Indian states.[41]

From 1966 to 2000, the creation of new states slowed down. The main reorganisation in this period took place in northeast India according to a different pattern than that seen elsewhere in India. This reflects the distinctiveness, as well as geographical isolation of the region. Here the new states of Mizoram, Meghalaya and Arunachal Pradesh were created by the central government to provide mechanisms of self-governance for hill tribes which had previously been part of Assam, and in response to secessionist movements in some instances.[42] But Sanjib

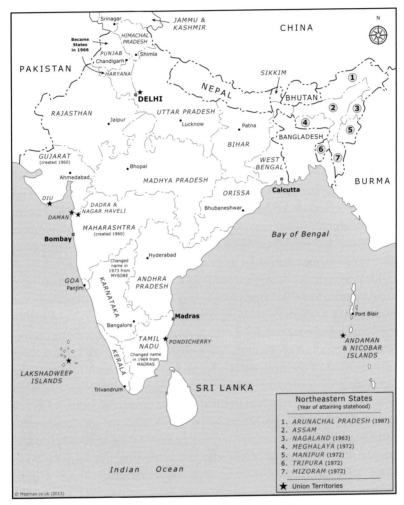

Map 4: Political map of India in 1975.

Baruah argues that state creation has often been a top-down affair in the northeast, driven by national security concerns more than being prompted by sustained political mobilisation in the case of states such as Arunachal Pradesh or Meghalaya. This has created what Baruah calls a more 'cosmetic federalism', masking the intention of increasing national control over this border region—especially after the 1962 war with neighbouring China—by creating small states that are financially dependent on New Delhi.[43] Practices of state creation have also enshrined strong measures of protective discrimination for 'local' populations against the consequences of migration into these geographically remote regions that have been subject to protective legislation since the nineteenth century.[44] These constitutional provisions in the northeast have privileged identities based on indigeneity to structure access to political and economic resources in the region.

The fixity of borders in the Hindi-speaking 'heartland'

One region remained outside most of the reorganisation of states until 2000. This was the so-called Hindi-speaking heartland of north and central India. The undivided, predominantly Hindi-speaking states of Madhya Pradesh, Rajasthan, Uttar Pradesh and Bihar ranked first, second, fourth and eighth respectively in total geographical area of all the states of India before 2000. In terms of population they ranked sixth, ninth, first and second respectively. The main change that took place in this region was the creation of Madhya Pradesh in 1956. This reinforced the tendency towards larger, composite states in this region. There are two major reasons why large and populous states were preserved in the Hindi heartland. Firstly, size was not made a criterion for deciding state borders by the States Reorganisation Commission in 1955. The States Reorganisation Commission generally favoured larger over smaller states, citing economies of scale and the virtues of broad-based economies. The Congress leadership also intervened to quash suggestions that Uttar Pradesh—the country's most populous state—should be divided to create smaller units. As Gyanesh Kudaisya suggests, Nehru and colleagues such as G.B. Pant saw the maintenance of the existing borders of states in the north as part of a strategy to contain further demands for state creation, and to limit them to the linguistic principle.[45]

The second reason that Hindi-speaking states were not sub-divided further lies in the nature of state politics in north India compared to the linguistic states created in south and west India in the 1950s. In the 1950s and 1960s, the borders of north Indian states were underpinned by a mixture of upper caste and Congress Party dominance. The rhetorical defence of the existing boundaries of the state of Uttar Pradesh, in particular—against calls for its reorganisation in the 1950s (and after)—

drew strongly on a sacred geography. The political pre-eminence of a vision of Uttar Pradesh's unity which drew upon a sacred geography was given strength by the upper caste dominance of politics in the state. The maintenance of the borders of Uttar Pradesh and Bihar was deeply entwined with the upper caste dominance of politics in these regions.

We will first turn to the question of why the States Reorganisation Commission (SRC) and Congress leadership in the 1950s favoured the continuation of the large states of north India. Not only did the SRC sanction the continuation of large states in terms of area and population, it proposed the creation of the new entity of Madhya Pradesh as an amalgam of former princely states and Hindi-speaking districts of the Central Provinces. This new Hindi-speaking state was to become the largest state in India in terms of geographical area. The SRC was clear that it did not consider size to be a criterion by which decisions about statehood were to be made. The SRC even predicted that Madhya Pradesh may become 'one of the richest states in the Indian Union' because its large borders encompassed diverse agriculture (both wheat- and rice-growing regions), and planned investments in industry across the state, including the Bhilai Steel Plant in today's Chhattisgarh.[46]

There was a vigorous debate about the size and borders of Uttar Pradesh during the SRC's deliberations. A submission to the SRC, claiming the support of 97 of 127 MLAs in the western districts of Uttar Pradesh recommended that this region be merged with Delhi. A separate demand had been made for a hill state (in present-day Uttarakhand).[47] It was also suggested that the state was too large to be administered effectively. The SRC disagreed in its report, stating: 'It cannot well be claimed that mere size as such is undesirable and there is in fact no clear or necessary connection between the size of a State and the quality of its administration'.[48] The Commission also noted the absence of strong popular support within the state for Uttar Pradesh's division. In a dissenting note to the States Reorganisation Commission report published in 1955, K.M. Pannikar (one of the commission's three members) expressed his opposition to the conclusions of the SRC about Uttar Pradesh, arguing that the units of a federation should be of similar size, and that Uttar Pradesh's size undermined its efficient administration. But Pannikar's intervention was dismissed not only by the SRC, but by a range of senior Congress politicians. On the whole the SRC favoured larger states on the grounds of 'administrative efficiency and co-ordination of economic development and welfare activity'.[49]

The advocates of Uttar Pradesh's unity drew on what Kudaisya describes as a 'heartland' theme or motif that has been made and remade throughout the colonial and postcolonial history of Uttar Pradesh, as a result of a close relationship between the region and ideas of the 'nation'.[50] So for Shiva Nath Katju, a member of the state's legislative assembly, the unity of Uttar Pradesh while achieved through 'administrative processes' was not artificial: '[it] merely clothed a region that was well knit linguistically, geographically and by diverse other ties into a single administrative unit. What is more, the state of Uttar Pradesh is truly the heart of India.'[51] The clear implication of such assertions was that the division of Uttar Pradesh would promote separatism across the country, not only because it would provide a licence for other statehood demands based on principles other than language but because Uttar Pradesh's unity itself was a fundamental bedrock of India's national unity. In making this point, it was common for supporters of Uttar Pradesh's current borders to draw on the state's sacred geography, which both provided a rationale for the positioning of its borders and made the state central to imaginings of India. Dr Ishwari Prasad, a historian and member of Uttar Pradesh's Legislative Council, thus employed the kind of physiological metaphor of an organic Hindu social order represented in the *varna* system, prominent in Hindu nationalist thought,[52] to emphasise Uttar Pradesh's unity: 'The state is an organism like the human body. It consists of large and small limbs but they must all function harmoniously in order to produce good results…The cultural and regional ties bind us together. The holy cities of Ayodhya, Mathura, Brindaban, Kashi, Hardwar, and Prayag are the repositories of those spiritual influences which lead to homogeneity and oneness on the higher plane'.[53]

Such imagery was associated with a Brahminical vision of social order, and it spoke to a vision of the Hindu cosmos which imagines the universe as a living organism, in which each part is linked integrally to the life of the whole. As Eck suggests, sacred geography of 'mountains, forests, rivers, hilltop shrines and sacred cities' became a legitimating myth of a longer term national unity.[54] Even the Chief Minister of Uttar Pradesh, G.B. Pant, drew on this sacred imagery to quash calls to reorganise his state, asserting: 'No power on earth can cut up the land of Rama and Krishna, of Ganga and Yamuna, which has been shaped by nature to be indissoluble. Our culture dates back to the times of the Vedas. We have been the soul of Aryavarta. Our culture and language envelop Bharat'.[55] Several months later, in December 1954, Pant became Union Home Minister and assumed responsibility for the issue of states' reorganisation at the Centre.[56]

The mythology deployed to provide a rationale for Uttar Pradesh's unity glossed over the composite culture of the state's Hindu-Muslim heritage. According to its critics, the imagery also supported the maintenance of caste hierarchy, as well as bolstering the political dominance of Uttar Pradesh within India more generally. The projection of Uttar Pradesh's wholeness provided a supposedly sacred justification of an uneven distribution of political power with real effects in the world of the profane. It was precisely the attempt to cast Uttar Pradesh as the dominant heart of India that inspired the call by K.M. Pannikar for the state to be divided in two in order to create a more even balance in size between the units of the federation. In his dissenting note to the SRC, he wrote:

The consequence of the present imbalance, caused by the denial of the federal principle of equality of units, has been to create feelings of distrust and resentment in all the States outside Uttar Pradesh. Not only in the southern States but also in the Punjab, Bengal and elsewhere the view was generally expressed before the Commission that the present structure of government led to the dominance of Uttar Pradesh in all-India matters.[57]

Furthermore, as B.R. Ambedkar, Dalit lawyer and the architect of India's constitution, argued, the dominance of Uttar Pradesh in India— and the large states of north India more generally sanctioned by the SRC—implied the political dominance of a conservative hierarchial social structure and culture. 'There is a vast difference between the North and the South', he wrote:

The North is conservative. The South is progressive. The North is superstitious, the South is rational. The South is educationally forward, the North is educationally backward. The culture of the South is modern. The culture of the North is ancient.

Did not Prime Minister Nehru on the 15th of August 1947 sit at the yajna [sic] performed by the Brahmins [sic] of Benares to celebrate the event of a Brahmin becoming the first Prime Minister of free and independent India…? How can the rule of the North be tolerated by the South?[58]

In order to overcome the dominance of the north, Ambedkar proposed that the north Indian states of Uttar Pradesh, Bihar and Madhya

Pradesh each be divided into a number of smaller units: three states in the case of Uttar Pradesh, two in Bihar and two in Madhya Pradesh.

Ambedkar moreover argued that large states were likely to consolidate the power of majorities and to 'crush' minorities (including 'Untouchables'):

> The consequences of too large a State on the minority living within it are not understood by many. The larger the State the smaller the proportion of the minority to the majority…A small stone of a consolidated majority placed on the minority may be borne. But the weight of a huge mountain it cannot bear. It will crush the minorities. Therefore creation of smaller States is a safeguard to the minorities.[59]

The greater demographic weight of upper castes in north India,[60] the more complete caste structure,[61] along with the strong overlap between structures of land ownership and the caste structure, helped to entrench upper caste dominance of Congress Party politics.[62] Lower castes and classes had been more progressively incorporated into Congress in the south and west, than in the north.[63] In the first two decades after independence, the Congress organisation throughout India relied on a 'complex pyramiding of vertical factional alliances' led by dominant landowning castes.[64] The stronger correspondence of landownership with upper caste status in the north underpinned a situation of social and political inequality. It impeded the development of horizontal political coalitions on a regional basis, and bolstered legitimations of Uttar Pradesh's expansive boundaries. In the south, the *ryotwari* system of land tenure, in addition to social reform movements before independence, had led to the earlier assertion of landowning middle castes who became core support bases for Congress and later regional parties. These 'forward' castes dominated the calls for linguistic states and playing a leading role in the politics of states in the south and west after linguistic reorganisation.[65]

Yet the objections of Ambedkar and others to the large states of north India on the grounds that they were likely to reinforce upper caste dominance were overruled. Once the matter of the reorganisation of Uttar Pradesh had been laid to rest with the implementation of many of the SRC's recommendations via the States Reorganisation Act in 1956, the question of the state's borders achieved a certain inviolability. The dominance of politics by the Congress Party until the 1980s helped to further marginalise debate about the borders of Uttar Pradesh.

The debate about Uttar Pradesh's size set the tone for discussions about other Hindi-speaking states. Bihar was the only Hindi-speaking state which had seen a serious popular challenge to the legitimacy of its borders—the movement for Jharkhand. The SRC categorised this statehood demand as lacking widespread support and again argued that there were other virtues to Bihar's present size, namely a composite agrarian and industrial economy. The advice of the States Reorganisation Commission (SRC) on the demand for Jharkhand was to reject the call for a separate state because of the volume of opposition within, and outside, Chotanagpur and Santal Parganas:

Even if it is assumed that Adivasis are solidly in favour of the formation of a Jharkhand State, a major issue of this kind cannot, in our opinion, be decided on the basis of the views of a minority. There seems to be no warrant, however, for the assumption that even Adivasi opinion can be considered to be unanimous on this point.[66]

Identities grounded in claims to indigeneity were not recognised as legitimate bases for claiming statehood. The report noted that the total tribal population is only 'little more than one-third of the total population and is divided into several language groups'.[67] The SRC noted in the case of Jharkhand that the 'ultimate objective' should be to remove the distinctions between *adivasis* and other citizens in so far as they impede the 'ecoomic and political advancement of the tribal areas'.[68] The Commission also rejected the complaint made by the Jharkhand movement of 'lopsided economic development', and said that it was 'natural and inevitable' that irrigation be favoured in north Bihar and industrialisation in the south. Furthermore they noted that the rest of Bihar could not afford to lose the benefits of the coal, industries and thermal power stations situated in Chotanagpur. In Bihar, appeals to a sacred geography were weaker than in Uttar Pradesh; more important was the volume of opposition in north Bihar to the state's bifurcation. From the vantage point of north Bihar the borders of the state were not open to change, and this coincided with New Delhi's reluctance to accept any case for state subdivision in predominantly Hindi-speaking states where language did not provide a rationale for statehood.

*Post-linguistic Reorganisation: New Challenges to Borders
in the Hindi Heartland from the Late 1960s*

The idea of increasing the number of states in Hindi-speaking areas had been effectively sidelined in the first two decades after independence. But by the late 1960s and early 1970s, a new generation of regional demands emerged that highlighted economic inequality, rather than identity, as a reason for territorial reorganisation. In the context of the weakening of the Congress Party's dominance of electoral politics, the shift of political leadership at the national level under Indira Gandhi and awareness that two decades of economic planning had not achieved hoped-for dividends, a new set of debates opened up about the organisation of the federal system. Regional demands and federal debates were drawn into an emerging landscape of non-Congress opposition politics.

In this section I examine how major changes in India's political life and political economy since the late 1960s are linked to the history of federal thought, specifically to debates about territorial organisation. My purpose is to show how state boundaries in Hindi-speaking states went from being well-institutionalised and underpinned by prevailing patterns of social and political power, to being questioned by important actors at the sub-state, state and national levels. These processes are at the heart of the next four chapters of the book.

The decade from 1967 saw two important sets of developments: the first occurred inside the Congress Party, under the leadership of Indira Gandhi; the second occurred outside Congress, and in opposition to it. Indira Gandhi had taken over as Prime Minister in 1966, following the two-year rule of Lal Bahadur Shastri after Nehru's death. Changes in social and political mobilisation in this period had implications for India's party system and, by extension, debates about the design of its federal system. From 1967 onwards, there was a gradual increase in coordination among opposition parties at the state level, which helped to consolidate space for a non-Congress politics to emerge.[69] At a national level, anti-Congress parties increasingly shared a common stance on centre-state relations and a critique of of a trend towards the centralisation of power under Indira Gandhi. The Jana Sangh reversed its approach to regional demands, moving away from its earlier emphasis on national integrity and, by 1973, had committed itself to the creation of new states as a matter of principle (before it offered its support for specific demands). It did so, as analysed below, as part of its critique of centre-state relations under Indira Gandhi in the early 1970s.

From the outset, Indira Gandhi led a Congress Party in transition. In the 1967 state elections, the Congress Party—for the first time—suffered defeats in large parts of the country at the hands of a mixture of regional and national opposition parties. In Madras it lost to the DMK, in Kerala to a left alliance, in West Bengal to a United Front-Left Front alliance (comprised of Communist Party of India [Marxist] and Bangla Congress), in Orissa to Swatantra. In most of north India, Congress won only small majorities, leading to instability, a swathe of defections and the formation of 'SVD' (Samyukta Vidhayak Dal, or United Legislators Party) governments in Bihar, Madhya Pradesh, Haryana and Uttar Pradesh (consisting of a combination of Jana Sangh, Socialists, Swatantra Party, local parties and Congress defectors).[70] Indira Gandhi also found her leadership of the party under challenge from old party bosses known as the Syndicate.

Mrs Gandhi began to identify the Congress Party organisation as a hindrance to the consolidation of her leadership, and as an obstacle to the achievement of the more radical goals of social and economic revolution that the Constituent Assembly had set for itself at independence.[71] She responded by leading a split in the Congress Party in 1969 to assert her control over the old party bosses, shifting rhetorically to the left and allying with the party's socialist factions. She also adopted a more populist style of leadership by appealing directly to the poor peasantry, in a bid to bypass the local elites that Congress had traditionally relied on in the countryside, as well as her opponents in the party hierarchy. This culminated in the 1971 elections, defined by Indira Gandhi's *garibi hatao* (eradicate poverty) call, in response to the opposition's rallying cry *Indira hatao* (get rid of Indira). She abandoned intra-party democracy, and loyalty to Indira Gandhi increasingly became the arbiter of political promotion. The result was a more and more atrophied Congress Party under a centralised leadership. Congress under Nehru had been a vehicle founded on 'stable linkages' with the electorate, and an unrivalled machine for the distribution of patronage.[72] Under Indira Gandhi, Congress strengthened its electoral mandate in the 1971 general elections and the 1972 state elections. But Congress' linkages with the electorate became increasingly unstable and reliant on the projection of its leader's personality.

Outside the Congress Party, two types of new opposition movements came to fruition. New regional parties were formed and tasted power, in many places for the first time, in 1967. In north India the Socialist Party, led by Rammanohar Lohia, and regional outfits such as the Bharatiya Lok Dal, organised around overlapping agendas of agrarian interests and the mobilisation of lower castes—qua castes—for access to political power and affirmative action in government employment and education. As Congress became increasingly reliant on what Paul Brass labelled a 'coalition of extremes' in north India,[73] drawing support from upper castes and Scheduled Castes, the party had become more vulnerable to mobilisation in the 'middle'. These intermediate peasant castes, many of whom had become landowners as a result of the abolition of tenant farming in the 1950s and benefited from the Green Revolution in the 1960s, became critical players in reshaping the political arena as they sought access to state power that corresponded with their economic status.[74] The Bharatiya Lok Dal, formed in 1967 by former Congress politician Chaudhury Charan Singh, the architect of *zamindari* abolition in Uttar Pradesh in the 1950s, drew support from owner cultivator classes in western Uttar Pradesh, and became a central player within the opposition Janata coalition formed in the 1970s.

Some, but not all, of these peasant castes were also *shudras* and part of the broad category of 'Other Backward Classes' that formed the backbone of caste-based political mobilisation pursued by the Socialist Party. Both Charan Singh and Karpoori Thakur, a Socialist leader who went on to become Bihar's Chief Minister for the period 1977–79, believed there was an 'overlapping constituency of progressive farmers and Backward castes', and built their political strategies around a combination of advancing the class interests of owner-cultivators and promoting the cause of the Backward castes for social justice.[75] The deeper participation of large numbers of OBCs in electoral politics in the late 1960s was described by Yogendra Yadav as India's 'first democratic upsurge', and heralded the beginning of India's second electoral system in which Congress remained in power at the centre, but was no longer the dominant party it had been in the 1950s and early 1960s.[76]

Beyond the confines of party politics, a host of social movements appeared on the scene in the early 1970s. In 1972, the Jharkhand Mukti Morcha (JMM), the All Assam Students' Union, Self Employed Women's Association, and farmer organisations such as the Zamindari Union of Punjab, Tamilnadu Agriculturalists' Association and Khedut Samaj in Gujarat were all founded. In 1973, the Akali Dal in Punjab published the Anandpur Sahib resolution calling for greater regional autonomy, and Chipko, the people's forestry movement began in the Uttarakhand Himalayas. The Chhattisgarh Mines Shramik Sangh, a new form of trade union, was set up in 1977 (and subsequently established a political wing, the Chhattisgarh Mukti Morcha [CMM]) and worked among the informal labour force of the iron ore mines near the Bhilai Steel Plant. The formation of the Dalit Panthers, an organisation of Dalit youth in Maharashtra, also marked the beginning of a new wave of anti-caste movements.[77] In addition, Maoist-inspired uprisings among the rural poor took place in Naxalbari, West Bengal—leading to the term 'Naxalite'—and in the Telangana region of Andhra Pradesh. Looking ahead, in each of the regions that became states in 2000—Chhattisgarh, Jharkhand and Uttarakhand—the new social movements formed in the early 1970s raised questions about the role of the state in the management of natural resources and the rights of local communities to meaningful economic citizenship.

Many of the new social movements were based in urban areas but they raised concerns about natural resource management and the agrarian economy, and patterns of state-directed industrial development. In particular they highlighted the marginalisation of 'peripheral' regions, and certain groups within these regions, in a centralised, national system of industrial planning. In all three of the new states, the state's control of forests was also a major source of discontent. The actual forms of social movement that were formed in Chhattisgarh, Jharkhand and Uttarakhand and their relationship with new ideas of political region are analysed in the next two chapters. What is important to note, here, is the broader context into which these movements were born. As Rajni Kothari observed, the emergence of new movements or what he described as 'non-party political formations' in the 1970s was linked to a shift towards a more participatory vision of decentralised democracy and development, in which grassroots issues became the subject of political activism.[78]

This was a period of economic stagnation and high inflation. Indira Gandhi's populist turn had itself encouraged the deepening participation of the poor in electoral politics, but frustrations with government grew. In 1973 and 1974, a series of demonstrations took place against food shortages and rising prices. In Gujarat, students began campaigning for the dismissal of the corrupt Congress government, inspiring a similar movement in Bihar. In March 1974, veteran Gandhian socialist Jayaprakash Narayan took over the leadership of the movement in Bihar and called for a countrywide movement against corruption and Indira Gandhi's increasingly authoritarian rule. He later called for 'total revolution' to fight for a 'real people's democracy'. By late 1974, what became known as the JP movement had become more national in scope and was drawing together much of the major political opposition to Indira Gandhi: the Jana Sangh, RSS and its student wing Akhil Bharatiya Vidyarthi Parishad, the Socialists, and students.

The confrontation between Indira Gandhi and these multiple new opposition forces came to a head with the declaration of the Emergency and suspension of democracy in June 1975. Indira Gandhi justified the move as a means of leading the campaign against poverty that she saw being stymied in the political climate of the 1970s. But despite this rhetoric, the period of Emergency rule did little to enhance the capacity of government institutions to oversee social or economic change, or indeed their legitimacy.[79] In January 1977, Indira Gandhi suddenly announced an end to Emergency rule and elections were held in March, bringing to power the first non-Congress government in Delhi. The Janata government was a somewhat unlikely combination of the Bharatiya Jana Sangh (led by Atal Bihari Vajpayee, with the largest number of seats), Bharatiya Lok Dal (led by Charan Singh), Congress (O) (led by Morarji Desai), the Socialist Party, and the Congress for Democracy (led by Jagjivan Ram). The constituent parties were united mainly by their opposition to Indira Gandhi, but had also signed up to a programme of 'Gandhian socialism' founded on political and economic decentralisation.[80] The government did not, however, last long. Morarji Desai was dethroned as prime minister in July 1979, and Charan Singh briefly became Prime Minister with the support of Indira Gandhi's Congress before fresh elections were held in 1980.

Political Change and Territorial Thinking

Throughout this period the Jana Sangh was seeking to establish itself as part of the 'legitimate opposition'. The central government took a tougher line against Hindu nationalists following several major communal riots between 1967 and 1970.[81] We see at this time the origins of the party's later thinking about the territorial organisation of India's federal system. The Jana Sangh responded to the government's tougher line against Hindu nationalism, the new landscape of oppositional movements and the shift in political communication under Indira Gandhi by attenuating its emphasis on Hindu militancy and themes of national strength and unity. Under Atal Bihari Vajpayee's leadership, from 1968–73, the Jana Sangh gave greater prominence to socioeconomic themes. As the party sought to integrate itself further with the legitimate opposition, firstly as part of the JP movement and then as part of the Janata Party, it increasingly downplayed Hindu nationalism. Instead it paid more attention to themes of political and economic decentralisation which were in keeping with the JP movement's 'Gandhian socialism'.[82] L.K. Advani, who took over from Vajpayee as President of the party in 1973 was a staunch advocate of decentralisation. The emphasis on decentralisation by the Jana Sangh—and the Janata Party more broadly in the late 1970s—was offered as a counterweight to the increasing centralisation seen under Indira Gandhi.[83]

The Jana Sangh also began in this period to offer limited support for the reorganisation of state boundaries. It did so for two reasons: firstly as a pragmatic response to a movement for statehood in Telangana and the assertion of new regional movements in other areas, and secondly as a means of aligning itself with different strands of anti-Congress movements across India. By the late 1960s and early 1970s, a new set of demands for statehood had been raised on the grounds of regional inequality or what some commentators labelled 'internal colonialism'. These included the demands from Telangana and a new turn in the statehood demand for Jharkhand. The development of peripheral nationalist or regional movements was not unique to India in this period. Indeed the appearance of such movements in advanced industrial countries including the UK, Canada and Spain led to a spate of new theories about regionalism, frequently relating the rise of political regionalism to geographically uneven trajectories of capitalist development. At their most basic, such theories argued that relative socioeconomic deprivation was the cause of regional movements.[84] The school of internal colonialism, by contrast, held that 'ethnoregional movements are most likely to occur in economically dependent territories with ethnically distinctive populations that are characterised by hierarchical cultural divisions of labour.'[85] An instrumental approach to the mobilisation of regional identities suggested that the strength or success of demands arising from the perception of regional neglect or internal colonialism depended on the extent to which elites could fuse cultural or ethnic identities with a sense of a 'backward' developmental profile to create a distinctive political identity.[86]

The Jana Sangh's thinking about federal structures developed in light of these new regional movements, especially that in Telangana. The Telugu-speaking regions of the domain of the Nizam of Hyderabad had been amalgamated with Andhra Pradesh in 1956, but they were a dry agricultural zone in contrast to the well-irrigated coastal districts of the state.[87] The regional agitation that began there in 1969 was driven by discontent among teachers and government officers about competition from better qualified coastal Andhrans, as well as the immigration of farmers from coastal regions to Telangana where they could buy land more cheaply.[88] In an April 1969 resolution, the Jana Sangh said: 'Admitting the validity of the reasons for the current agitation for a separate Telangana, Jana Sangh feels concerned about it.'[89] Only two months earlier, the Central Working Committee had resolved that the party 'disapproves of the separate Telangana demand and urges the people of both regions to exert jointly for the welfare of the State'.[90]

Four years later, as part of a lengthy resolution on the country's 'Internal Situation' in the Kanpur meeting of the Jana Sangh in February 1973, the party demonstrated its aim to harness certain types of regional movement as part of an oppositional strategy against Congress. Recognising the spreading public unrest in many parts of the country as the JP movement gathered pace, the Jana Sangh highlighted the movement in the Telangana region of Andhra Pradesh and called for the immediate bifurcation of the state. This was the first time that the Jana Sangh had explicitly supported any demand for statehood. The Jana Sangh used the symbolism of the Telangana agitation—in a region of India's first linguistic state, Andhra Pradesh—to challenge the idea of states organised according to ethnicity or language. The party argued that the 'powerful mass movement' in Telangana was evidence of the 'undue importance given to language and the indifference shown to considerations of economic development and administrative efficiency in the re-organisation of states'.[91] By supporting the creation of Telangana, the Jana Sangh reasserted its opposition to multinational federalism by arguing that economic imbalances should be the foremost reason for creating states and not distinct regional (linguistic or religious) identities. The party went on to call for the establishment of a second, impartial States Reorganisation Commission to examine other pending demands for statehood keeping in view the 'considerations of economic development and administrative convenience'.[92]

The creation of new states was not part of the Janata Party's official platform when the coalition came to power in 1977. The party's manifestos clung strictly to the theme of decentralising economic and political power to the village level, as well as the desirability of smaller districts and development blocks. They did not mention new states.[93] Yet several senior leaders within the Janata Party—especially from the Jana Sangh and Choudhury Charan Singh's Bharatiya Lok Dal (with its stronghold in western Uttar Pradesh)—were known to be sympathetic to the idea of dividing large states. Jayaprakash Narayan had also given his blessing to the division of Bihar and Uttar Pradesh.[94] This emboldened Janata politicians while new state governments were in office in 1977 to promote the idea of statehood in all three of the Hindi-speaking states that were eventually split in 2000: Bihar, Madhya Pradesh and Uttar Pradesh. In Jharkhand, Jana Sangh politicians and a handful of others (beyond the existing Jharkhand parties or movement) began calling for statehood for south Bihar; in Chhattisgarh, Socialist politicians called for statehood, and in Uttar Pradesh, Janata politicians called for statehood in Uttarakhand. These calls for statehood, which will be discussed in chapters three to five, were not pushed by the state-level Janata leadership in any state. In Bihar especially they became a source of tension between alliance partners within the Janata coalition. But in general they demonstrated a growing willingness among politicians in different non-Congress parties to question the existing boundaries of Hindi-speaking states.

1980s: Regional Conflicts and Rising Hindu Nationalism

Although Indira Gandhi returned to power in the 1980 elections, Congress' continued ability to form national governments across the decade provided a misleading impression of the party's strength. After the fleeting opposition unity seen in the 1970s, it was fragmentation among opposition parties that gave an advantage to Congress in the 1980s.

India, in this period, was characterised by political scientists such as Manor and Kohli as suffering from a 'crisis of governability', in which political institutions struggled to respond to the increasing demands placed upon them, and were unable to contain violence.[95] One response to this new situation by Indira Gandhi was to appeal to Hindu chauvinism and national unity. This was in part an attempt to communicate with voters of northern and central India in the absence of a well-functioning party organisation able to dispense patronage.[96] It was also another example of Indira Gandhi seeking to undermine the non-Congress opposition by adopting their clothes: in 1969 this had pushed her towards the space occupied by the Marxist left. In the early 1980s, this meant adopting the language of Hindu chauvinism and positioning herself as the defender of national unity.

The Bharatiya Janata Party was formed on 5 April 1980 by former Jana Sangh members. While ex-Jana Sanghis comprised the bulk of the membership of the new party, the BJP also welcomed Janata Party leaders with no prior association with Hindu nationalism and claimed to be committed to upholding the Gandhian socialist part of the Janata Party's programme.[97] There was some agreement among observers of Indian politics in the early 1980s that the BJP represented a genuinely new party, less uncompromising in its tactics and more porous than the Jana Sangh.[98] Some distance was established between the RSS and the BJP in this period, and themes of Hindu nationalism and national unity were since less prominent. There was also some continuity with the Jana Sangh's shift to emphasise socioeconomic issues in the 1970s. When it came to regionalism, the BJP built on the Jana Sangh's evolving and opportunistic policy platform. Their policy initially evolved in reaction to the recentralising moves of Indira Gandhi after she returned to power in 1980, and later in response to the more accommodating stance of Rajiv Gandhi in the early years of his premiership. By the late 1980s the party came to set out a more consistent platform. It promoted the rights of states vis-à-vis the central government but increasingly also called for a federal system that reflected the idea of India as a 'Hindu nation'. Support for new states and non-secessionist regional movements became part of this platform.

In 1982, the Congress (I) under Indira Gandhi sought to weaken the opposition governments of several states by talking up the threats to national unity from 'anti-national' minorities, using a language that had been more associated with the Jana Sangh and Sangh Parivar in previous decades. She took an especially hard line against regional movements in Punjab and Kashmir, with the result of substantially inflaming secessionist sentiment.[99] The central government also abandoned its previous position of relative neutrality towards regional conflicts.[100] Indira Gandhi was especially preoccupied with the supposed threats to Congress dominance posed by the mainly Muslim National Conference government in Jammu and Kashmir, and the Sikh-led Akali Dal in Punjab. In Punjab her strategy since the late 1970s had been to patronise Sikh extremists (especially Jarnail Singh Bhindranwale) in a bid to weaken the Akali Dal, leading ultimately to the ill-fated Operation Blue Star in which security forces entered the Golden Temple in Amritsar to clear it of militants. In the 1983 state elections in Jammu and Kashmir, the Congress campaigned against the discrimination shown towards the Hindu south of the state, as well as the 'anti-national' role of the National Conference leader Farooq Abdullah.[101] In 1984, however, Indira Gandhi was assassinated at the hands of her Sikh bodyguards and Rajiv Gandhi was elected in the ensuing elections.

For the first eighteen months of his premiership, Rajiv Gandhi was more accommodating of both opposition parties and regional movements than his mother had been. This was exemplified by a 1985 accord in Assam, an agreement with Mizo leader Laldenga to form the state of Mizoram (which came into being in 1987, along with Arunachal Pradesh), accommodative overtures to the Akalis in Punjab and statements on Gorkhaland and Jharkhand.[102] But from 1986 he too changed tack. Important events, in this respect, included the Shah Bano case, following which Rajiv Gandhi introduced the Muslim Women Bill in 1987 as a concession to conservative Muslim opinion; renewed Sikh militancy in Punjab; and the beginning of a new phase of militancy in Kashmir, following elections which were widely held to have been rigged. Rajiv Gandhi's authority was further brought into question by the Bofors corruption controversy in 1986 and stalled attempts to undertake limited steps towards economic liberalisation. As Brass argues, ongoing crises in Punjab, Kashmir and Assam highlighted a major structural tension in the Indian political system between the centralising drives of the state 'in a society where the predominant long-term social, economic and political tendencies are toward pluralism, regionalism and decentralisation'.[103] The divergent responses of the BJP and other non-Congress opposition parties to such crises began to set out the dividing lines for political competition from the 1990s. The topic of centre-state relations, and, especially, critiques of Congress' centralising tendencies, provided areas of agreement among the opposition. However, the growing assertion of a Hindu nationalist platform by the BJP in the second half of the 1980s created stronger dividing lines among opposition parties.

In the early 1980s, the BJP had maintained some distance from the Sangh Parivar.[104] It also became a stronger proponent of states' rights in India's federal system and emphasised the need for a decentralisation of power. It did so in a way that was consistent with its earlier opposition to the idea of 'multinational' federalism and its preference for a strong central government. In its 1980 founding policy document, *Our Five Commitments*, the BJP set out a critique of the rise of 'authoritarian forces' (the Emergency and subsequent dissolution of several state assemblies) stating that it is a weak Centre which 'has a tendency to become corrupt and authoritarian'. The BJP supported a strong Centre, but also asserted that a strong Centre on its own is not a bulwark against authoritarianism. Instead, what was needed was for states to also possess adequate powers: both the Centre and states must be powerful.[105] To support the strengthening of the Centre and the states, the party proposed a further reorganisation of states:

Most of the major States of India, which are relatively underdeveloped, are too unwieldy for efficient administration and integrated planned development. The Indian experience is that, generally speaking, whenever big States were broken up and formed into smaller States, development picked up momentum. BJP strongly supports the demand for smaller viable States and will work for creating a consensus on the subject so that a smooth territorial transformation can take place.[106]

In a 1983 resolution on Centre-State relations, the party again reiterated its support for creating new states. The resolution suggested the 'reorganisation of some unwieldy states into smaller, more manageable states for better administration and quicker economic development'.[107] It also recommended an increase in the devolution of funds to the states, for example by raising states' share of central excise, corporation tax and customs duties. The party's national executive argued that protecting states' rights did not mean accepting the idea of India as a multinational federation. The party leadership criticised the fact that 'the Centre has all along weakened the states in gross violation of the letter and spirit of our Constitution', as well as asserting that:

The existence of states cannot...be allowed to dilute the sense of 'Indianness' and total loyalty to a single entity identified in national consciousness as 'Bharat Mata'. States must be recognised as vital political units, but there is no question of their becoming centres of parallel or conflicting loyalty.[108]

This resolution was passed shortly after the central government had appointed the Sarkaria Commission to review centre-state relations.[109] By raising the idea of creating new states, the BJP built on the Jana Sangh's 1973 policy shift embodied in the recommendation for a second States Reorganisation Commission and further drove home two key points that made the party's position distinctive. Firstly, they emphasised the ideological consistency between support for regional movements and the party's wish to make state and nation congruent. The BJP's vision emphatically rejected a view of Indian federalism as a structure that recognised multiple 'nations' within India, although it did tone down some of its more assimilationist rhetoric towards minorities before the 1984 elections.[110] Secondly, the party appeared willing to use support for regional movements opportunistically as part of its oppositional strategy. Centre-state relations had become an increasingly important dividing line between the Congress (I) and opposition parties. Opposition to Congress during the heyday of the 'Congress system' had been confined to particular regions, helping to preserve Congress dominance. What was new in this period was that national parties—and newer regional parties—were increasingly seeking to make links between regional oppositional spaces at an abstract, all-India level. Support for small states as a matter of principle thus became an increasingly prominent part of the BJP's stand on centre-state relations from 1980 onwards because it helped to make links between geographically separate regions for which statehood was proposed. But at this stage the party had not offered its official support to any specific demands for statehood and was no longer raising the issue of Telangana at the national level.

The BJP's thinking on territorial reorganisation took further shape following their disastrous performance in the 1984 elections when they won only two parliamentary seats. As L.K. Advani recalls, one significant recommendation of the working group set up to assess the reasons for the BJP's losses in the 1984 elections, was the assertion of the need to strengthen and broadcast the party's distinct ideological appeal.[111] This specifically meant reinforcing Deendayal Upadhyaya's philosophy of 'integral humanism' as the party's basic philosophy. This was a vision of society that stressed its organic unity, harmony and absence of conflict. If at all the party had toned down its assimilationist rhetoric towards minorities in its 1984 manifesto by recognising the composite nature of the Indian nation, the reassertion of integral humanism after the elections put the emphasis back on the unity of 'unity in diversity'. The working group asserted:

Long back the ancient Indian genius had enunciated the principle *Yat Pinde Tad Brahmande* ('That' what is in whole is also in parts, or the 'part' and the 'whole' are manifestations of one and the same reality).[112]

From 1986, when L.K. Advani had taken over again as party president, the party returned to more explicit communal modes of mobilisation. In addition to what Christophe Jaffrelot and Paul Brass call the instrumentalist use of ethno-religious themes to bolster a sense of Hindu community,[113] the rise of the BJP was supported by social changes that had been occurring in preceding decades, not least the politicisation of the lower castes and rise of a larger middle class. As Corbridge and Harriss write, the BJP found increasing support as a result of the growth of a middle class straddling town and countryside and a sense of the 'weakening of "traditional authority" [as a result of lower-caste mobilisation] which has…built up a sense of a threatened social order for which the BJP seems now to provide the main defence'.[114] Thomas Blom Hansen agrees: 'The growing responsiveness within [urban middle classes] to Hindu nationalist discourses revolving around themes of the endangered nation was conditioned by what was felt as a sense of encroachment on their social world by ascending groups of peasants, traders and entrepreneurs.'[115]

In this period, its pronouncements on federalism and regional movements focused increasingly on the need for a federal system that reflected the idea of India as a Hindu nation. The idea of devolving greater powers to the states in order to check an authoritarian centre—which it (and other opposition parties) had discussed while Indira Gandhi was in power—was increasingly sidelined by the BJP. But it continued to call for the creation of smaller states. In January 1987, against the backdrop of renewed militancy in Punjab, L.K. Advani set out again the party's thinking on state creation in his presidential speech to the BJP's national council in Vijayawada. This is the fullest statement of the thinking that underpinned the BJP's theoretical support for creating more states within the federal system. Advani highlighted India's unusual constitutional provision which allows the central government to alter state boundaries on the basis of a simple parliamentary majority. He used this to argue that there was no constitutional basis for the idea of India as a multinational federation, or even as a federation at all. In this 1987 speech, he also first recommended a commission to examine the suitability of a presidential system to contain 'centrifugal tendencies'. He justified the creation of further states on the grounds of better administration:

One Country One People

Rajiv Gandhi's *volte face* on the Anandpur Sahib resolution, his agreement with Laldenga on Mizoram and his statements on Gorkhaland lend strength to that school of opinion which regards India not as a nation of many States, but as a State of many nations.

India is not a Multi-national state

The BJP rejects this thesis of a multi-national state. India is multi-lingual, it is multi-religious; but it is still one nation. Indians are one people. The Indian Constitution is also based on this acceptance. It is, therefore, that our Constitution-makers made the Indian Republic federal in form but essentially unitary in content. No Parliament of any real federation would be conceded the right to alter boundaries of any state, and even amalgamate two or more States into one. Article 3 empowers the Indian Parliament to do this, and that too, by a simple majority! Constitutional Pundits have, therefore, described India as *an indissoluble Union of destructible states*. Protagonists of the multi-nation-state theory (most advocates of 'true federalism' belong to this category) would very much like to see this appellation inverted.

Unity before Diversity

India is rightly proud of the fact that our nationhood is an example of unity in diversity. But this is also an unfortunate fact that while all through the freedom struggle and in the early years of independence, this dictum *unity in diversity* always had unity boldly underlined, these days everyone keeps emphasising *diversity*.

Advani went on to propose a comprehensive review of the constitution to consider, among other things:

The need to redraw the political map of India with needs of development and administration as the principal consideration; the ad hoc responses to agitations have resulted in having states varying in size from half a million to one hundred million. Some of the larger states are stagnating principally because of their unwieldy size.

What would contribute more to the strengthening of our nation-state; a centralised federal polity as we have at present, or a decentralised unitary set-up, with power decentralised not merely to 20 odd states but to some 60 or so janapadas, or provinces?[116]

The BJP's subsequent 1989 general election manifesto argued that:

Indian constitution is quasi-federal. It envisages strong states with a strong Centre. The BJP also recognises that regional imbalances have developed in some states because of their size. The party stands for the formation of smaller states that are economically and administratively viable.

For the first time the party called specifically for the creation of Uttaranchal and Vananchal, the granting of full statehood to Delhi and the status of Union Territory to Ladakh.

At the national level, the BJP's support for creating more states was projected as consistent with the doctrine of Integral Humanism, and it sat alongside the renewed emphasis on Hindu nationalism and national unity. At the regional level, as will be seen in chapters three and four, the politics that led local leaders of the BJP to support specific demands for statehood were frequently more pragmatic than the ideological pronouncements of the national leadership. However, the distinction between the language at both levels was not watertight. National leaders were not blind to the potential electoral advantages of supporting state creation. Indeed, the party's support for specific regional movements could be seen as a precursor to the party's later strategy of forming electoral alliances with regional parties in southern and eastern India in order to facilitate an expansion of the party's social base once the electoral limits of Hindutva had been reached.[117] To an extent, then, this was part of the process by which the BJP became more of a 'normal' party and compromised with local political conditions. The accommodation of diverse regional circumstances was in the spirit of a shift towards making the BJP 'more of an aggregative party with a strong ideological identity' favoured by L.K. Advani, and the working group set up to investigate the 1984 elections.[118] This accommodation also helps to explain how the regionalisation of politics that was taking place in this period did not pose an insurmountable threat to the expansion of the BJP. Indeed, tailoring the party to specific regions within states was an important step in the electoral expansion of the BJP. As E. Sridharan writes, the BJP had essentially been a 'sub-regional' (that is, sub-state) force until it formed its first state governments in Madhya Pradesh, Himachal Pradesh, Gujarat and Rajasthan in 1990.[119]

The need to give greater autonomy to the states was pursued more vigorously by other non-Congress opposition parties such as the Janata Dal, CPM and various regional parties in the late 1980s, as well as some in Congress and other opinion makers in the media and academia.[120] Thus, clearer dividing lines began to appear between the BJP and other non-Congress parties about centre-state relations and the appropriate response to the regionalisation of the polity. Despite the divergent emphases of the BJP and other opposition parties, however, the 1989 Lok Sabha elections were fought under an umbrella of opposition unity that, as Nirmal Mukarji and George Mathew write, was 'basically an effort to reflect India's essentially federal polity'. The elections became a contest between a ruling party (Congress) that had come to embody 'unitary and centralised governance' and an opposition grouping which projected a 'federal alternative'.[121]

The New Federal Political Order from 1989

In 1989, India entered its third electoral system.[122] Since 1989, Congress has no longer been the 'natural party' of government, and no single party has won enough seats to form a government on its own at the national level. The decade from 1989 to 1999 saw a succession of relatively unstable national regimes, with six general elections held in total. From 1999 onwards, two national alliances led by the BJP (1999–2004) and Congress (2004–09; 2009–) with a variety of regional allies have formed governments.

Three major trends have dominated the period since 1989. The first is connected to a further deepening of the social basis of democratic participation and the rise of lower caste parties and political mobilisation in north India. After the 1989 elections, a National Front government led by the Janata Dal came to power in New Delhi. The Janata Dal brought together Socialists and the inheritors of Charan Singh's agrarian politics around a common agenda of social justice for lower castes.[123] It was at this point that in two major states of the Hindi belt—Bihar and Uttar Pradesh—lower caste Chief Ministers came to power: Mulayam Singh Yadav in Uttar Pradesh in 1989, and Lalu Prasad Yadav in Bihar in 1990, marking the beginning of new party systems in both states in

which Congress dominance was decisively challenged. The implementation of the Mandal Commission recommendations for affirmative action
in government employment for OBCs in 1990 heralded the crystallisa-
tion of a lower caste political front. Yadav describes a 'second democratic
upsurge' that took place in the 1990s, as lower castes and classes became
as, and in some states more, likely to participate in politics than their
more socioeconomically privileged counterparts.[124]

The second trend after 1989 was the intensification of a Hindu
nationalist politics, symbolised in the destruction of the Babri Masjid
(mosque) in Ayodhya and the continuing campaign to build a Ram
Mandir on its site. The prominence of the politics of Mandal and Mandir represented two attempts to define new national political blocs.
Neither has succeeded on its own terms at an all-India level, but parties
representing lower castes have become important in states such as Bihar
and Uttar Pradesh, while the BJP has been a major challenger at a
national level since 1989, forming its first state governments in 1990.
The third trend is associated with economic liberalisation, which has its
roots in policy changes in the 1980s, but was confirmed in 1991, with
a more determined shift towards the reform of trade and industrial
licensing systems in the face of economic crisis.

One of the most important consequences of these trends—especially
the first and third—has been the rise in the prominence of the state level
in India's political arena. As Yogendra Yadav and Suhas Palshikar write,
'In the last two decades, state politics has broken free of the logic of
national politics and has acquired a logic of its own…If the people voted
in state assembly elections held in 1970s and 1980s as if they were
choosing the prime minister, they now vote in the parliamentary elections as if they are choosing their chief minister.'[125]

Since 1989, national election results have been best read as the amalgamation of multiple state-level contests. Not only have states been the
major locus of lower caste politics, they have also become increasingly
powerful economic actors. India's fiscal federal relations have seen a shift
from 'cooperative federalism' based on cooperation between the central
government and states towards 'inter-jurisdictional competition', as
states compete with each other to attract investment.[126] Thus political
and economic decentralisation have worked in tandem.

In terms of the story of federal reorganisation from 1989 onwards,
the increasing importance of the state level is most notable. In the con-

text of new patterns of political competition in Hindi-speaking states in north and central India, the idea of changing state boundaries or subdividing states began to receive greater political attention within state capitals, as well as within regions for which statehood was proposed. This was a result of attempts by regional parties and regional outfits of national parties to politically mobilise or incorporate lower castes. Because of the mismatch between the geographical spread of particular clusters of lower caste *jatis* and the existing borders of north Indian states, new political leaders made regionalised appeals that either reached out to particular social groups concentrated in one part of their state, or implicitly or explicitly excluded voters in another part of the state. In Bihar, Madhya Pradesh and Uttar Pradesh, changing electoral geographies meant that the idea of changing state borders became a subject for political discussion within the parent states as a whole—not only in the regions for which statehood was demanded. The 1980s had seen the BJP—a national party—adopt a clear policy in favour of states reorganisation in the abstract, and of statehood for specific regions. In the 1990s, however, it was dynamics at the state level that were arguably most important in pushing forward the idea of dividing of Bihar, Madhya Pradesh and Uttar Pradesh in 2000. These shifts destabilised earlier rationales for the size of states in the Hindi heartland and opened up the possibility of a wider restructuring of political and economic life via a change in state boundaries.

Conclusion

Patterns of social, economic and political power underpin maps of the internal borders of the federal system. This chapter has demonstrated how processes of political and economic change helped first to establish and then to unsettle the stability of state boundaries in the Hindi heartland, introducing new forms of political discourse and mobilisation that brought the territorial structures of federal institutions into question. The role of the BJP was of central importance in the story of state creation in 2000. Yet its thinking about federalism was crafted as a compromise between ideologies of Hindu nationalism and the political environment in which it negotiated its rise to political power from the 1970s onwards. Changes to state-level politics, especially the decline of upper caste political dominance as a result of the political mobilisation of lower castes in north and central India, were also necessary conditions for state creation. They encouraged political leaders at the centre of the states of Bihar, Madhya Pradesh and Uttar Pradesh by the 1990s, to countenance their bifurcation: something, as will be analysed in chapter five, that their predecessors would not have done. First, however, we must turn to the regions of Jharkhand, Chhattisgarh and Uttarakhand themselves in order to understand the forms of social mobilisation and politics in these regions and how they connect to the discourses of federal political thought at the all-India level, outlined in this chapter.

3

SOCIAL MOVEMENTS, POLITICAL PARTIES
AND STATEHOOD[1]

JHARKHAND AND UTTARAKHAND

Of the three regions that attained statehood in 2000, Jharkhand had the longest running movement for statehood. Multiple parties, outfits and actors had campaigned for a separate state, employing different tactics, arguments and with different degrees of intensity. In the 1970s, the Jharkhand Mukti Morcha, like the Chipko movement in Uttarakhand, carved out a new space of social activism focused on social and economic issues. In their early years, they both operated largely independently of electoral politics and political parties The JMM built on a much longer history of a demand for a tribal state led by the Jharkhand Party. But, in the 1970s statehood was not the movement's sole goal; it pursued a wider agenda focused on the marginalisation of local people within the region's fast growing industrial economy. By the 1980s, increasing competition within social movements and interactions between political parties, social movements and the state, in both its accommodating and coercive guises, began to encourage the renewed and more determined pursuit of statehood.

Social movements therefore played a leading role in demanding statehood in Jharkhand. By contrast, in Uttarakhand, the Chipko movement that began in the hill region in the early 1970s as a protest against commercial forestry and the state's management of forests did not align itself strongly with the idea of statehood at all. Indeed social movement activists in Uttarakhand were at first hostile to the idea of statehood, seeing it as an idea pushed by political parties from outside or not a fitting solution to the issues they raised. Yet in Uttarakhand too, statehood became a more pressing priority from the 1980s onwards as a result of the interactions between social movements and political parties, in the context of changing policies towards forest management and the increasing commercial penetration of the hills. Some groups within the social movement sphere began to take up the demand for statehood as a means to secure greater local control over the hill economy. They were joined by a new political party, the Uttarakhand Kranti Dal, which campaigned for statehood on the grounds that the region was being neglected within Uttar Pradesh and that policy-makers in the plains did not understand the unique needs of the hills. It was in 1994, however, in the context of the consolidation of lower caste political mobilisation in the plains of Uttar Pradesh that statehood became the subject of mass mobilisation across the hills. A protest movement drew together in 1994–95 a diverse coalition of social groups including students, ex-servicemen, government officials and women's organisations in months of protests, blockades and disruption of local services.

This chapter looks at why statehood became a singular objective for social movement actors from the late 1980s onwards, and why some political parties, especially the BJP, also adopted statehood as a goal. In both Jharkhand and Uttarakhand, unlike Chhattisgarh, where no popular movement emerged, social movement actors and political parties came to focus more single-mindedly on the achievement of statehood as a priority in itself and as a means of achieving control of the state. I will show that interactions between social movement actors, political parties and the state helped to produce a focus on statehood that functioned as a lowest common denominator among actors with divergent interests. The relative local consensus in favour of a new state thus can be seen as a compromise which developed within specific regional contexts, but against the larger backdrop of political and economic change across India outlined in the previous chapter.

Social Movements and Political Parties

Popular mobilisation via social movements in Jharkhand and Uttarakhand rose and fell in intensity, shifting in site and even in target. However, there were definable historical movements drawing on shared repertoires of action, and embedded within their respective local political economies. Specific factors of context and contingency were important. There were nonetheless common elements in the transmission of the idea of focusing on a demand for statehood from social movements to electoral politics in both Jharkhand and Uttarakhand.

The new forms of social movements that were formed in the 1970s have typically been analysed in isolation from electoral politics. This is in part because they presented a critique of established political parties and their failure to represent issues affecting the poor and those marginalised within prevailing processes of development. Authors such as Gail Omvedt and Smitu Kothari have argued that the new social movements of the 1970s in India were a response to the failures of established organisations of the left such as political parties, trade unions and intellectuals to represent such issues.[2] However since the 1970s there has arguably been a symbiosis between the development of social movements, the transformation of the Congress Party from the dominant party of Indian politics, and the emergence of new political parties. Political parties have, at times, adopted characteristics of social movements, developed alliances with them or co-opted some of their goals and members. Social movements themselves have been influenced by their interactions with political parties and the electoral sphere. In developing such an argument in this chapter, I extend the insights of a recent body of literature about social movements that emphasises the porosity of the boundary between institutionalised and non-institutionalised politics, or between social movements, political parties and the state.[3] As Jack Goldstone has argued, social movements in most of the world have become an essential part of 'normal politics' whose 'actors, fates and organisations' are often closely intertwined with political parties. They are not simply 'challengers' outside the polity.[4] Actors within social movements change their strategies, and sometimes their goals, in light of the political context within which they operate.

Social movements comprise multiple organisations whose prominence and activities vary over time. As Mario Diani suggests:

Social movements cannot be reduced to specific insurrections or revolts, but rather resemble strings of more or less connected events, scattered across time and space; they cannot be identified with any specific organisation either, rather, they consist of groups and organisations, with various levels of formalisation, linked in patterns of interaction which run from the fairly centralised to the totally decentralised, from the cooperative to the explicitly hostile.[5]

Social movements can be seen as consisting of a 'process whereby several different actors…come to elaborate, through either joint action and/or communication, a shared definition of themselves as being part of the same side in a social conflict'.[6] Organisations or actors within social movements frequently vary in their positions on issues, tactics and relationships with other 'non-movement' actors.

Situating the Jharkhand Statehood Demand

The demand for a Jharkhand state is one of the oldest movements for regional autonomy in India. 'Jharkhand' literally means 'forest region', denoting the thick forests that cover almost 30 per cent of the state's geographical area. The demand for statehood has gone hand in hand with the articulation of *adivasi* identity and the development of the region as India's first hub for heavy industry. The new state of Jharkhand is comprised of the former Chotanagpur and Santal Parganas districts of south Bihar. The Chotanagpur plain contains as much as 40 per cent of India's mineral wealth and has been at the heart of industrial development in India since the extension of the railways to reach its coalfields in the late nineteenth century. In 1907, Jamshedji Tata set up a steel plant in what came to be called Jamshedpur, a company town. After independence, industrial towns such as Rourkela, Ranchi and Bokaro were developed, as well as a number of projects to harness the power-generating potential of Jharkhand's supplies of coal and water, including the Damodar Valley Corporation, Patratu Thermal Power Project, Koel Karo Hydel Project, Subarnarekha Multipurpose Project. Agriculture in Jharkhand is predominantly rain-fed, with the bulk of investment in irrigation having been directed historically towards north Bihar. Writing the history of Jharkhand's ethno-regional movement, tribal politics and political economy has become a mini-industry in its own right.[7] In this chapter, I seek to build on the insights of existing literature rather than replicating it, while adding a new emphasis on the operation of political parties and their intersection with the Jharkhand movement.

The first demand for an *adivasi* state surfaced in the 1920s at the time of the Simon Commission (appointed to examine India's constitutional situation). The history of tribal rebellion in Chotanagpur, however, goes back to the nineteenth century. From 1910, several organisations led by missionaries and Christian tribal youth such as the Chotanagpur Unnati Samaj (Chotanagpur Improvement Society) sought to promote education and economic development among *adivasis*. These organisations came together in 1937 after the first provincial elections, held in 1935, to form the more militant Adivasi Mahasabha, led by Jaipal Singh, as an alternative to Congress.[8] The Mahasabha was renamed the Jharkhand Party after independence and became the main opposition party in Bihar in 1952, contesting elections on the platform of statehood for Jharkhand. The tribal state demanded by the Jharkhand Party (and some later political formations) included not only the Chotanagpur and Santal Parganas districts of Bihar but, as Map 5 shows, neighbouring tribal-dominated districts of Central Provinces (today's Chhattisgarh), Orissa and later West Bengal. The support base of the Jharkhand Party was largely urban, with a leadership drawn from a tribal elite in the Chotanagpur region. Its influence started to wane in the late 1950s, however, and in 1963 Jaipal Singh agreed to a merger with the Congress Party.

Until this point, Jharkhand regionalism had been closely associated with the assertion of an *adivasi* identity, aimed at forging a group sentiment among Mundas, Oraons, Santals, Hos and dozens of smaller tribal communities, as distinct from caste Hindus in the plains or *dikus* or exploitative 'outsiders'. Much has been written about the assertion of identities based on indigeneity from the nineteenth century until the present in Chotanagpur, which underlaid the demand for a tribal state made by the Jharkhand Party.[9] Intimate connections were posited between tribal communities—or *adivasis*—and the local forest environment that had been disrupted by the colonial state, landlords and moneylenders. Local communities had protested against such incursions in Tamar in 1816, in the Birsa Munda uprising in the 1890s, the Tana Bhagat movement in the early twentieth century and at other moments. As Vinita Damodaran suggests, the mapping of the *diku* or 'outsider' in these resistance movements helped to provide a new sense of community and more radical consciousness. The term '*adivasi*' came into usage in the early twentieth century. Colonial writings and systems of census classification, together with the activities of missionaries, also helped to reinforce a notion of difference between tribals and plains Hindus.[10]

However, as Corbridge has shown, economic differentiation among *adivasis* as well as the changing demography of the region, especially the

Map 5: Jharkhand, showing Greater Jharkhand.

declining concentration of Scheduled Tribes in the population, helped to fracture the Jharkhand movement, and weaken the claim for statehood on the basis of tribal identity alone.[11] Along with the changing government classification of tribes and non-tribes, migration altered Jharkhand's demography.[12] Industrial development attracted migrants from the plains of Bihar and elsewhere, and large numbers of *adivasis* migrated for work outside Jharkhand. By 2001, only 26.3 per cent of Jharkhand's population were officially categorised as Scheduled Tribes in the census.[13]

JHARKHAND AND UTTARAKHAND

By the late 1960s and early 1970s, in this changing context, a new phase of mobilisation began. Several organisations were formed in the late 1960s in the vacuum that remained after the Jharkhand Party's merger with Congress. But it was the establishment of the Jharkhand Mukti Morcha (JMM) in 1972 that proved the most consequential. The JMM had a radical agrarian programme, working among Santal *adivasis* beyond the traditional areas of Jharkhand Party activity in Chotanagpur, and non-tribal Kurmi-Mahatos. This was combined with attempts to organise local mine workers who had been threatened with unemployment in the aftermath of the nationalisation of coal mines in 1971.[14] It attempted to redefine 'Jharkhandis' as oppressed working classes regardless of ethnicity; arguing that Jharkhand was treated as an 'internal colony' of Bihar in which local Jharkhandis were exploited in the service of Bihar—and India's—overall development.[15] A common refrain of supporters of statehood of many persuasions was that 70 per cent of Bihar's revenues came from Jharkhand, while only 30 per cent were invested in the region. This precise assertion has always been difficult to substantiate because of data limitations, but there is fairly strong evidence to suggest that the districts of south Bihar contributed a disproportionate amount to the tax base of the former state government.[16] While in the 1970s, statehood had not been the sole focus of the JMM, in the 1980s it was given a fresh pre-eminence by various parts of the Jharkhand movement. This reflected competition within the movement more than a united agenda. By the late 1980s, statehood had gained support from a wider range of actors, including, most prominently, the BJP.

All groups that have organised under the banner of Jharkhandi regionalism have had to find ways to come to terms with the contradiction thrown up by the reality of a differentiated regional economy and society, and yet the persistence of an 'ideal' of *adivasi* political community. Such an ideal is supported by the perpetuation of official categories and legislation that recognise and give meaning to 'scheduled tribes' and 'scheduled areas', as well as the strong cultural association of the idea of Jharkhand with a history of *adivasi* movements. The endeavour to project an *adivasi* politics in Jharkhand is quite different from the situation in neighbouring Chhattisgarh, where no such pan-*adivasi* identity has been well mobilised or linked historically to a statehood demand.

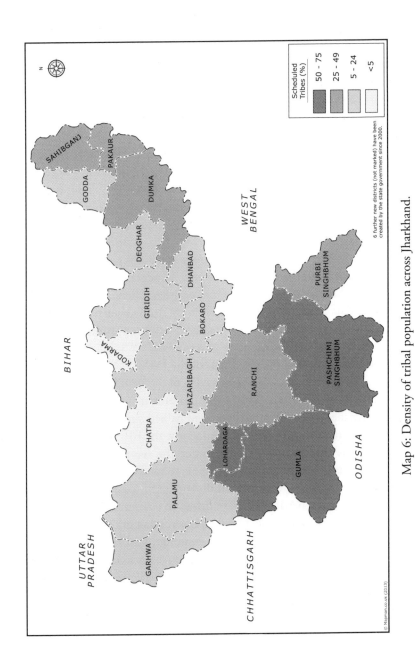

Map 6: Density of tribal population across Jharkhand.

New Social Movements and Non-electoral Politics in Jharkhand

The Jharkhand Mukti Morcha (JMM) thus emerged at a time of transition for the older Jharkhand movement. After the 1963 merger of the Jharkhand Party, the movement for Jharkhand had gone into decline. As Corbridge argues, this reflected the increasing economic differentiation among *adivasis*, in addition to the migration of non-tribals into the region, and the difficulties of maintaining a coherent 'tribal' politics in such a context.[17] A number of more radical local organisations emerged in the late 1960s but none with the profile that the JMM was to develop. The arrival of the JMM marked an important turning point for Jharkhand, introducing new forms of mobilisation around socioeconomic issues and a broader conceptualisation of Jharkhandi identity that deliberately appealed to the common class interests of tribal and non-tribal workers in the region.

The JMM was formed in late 1972 by the Bengali Marxist trade unionist A.K. Roy, Santal tribal leader Shibu Soren and Kurmi-Mahato leader Binod Bihari Mahato. A.K. Roy sought to create what Gail Omvedt heralds as India's first 'red-green movement' uniting urban trade union activities in the coal mining industries of Dhanbad and movements of the peasantry in neighbouring rural areas.[18] The JMM's agitations took place against a backdrop of stagnation across the agrarian sector, the transfer of land for industry and mining, the apparent flouting of land alienation laws, in addition to migration into the region. The JMM encouraged traditionally more prosperous groups (such as Kurmi-Mahatos) to make common cause with Santal *adivasis*—especially in areas which had not been strongholds of the old Jharkhand Party.[19]

Land was a major issue for the JMM. The Chotanagpur Tenancy Act 1908 had made the sale of tribal lands to non-tribals illegal, but considerable tribal land had changed hands nonetheless. A 1969 amendment mandated the restoration of lands that had been alienated in circumvention of the Act, but exemptions to the amendment and state indifference meant that little land was restored.[20] Groups of Santal *adivasis*, together with Kurmi-Mahatos, organised as part of Binod Bihari Mahato's Shivaji Samaj responded to this by forcibly harvesting paddy from land that had been alienated from tribals in what they called a *dhan katao andolan* ('cut down paddy' movement). They sought thereby to reclaim tribal land. The *dhan katao andolan* and land reclamation movements reached a climax in the harvests of 1974–75. Shibu Soren established an *ashram* in Tundi block of Giridih district, which became the centre of his agitations. The JMM, and Shibu Soren in particular, became known for delivering summary justice against landlords and moneylenders, even holding their own courts.[21] By the end of the Emergency, Shibu Soren had a number of cases registered against him, including an accusation of murder (along with scores of other defendants) in a notorious case in which a mob attacked a village to drive away outsiders.[22] In Tundi, where the JMM was best organised, it also introduced collective farming and encouraged collective action to reclaim wastelands. By early 1975, R.N. Maharaj and K.G. Iyer identified five villages covering 125 acres engaged in collective farming and wrote that through mass mobilisation the JMM had brought about a 'transformation in the social, economic and cultural milieu of the countryside'.[23] This may be an overstatement, but it is an indication of the reputation of the JMM in its early days. More generally the JMM, especially A.K. Roy, railed against Jharkhand's position as an 'internal colony' of Bihar, complaining about the marginalisation of local people in the fast developing industrial economy.[24]

In the late 1970s, the JMM took a leading role in protests against state forestry policies in Singhbhum. The Bihar Forest Development Corporation, established in 1975 to improve the management of forests, had started to cut down natural forest in Singhbhum and replace it with teak, a more profitable type of timber. The planting took place at first in areas where *adivasis* had few rights to land, but gradually also began in *khuntkhatti* forests in which *adivasis* supposedly had complete rights.[25] The Jharkhand Party led a one month protest against the teak plantations, calling for the protection of the traditional forest and sought to open negotiations with the government. When their negotiations failed, the JMM took over the protest and backed a *jungle katao andolan* ('Cut down the forest! movement'). The JMM encouraged the cutting down of teak trees with the aim of reclaiming land for cultivation.

Some writers and activists, including the Jharkhand Party, have played up the cultural dimensions of the *andolan*, emphasising the symbolic importance of the naturally growing *sal* trees to *adivasi* lifestyles. But other leaders involved in the *jungle katao andolan* stress that they saw the movement as being driven by opposition to the plantations, more than the protection of *sal* versus teak on cultural grounds. They saw the teak plantations as a continuation of a colonial mentality by the the Forest Department which used the forests as a source of revenue.[26] The police and the Forest Department repressed the movement forcefully, with several incidents of police firing on protestors—in Ichahatu on 6 November 1978, Serengda on 25 November 1978, and a brutal incident in which nine injured *adivasi* protestors were shot dead at a hospital in Gua on 8 September 1980.[27] Alongside the agitations associated with the JMM, a number of other protest movements took shape in this period, including the activities of Kisan Samitis of the far-left CPI (ML), sympathetic to the Naxalbari movement in neighbouring West Bengal. Protests also ensued against the displacement and alienation of tribal land to be entailed by major 'development' projects, notably the Koel Karo dam and the Subarnarekha River multipurpose project.

The JMM also demanded statehood, but this was not a primary tool of mobilisation. As has been shown, the JMM sought to provide leadership to existing protest movements and to mobilise people around a common identity of Jharkhandis as 'workers'. But the idea of Jharkhandi nationality did provide a useful frame to unite disparate threads of the movement. As a correspondent for the Indian journal *Economic and Political Weekly* wrote, what distinguished this turn of the Jharkhand movement was its use of direct action more than its commitment to achieving a concrete state:

None of the organisations, not even the Jharkhand party, is in great haste to get a separate state. The reason for the revival of the movement, according to Horo [leader of the Jharkhand Party], is to help the oppressed train themselves in mass struggles. Shibu Soren, the general secretary of Jharkhand Mukti Morcha, has a similar view: "Even if Jharkhand does not come into being in my lifetime, why should I be bothered? Our first concern is to chase away the bloodsuckers and help the people lead a respectable, quiet and fraternal life." According to A. K. Roy, the leader of Marxist Co-ordination Committee and Colliery Kamgar Union who is experimenting with the application of Marxism-Leninism "in its true spirit" in Dhanbad area, the Jharkhand movement is important because "the emancipation of the working class is impossible unless it is linked with the aspirations of the subjugated nationalities of Chotanagpur". It is clear that if Jharkhand comes into being, these organisations, which will then form the government, will take steps to "liberate" the people from the exploiters. But it is not that until Jharkhand is attained, the "liberation" should be postponed; what they would do as the government, the organisations are doing meanwhile, by mass struggles. That is when, as already pointed out, the current movement radically differs from Jaipal Singh's agitation. *To sum up, the current movement is basically for a political Jharkhand, and not for a territorial Jharkhand,* though this aim is never to be lost sight of. This is proved also by the latest trend of the movement to take into its fold also the adivasis of "Uttaranchal" (North Bihar). A committee called "Uttaranchal Bhartiya Adivasi Sangharsh Samiti" has recently been formed, under which banner the adivasis of Katihar, Purnea and other north Bihar districts are to organise themselves against the oppression of the landlords, moneylenders and the police. North Bihar is not to come within the boundaries of the proposed Jharkhand; and yet the leaders of Jharkhand nationalism have chosen to orga- nise the adivasis in that area (emphasis added).[28]

The JMM had a strong history of regional protest to draw on with a pre-existing claim to statehood on a cultural or ethnic basis. JMM lead- ers were quite aware of this. As Shibu Soren explained to me: 'At the beginning I told the others that establishing the JMM wasn't enough— we have to do something to unite the people. And the Jharkhand *andolan* is very old so we should support it and we should demand a new state.' He went on to suggest that a link to the Jharkhand move- ment was something of an act of translation, a bridging mechanism between the ideals of the JMM and the sphere of reference of the local people: 'I used to tell Roy-ji [A.K. Roy]…that the people in Jharkhand understand the language of Birsa Munda, Tilka Manjhi, Sidhu and Kanhu Murmu and Shekh Bhikhari [leaders of eighteenth and nine- teenth century revolts]. They don't understand the language of Lenin. People here have a right to land, forest and water.'[29] Furthermore, as another former JMM politician recollected, the JMM campaigned around local issues which had greater resonance in some areas than oth- ers, whereas statehood was popular throughout: 'We raised all these issues [forestry in Singhbhum; land alienation in Santal Parganas] but not in an organised way so we didn't get a good response in the Chotan- agpur region. But everyone supported the creation of Jharkhand.'[30] Yet despite consciousness of this framing, a push for statehood was not the driving force of the JMM's activities in the early 1970s. The turn (or return) towards a more determined focus on a 'territorial' Jharkhand by some actors in the movement requires explanation.

Reassertion of Statehood Demand

Three main factors explain why the demand for statehood was pushed with increasing determination, sometimes to the exclusion of other parts of the agenda of Jharkhand's social movements. In the first place, the election of a non-Congress government in Bihar after the Emergency in 1977, and of ex-Jana Sangh politicians in Jharkhand as part of this government, created space in electoral politics for a reconsideration of the Jharkhand demand. Secondly, competition within the Jharkhand movement itself, in light of Congress attempts at co-option from 1980 onwards, produced a new, more radical, youth wing of the movement and a cultural revivalist flank. Members of these new formations increasingly laid emphasis on the need for statehood for Jharkhand. Lastly, from the late 1980s, the BJP began to consolidate its electoral presence in Jharkhand at a time when it was expanding nationally. It enhanced its position in Jharkhand in a period in which Lalu Prasad Yadav's government came to power in Bihar, with its social base centred in north Bihar—outside Jharkhand. In the context of these three competing processes, statehood emerged as a common focal point. But the effective agreement about the institutional form—a new state—only papered over the conflicting agendas of those involved.

New Electoral Space

One factor that proved important in recentring the demand for a separate state was the defeat of Bihar's Congress state government after the Emergency and the election of a Janata government (1977–79) led by Chief Minister Karpoori Thakur. Thakur's politics consolidated the emergence of a backward-forward caste divide in Bihar's politics.[31] When he became Chief Minister as head of the Janata government in 1977, Thakur—from a Nai (barber) caste—reserved a proportion of posts in government and educational institutions for OBCs, and for the first time his ministry had more backward than forward caste ministers.[32] Though his government collapsed after the Jana Sangh pulled out, this period foreshadowed the political empowerment of the lower castes that was to have such a strong impact on the politics of Bihar and challenge the grip of upper castes on power. Karpoori Thakur was stridently opposed to the creation of Jharkhand while he was in office, even though—as shown in the previous chapter—various national Janata Party leaders had floated the idea of dividing the large states of north India. But the apparent support of the national leadership emboldened Janata politicians in Jharkhand, the largest number of whom were ex-

Jana Sangh (unlike Janata politicians in north Bihar), to make overtures of support to the Jharkhand movement. The ex-Jana Sangh politicians were also opposed to Thakur's reservation policies, giving them an additional reason to go against his line on Jharkhand. They set up a 'Sangarsh Samiti' (Struggle Committee) under the leadership of a non-Christian tribal, Lalit Oraon, and passed a resolution calling for the establishment of a state in Chotanagpur and Santal Parganas in September 1977. Significantly, the Sangarsh Samiti proposed a state comprised only of south Bihar—not the tribal dominated Greater Jharkhand traditionally demanded by the movement.

The Jana Sangh had begun to develop a presence in Jharkhand from the 1960s. The party's core constituency had been among the non-tribal population (those called *dikus* or 'outsiders' by the Jharkhand movement, and *sadans*—long-resident non-tribal locals). Local BJS leaders gradually began to support the idea of statehood as part of their attempt to stem the spread of Christianity and to build a support base among non-Christian tribals. The overriding concern of early Jana Sangh and RSS leaders in the region was the strength of the Church's association with the traditional Jharkhand movement as led by Jaipal Singh's Jharkhand Party.[33] The RSS expanded its presence and social welfare organisations in tribal areas through the Vanvasi Kalyan Ashram and Ekal Vidhyalaya (one teacher schools) in the 1960s in order to compete with Church welfare organisations. Devdas Apte, an RSS organiser, was sent to Jharkhand by the Jana Sangh in 1970. The party had won a handful of seats in Jharkhand in the 1967 and 1969 assembly elections, but Apte made a more concerted effort to encourage new tribal politicians to join the Jana Sangh in the former heartland of the Jharkhand Party. An important local leader was Karia Munda, from a family of farmers, who first contested elections after the death of Jaipal Singh in 1970, stepping into what he perceived was a 'political vacuum'.[34] He won his who first election in 1977—the first time a non-Jharkhandi party had won the parliamentary seat of Khunti, the earlier stronghold of the Jharkhand Party.[35] While seeking to build the party's base among non-Christian tribals, local Jana Sangh politicians began to favour the idea of statehood. But despite support for the idea of statehood from its local leadership, the Jana Sangh's national and state party leadership remained opposed in the 1970s.[36]

The Jana Sangh was not the only party to exploit apparent divisions between non-Christian and Christian tribals, reflecting in part growing socioeconomic differentiation within the tribal population. Congress leader Karthik Oraon campaigned for reservations to be confined to non-Christian tribals because—he argued—Christians had cornered the benefits to date.[37] Other political actors in this period sought to build bridges between migrants and local Jharkhandis. Subodh Kant Sahay, then a Janata Party (but not ex-Jana Sangh) politician, explained that in the late 1970s he had tried to encourage non-tribal migrants to support the Jharkhand demand. He began to work in non-tribal coal mining areas where migrant workers had led protests against the idea of Jharkhand. He appealed to recent migrants to think about the second generation of migrants who had been born in Jharkhand and would be advised to think of themselves as Jharkhandis rather than outsiders in order to protect their rights in the future.[38] Thus, changes in electoral politics in the 1970s, and attempts by politicians from outside the historical Jharkhand movement to forge a base in the area, led to a reconsideration of the statehood demand and its extension to new social groups by a fresh set of actors.

Intra-Movement Competition

The second factor that explained a growing emphasis on statehood was competition within the Jharkhand movement itself. After Congress returned to power in Bihar and nationally in 1980, it sought to lessen the challenge posed by the JMM's radical activities in Jharkhand by drawing its less ideologically driven wing into electoral politics. Shibu Soren is thought to have struck a deal with Indira Gandhi via the then Congress Chief Minister of Bihar, who promised him immunity from future prosecution relating to his earlier underground activities in return for cooperating with the government. He agreed to a seat-sharing arrangement with Congress in the first elections contested by the JMM in 1980. The deal with Congress was strongly opposed by the more left-wing leaders of the JMM, A.K. Roy and Binod Bihari Mahato, who had both gone to jail during the Emergency. After the elections, the splits between Marxist and Soren-led wings of the JMM worsened. The JMM's success in the elections when it won eleven seats emboldened the Shibu Soren-group. At the end of 1984, the JMM formally split for the first time, when Mahato left to form a breakaway 'real' JMM, accusing Soren of having been bought by Congress.[39]

For a time, a traditional Congress strategy of co-opting its potential opponents appeared to have achieved its objectives. What now appeared to be the more radical wing of the JMM had broken away, but its most charismatic leader Shibu Soren remained within the orbit of Congress. Soren was the only JMM leader with claims to a serious mass appeal especially among *adivasis*. In the 1984 general elections, against the backdrop of increasing divisions within the Jharkhand movement, Congress won all fourteen parliamentary seats in Jharkhand, its best ever showing in the region. These elections had seen a pro-Congress wave across India following the assassination of Indira Gandhi. Within a year of taking over as Prime Minister, Rajiv Gandhi signalled a greater degree of sympathy toward regional movements in various parts of the country. He negotiated settlements of both the Assam and Punjab crises, and took a special interest in tribal regions, touring several in 1985. Congress MLAs and MPs from Jharkhand began to call for the Chotanagpur and Santal Parganas region of south Bihar to be declared a centrally administered Union Territory—a move short of statehood. Shibu Soren was reported to have said that if this were to be granted he would withdraw from the statehood movement.[40]

The Congress Party's strategy was derailed by the emergence of two new groups within Jharkhand, critical of the JMM's co-option, who resurrected a demand for statehood. The first was a more radical youth wing of the Jharkhand movement; the second, a grouping that reasserted and actively constructed an understanding of Jharkhand as a cultural region for which statehood should be granted. Competition between different actors within the Jharkhand movement helped to bring the question of statehood back to the fore. As McAdam, Tilly and Tarrow argue, nearly all protracted episodes of contentious politics produce a 'competition for power' with different effects. In the French Revolution, this led to polarisation and to the revolution 'devouring its children' under Robespierre; in the American civil rights movement it led more radical parts of the movement to challenge the leadership of Martin Luther King.[41] In the case of Jharkhand, it prompted a greater focus on statehood as a result of competition between actors in the Jharkhand movement, keen to prevent Shibu Soren and his allies from 'selling out' to Congress.

The new generation of student activists in Jharkhand were inspired by the students' movement in Assam, whose leader had recently become

Assam's Chief Minister. They set up a student wing of the JMM, the All Jharkhand Students Union (AJSU), in June 1986 under the leadership of Surya Singh Besra, a Santal *adivasi*. The murder in August 1987 of thirty-seven-year old Nirmal Mahato, president of the JMM, inspired the ire of Besra and his colleagues and strengthened their resolve to push for statehood.[42] Besra travelled to Assam as well as to Gorkhaland to learn from the tactics used by activists in these similar movements.[43] Unlike the JMM's increasing drift and divisions, AJSU focused squarely on achieving statehood. In September 1987, AJSU called a *bandh*, which Besra said had not been supported by JMM, who felt the student's organisation was too much a '*garam dal*'—i.e. a hot or violent group. In an interview Besra endorsed the JMM's reading and said of his more youthful self that: 'I totally believed that in the Gandhi-wadi way I cannot achieve Jharkhand. So I have to follow the Subhas Chandra Bose path.'[44]

A month after AJSU's formation, another group of local activists of diverse backgrounds established the Jharkhand Coordination Committee (JCC) in a bid to strengthen the Jharkhand movement by acting as an umbrella organisation for different groups and emphasising the cultural unity of the Jharkhand region. Ram Dayal Munda had become Vice Chancellor of Ranchi University in 1980 and established there a Centre for Tribal Languages and Literature. This became a centre of Jharkhandi cultural revivalism. The JCC sought to reconcile the contradictions inherent to a Jharkhand movement which sought to mobilise support predominantly from *adivasis*, in the context of an increasingly mixed population. Ever since the States Reorganisation Commission, the central government had argued against statehood on the basis that tribals were not a majority of the population. The JCC responded to this by bolstering a cultural Jharkhandi identity that encompassed both tribals and long resident non-tribal groups. The JCC argued that the Jharkhand question was not merely a 'tribal question' and discussed how to reach out to long-resident *sadan* communities who shared a common culture with *adivasis* (*sadan* communities included the Kurmi-Mahatos who had been descheduled in 1931).[45] This was partly a question of strategy: as Amit Prakash has argued, ethnic identity was deployed by the Jharkhand movement over time as a move to augment its bargaining power with the state.[46] The JCC also continued to link a statehood demand based on a Jharkhandi identity to the economic situation, arguing: 'The economic plunder of Jharkhand is directly linked with the suppression of Jharkhandi identity.'[47]

The founders of the JCC sought to sideline the more right-wing elements of the Soren-led wing of the JMM. Indeed, the greater focus on statehood by the JCC was in part a reaction to the JMM's proximity to Congress. The cosiness with Congress was reflected in Shibu Soren's apparent acquiescence in attempts made by Congress to redefine the Jharkhand struggle in terms of development and to find an institutional solution short of statehood. A participant in talks between several leaders of the Jharkhand movement and the central government in the late 1980s reported that during these talks, Shibu Soren had sought repeatedly to steer the conversation away from the movement's historical call for statehood for Greater Jharkhand and towards the issue of development. It seemed to this JCC member that Soren's 'kingmakers' in Congress had instructed him to do this. He went on to say that:

We had always said that this [the Jharkhand movement] was not just a question of development. We were demanding a political system and the right to decision making. This was the fundamental cause of the demand for statehood: it is not a question of development or law and order, these come after the creation of a state... we were in the majority in the meeting so we wouldn't let Shibu Soren continue in the way he wanted.[48]

Intellectuals in the JCC were also keen to counter the communal appeals that were being made more forcefully by the BJP and affiliated organisations in the Sangh Parivar, seeking to expand their base among Jharkhand's tribal population. They sought to prevent the BJP from capturing the political ground of the Jharkhand movement by promoting the idea of statehood. In December 1987, a delegation of the JCC (BP Kesri, SB Mullick, Surya Singh Besra, Santosh Rana and Md. Islamuddin Ansari) met the President of India and presented him with a memorandum demanding the formation of Jharkhand state from twenty-one districts of the four states of Bihar, Madhya Pradesh, Orissa and West Bengal: keeping the emphasis on a Greater Jharkhand state, rather than just Chotanagpur and Santal Parganas in south Bihar. Local leaders of the BJP were lobbying the party to support statehood for south Bihar. Movement activists in AJSU and the JCC therefore, in different ways, pushed statehood more aggressively in response to the JMM's closeness to Congress and to prevent the BJP from hijacking the movement.

At the same time, Jharkhandi activists also began to make links with an emerging international discourse around the protection of indigenous rights. From 1985, Indian activists participated in meetings of the United Nations Working Group on Indigenous Populations (UNW-GIP), seeking recognition for India's *adivasi* communities as indigenous. In 1987, Indian activists, most of whom came from Jharkhand (as Alpa Shah notes), represented a new Indian Council of Indigenous and Tribal Peoples at UNWGIP.[49] Thus, as the centrality of tribal identity to the territorial demand for Jharkhand was coming under increasing strain, Jharkhandi activists turned to new transnational modes of campaigning in an attempt to create political space for *adivasis* in Jharkhand (and nationally) on the basis of their claims to indigeneity. The effects of this appeal to a transnational discourse around indigeneity on the ability of *adivasi* communities to represent themselves are much debated.[50] Nevertheless, a communitarian discourse around tribal identity was kept alive, while it was also recognised that the case for a state in which tribal communities were to have preferential rights—either by virtue of their demographic weight, or by virtue of a political settlement privileging their special claims to recognition and representation—was receding. This must be understood as a critical contradiction in the history of state formation in Jharkhand. In the popular imagination the demand for a Jharkhand state was—and still is, as the section below illustrates—widely seen as a call for a tribal state. However, at an elite level, there was a pragmatic recognition that territorial reorganisation alone was unlikely to yield a state in which *adivasis* had a special status.

A series of focus group discussions held in villages in the assembly constituencies of Mandar and Torpa in the Kunti district, which were at the heart of the Jharkhand movement led by Jaipal Singh and his successors, illustrated the enduring tensions around the identity of the Jharkhand state.[51] Torpa was Jharkhand Party leader N.E. Horo's assembly seat until 2000, but was then won by the BJP. Mandar was held by Congress until 1990, and since then has reflected the enormous political fragmentation seen across the state. It has changed hands between the Janata Party, JMM, Congress and the 'United Goans Democratic Party' (a Goan party with a Christian base under whose auspices a small group in Jharkhand have competed). In Torpa block, a small group of Munda *adivasis* reflected the view that Jharkhand was a state that had been constructed for *adivasis*:

Respondent 1: The need for a state that would belong to us—the land-owners in this part was very important for me because somehow it was a question of my as well as all my *adivasi* brothers' and sisters' existence

Respondent 2: Jharkhand was supposed to be a dream every *adivasi* had, ever since we got independence, we felt unless we have a state of our own we are not truly free in the true sense.

Respondent 3: Jharkhand? A piece of a promised land that we had been waiting for ever since we got freedom, the land of Lord Birsa, the land of his beloved children, the *adivasis*. We don't want anyone's money, just respect and this was it.

The comments of Rajput respondents in Mandar when asked for their feelings about the new state, also reflected the converse sense that the state had not been created for them:

Respondent 1: I didn't have much interest, but still a little hope that a new state would give us roads, electricity etc. persisted in my mind. Nevertheless we knew that Jharkhand was supposed to be made for *adivasis*. Why would a *non-adivasi* consider it important?

Respondent 2: We don't have anywhere to go. The government is *adivasi*, the state is *adivasi*, and so are the officials. Who will listen to us?'

A local BJP worker in Mandar explained how the BJP has sought to build a social base that bridges *adivasis* and non-*adivasis* by supporting the demand for Jharkhand. He said, 'I still urge the people to vote for the BJP as it's the only party that thinks for the whole state not only the *adivasis*.'[52]

The BJP and Jharkhand

The third factor that explains the pre-eminence of the statehood demand in the 1980s was the rise of the BJP. In the 1980 elections to the Bihar State Assembly, the BJP won eleven seats (nine of its MLAs were first elected in the Janata regime of 1977–79). This was the same tally as the JMM, which also contested elections for the first time in 1980. The local leadership of the BJP pushed for the party to adopt the demand for statehood in order to be able to better compete with the JMM. Inder Singh Namdhari, state president of the BJP in Bihar between 1988 and 1990, played a particularly important role in soliciting official support from the party's national leadership for the demand for statehood. Namdhari came from a family of cloth merchants who moved to Palamau district of Jharkhand from Punjab at the time of partition. He explained that they moved to Palamau because, before partition, relatives of his family had previously travelled to the area during the rainy seasons in order to lend money to farmers.[53] His family roots therefore lay among groups that had been the target of earlier Jharkhand statehood movements. Namdhari, who studied engineering at college, said that he had joined politics out of an 'obsession' that there should be a separate state. For him, statehood would mean that 'nature's resources [could be] properly utilised' and the state could be the 'first' in the country since its natural resources were greater than any other region. It was Namdhari who coined a new name for the putative new state. He used the name 'Vananchal' as a means of distancing the BJP from the historical demand for statehood. Vananchal was different from the Jharkhand proposed by the historical movement in the region because it covered only those districts in south Bihar. The name Vananchal also drew on the Sangh Parivar's use of the term *vanvasi* (forest dweller) in preference to *adivasi* (original inhabitant). Namdhari explained:

The BJP and myself never treated the demand as a tribal demand: we wanted statehood for the rapid growth of the state…North Bihar leaders exploit Jharkhand but did not invest proportionately because North Bihar is affected by famine, floods and feuds…In the field of industry, there was no doubt that Jharkhand was ahead. The main complaint was that Jharkhand's money was spent in North Bihar. If money was spent here, the state would develop.[54]

The vision of statehood for Jharkhand proposed by many politicians within the BJP was also consistent with more assimilationist modes of thought. The Sangh Parivar present 'sarna' religious practice and the places of worship of *adivasis* as part of 'sanatana dharma', the idea of an eternal religion or law on which Hinduism is based.[55] This links to an assimilationist project that has sought to 'absorb' Scheduled Tribes into the Hindu 'nation', one that intensified with the more aggressive promotion of a *Hindutva* agenda from the late 1980s and 1990s.

By the late 1980s, new wings of the Jharkhand movement were leading a phase of more direct agitations, once again aggressively foregrounding the demand for statehood. To the consternation of BJP leaders in north Bihar, Inder Singh Namdhari saw support for statehood as an opportunity for the BJP to steal ground from the JMM in the electoral sphere. When Namdhari left the BJP in 1990 because of differences with the state leadership, he said 'It was owing to this [statehood] demand that we were able to compete with the JMM. But some leaders seem to be unable to swallow the idea.'[56] Most of the BJP's seats within the Bihar state assembly were located in south Bihar, and thus party leaders from the northern parts of the state were naturally suspicious of the statehood demand because it threatened to leave them high and dry—cut off from the main areas in which the BJP had an electoral presence. Nevertheless by the time he left the party, Namdhari had persuaded the BJP's National Council to make support for the statehood demand in Jharkhand (or Vananchal) official party policy.

The BJP's support for statehood tried to sideline the connection of a new state with any particular ethnic identity. The name 'Vananchal' distanced the BJP from the historical movement for an *adivasi*-dominated (Greater) Jharkhand. The BJP appealed to a constituency including regional industrialists, urban middle classes and *dikus*. This clearly contrasted with the case for statehood promoted by the Jharkhand Party, which had focused on tribal identity, and subsequently by the Jharkhand Mukti Morcha (JMM), which had grown initially out of agrarian and workers' struggles, or that of AJSU or the JCC who sought to link a cultural identity to the control of land and natural resources.[57]

Direct Action and Negotiating with the State

The BJP was not the only organisation pushing statehood more aggressively in this period. In 1988 and 1989, AJSU and the JCC—sometimes acting together, sometimes independently—organised a number of mass rallies and introduced a new tactic of economic blockades to the repertoire of the Jharkhand movement. In March 1989, they held a twenty-four hour economic blockade which stopped the transportation of minerals and forest produce. A forty-eight hour *bandh* (general strike) was called by AJSU and supported by the JCC on 20–22 April 1989. Surya Singh Besra described AJSU's tactics during the April *bandh*:

In that bandh there was violence—like Bodoland and Gorkhaland, the Jharkhand movement had become violent. All the train tracks were blasted, many trains derailed, all the minerals like iron ore, coal—their supply was blocked. All the necessities of the people—like water, electricity-supply were blocked.[58]

The increased use of direct action in pursuit of a more singular goal of statehood pushed the central government to engage more resolutely with the demand for regional autonomy. This also reflected a key difference in AJSU's view of the state compared to other parts of the historical Jharkhand movement. As one activist with deep experience of participation and leadership within the movement in Singhbhum said:

The turning point in the political history of Jharkhand was the formation of AJSU, because AJSU was able to negotiate with the state whereas all previous movements [alluding to two hundred years of struggles against colonialism, before and after the British left India] saw the state as antagonistic. Yes, AJSU called for an election *bandh* and so on but they were not opposing the existence of the state.[59]

In early May, when AJSU threatened to intensify the movement with a seventy-two hour *bandh*, the central government made contact with Besra and the first offer of talks was made.[60] After the threat of a further ninety-six hour *bandh* in June, the central government invited Jharkhand leaders for talks and this time lined up a heavy-weight team including the Home Minister and Bihar Chief Minister. These talks were attended by leaders of the JCC and AJSU, but not by the JMM. This was because leaders of the JMM, including Shibu Soren and Suraj Mandal, had urged their followers to reject the *bandh* calls led by AJSU, preferring to maintain a relationship with Congress and thereby positioning themselves for influence in a future state.[61]

Following a further meeting in August 1989 in Delhi, this time also attended by the JMM, the central government agreed to establish a Tripartite Committee comprising representatives from the Jharkhand movement, the central government and the state government. The Committee on Jharkhand Matters (COJM) was set up to investigate the case for a separate state with the remit that:

the Government desired that the tribal areas and tribal people should develop without hindrance to their cultural growth and, for the purpose, a solution to the problem should be found within the constitutional frame.[62]

However, the Rajiv Gandhi government dissolved soon after the formation of COJM and fresh parliamentary elections were elections were held in 1989, leading to the election of the National Front government led by the Janata Dal and supported from outside by the BJP. This interrupted negotiations with the central government over statehood.

Thus, by the late 1980s, a more militant wing of the Jharkhand movement, together with cultural revivalist activity, had put statehood back at the forefront of political activity in the region, alongside the more assertive presence of the BJP. The new articulation of the Jharkhand demand by the BJP, in addition to the new phase of activism in Jharkhand, eventually had the effect of helping to create a convergence of regional opinion in favour of statehood, because of a hollowing out of the meaning of 'Jharkhand'. The demand for statehood was loosened from a connection to a putative nationality group, as well as from a critique of natural resource usage and land alienation. Furthermore, the contraction to just those districts that fell into south Bihar necessarily reduced the centrality of tribal identity to the idea of Jharkhand, compared to Greater Jharkhand. The case for statehood made by the BJP reflected a vision for a particular kind of developmental state that could support industrial expansion and assimilate tribals into the 'mainstream'. This stood in contrast to the more communitarian vision of intellectuals in the JCC. It should be stressed that not all local activists involved themselves in the statehood campaign. Kaushik Ghosh, for instance, describes the distance between activists in the Koel Karo movement campaigning against the displacement threatened by a local dam and Jharkhand leaders involved in electoral politics.[63] This helps to highlight the fact that the emphasis on statehood in the late 1980s arose from the interaction between parts of the Jharkhand movement, the state and electoral politics.

The report of COJM, eventually tabled by the National Front government in 1990, noted that the Jharkhand parties had a weak electoral presence but that this did not accurately reflect the 'ground realities' of support for regional autonomy. These 'realities' included the formation of AJSU, JCC, the growing importance of non-tribal elements—'the Jharkhand movement is no longer ethno-centred', it noted—and there was near consensus among other political parties on the need for regional autonomy.[64] But rather than statehood, the Committee recommended the formation of a Jharkhand General Council elected by an electoral college of *mukhiyas* (panchayat leaders) and *gram panchayats*. Members of the Jharkhand movement submitted a dissenting note calling for full statehood for the greater Jharkhand region, arguing that the proposed powers for the Jharkhand General Council were inadequate because they excluded regional planning, a share of central gov-

JHARKHAND AND UTTARAKHAND

ernment allocations, control over police, revenue raising powers, and the ability to prioritise local people in employment.[65] Bihar's new Chief Minister Lalu Prasad Yadav responded to the publication of COJM's report by introducing legislation to create a Jharkhand Development Council, although the ordinance was blocked by Home Minister Subodh Kant Sahay because he believed that the proposed body lacked sufficient powers.[66]

Lower Caste Politics, the BJP and New Social Equations

In both Bihar and Uttar Pradesh, in the early 1990s, new state governments were elected and led by lower caste Chief Ministers who were committed to a dismantling of upper caste dominance in their states. This shift in state politics changed the context in which regional demands were made. The regions of both Jharkhand and Uttarakhand, as will be shown in the next section, lay outside the primary arenas of Mandal-era politics as a result of their distinct demography. This created new political equations within both states. The consolidation of Lalu Prasad Yadav's position in north Bihar only added to the consensus within Jharkhand around the need for statehood. In the 1990s, it was the BJP who saw increasing electoral support across Jharkhand. After the early years of the decade, popular mobilisation in the Jharkhand movement also receded and the question of statehood was pursued largely within electoral politics.

The JMM and BJP had both offered support to the new Bihar state government elected in March 1990 with Lalu Prasad Yadav as Chief Minister. They even began to flirt with a joint strategy to obtain statehood for Jharkhand,[67] but this did not last long. In October 1990, the BJP withdrew its outside support from the central government after the arrest of L.K. Advani in Bihar during his Rath Yatra. When Chandra Shekhar, supported by Congress, took over from V.P. Singh (an ally of Lalu Prasad Yadav) as Prime Minister there were reports that Lalu's leadership of the government of Bihar might have been in question. Sensing their enhanced bargaining position, the BJP stepped up their demand for statehood and said that they would not settle for anything short of it. Even north Bihar leaders such as Tarakhant Jha who had previously been hostile to the demand, appeared to change their position.[68]

In parallel, the JMM led a series of protests in the early 1990s, the largest being a ten day economic blockade in April 1992. After this blockade, the new Congress government at the Centre said that it would consider the issue of statehood only if the JMM withdrew from the Bihar state government. This precipitated another split in the JMM in July 1992 as twelve MLAs joined Shibu Soren in leaving the government.[69] From this point, the JMM (S) increasingly competed with the BJP to prove its credibility on the statehood issue. The ratcheting up of pressure for statehood by other actors within the Jharkhand movement, in addition to the BJP's support, pushed the JMM (S) to bolster its stand, by raising the question of statehood in parliament, for example. In September 1994, Bihar Chief Minister Lalu Prasad Yadav and Rajesh Pilot, Union Minister for Internal Security, signed an accord agreeing to the establishment of a Jharkhand Autonomous Area Council (JAAC). But the proposed JAAC had circumscribed powers and little financial autonomy, and the state government failed to follow even the provisions of this accord and repeatedly postponed elections to the council.

In the 1990s, the BJP captured increasing electoral space, winning a majority of Lok Sabha seats in Jharkhand from 1996 onwards and increasing numbers of state assembly seats. Two explanations for this stand out: firstly, a wider strategy of 'social engineering' within the BJP, and secondly, the party's ability to gain ground due to increasing corruption among the JMM leadership. In the early part of the decade, a new local leadership was promoted within the BJP to replace Inder Singh Namdhari and his allies. Key support in building this new leadership came from BJP General Secretary Govindacharya, the architect of the party's 'social engineering' strategy to promote lower castes within the party organisation. This was a conscious effort—not accepted across the party—to expand the party's social base away from its predominantly upper caste, north Indian core. Regions such as Jharkhand—and Chhattisgarh—were a central part of the *adivasi* belt which the BJP made a priority for its expansion. The party built on the groundwork laid by the Sangh Parivar in the 1960s and 1970s, but also sought to expand in new parts of Jharkhand. Govindacharya also happened to be the BJP's new party official 'in charge' of Bihar. As well as encouraging new leaders in Jharkhand, he helped to promote a new group of leaders in north Bihar who began to articulate a positive case for north Bihar to separate from Jharkhand (moving away from the outright opposition of their predecessors).[70] In this period, then, the party-building strategies of the BJP's national leadership came to the fore, over the heads of the former Bihar state leadership.

JHARKHAND AND UTTARAKHAND

Table 3.1: State assembly seats won by BJP in Jharkhand, 1980–2000.

Year	1980	1985	1990	1995	2000
Assembly seats (of 81)	11	12	21	21	32

Table 3.2: Lok Sabha seats won by BJP in Jharkhand, 1980–99.

Year	1980	1984	1989	1991	1996	1998	1999
Lok Sabha seats (of 14)	0	0	5	5	12	12	11

Source: Election Commission of India.

Within Jharkhand, this new phase was symbolised by the rise of Babulal Marandi. Marandi, a Hindu Santal *adivasi*, had joined the Vishwa Hindu Parishad (VHP) in the early 1980s. In 1990, he was convinced to join the BJP and became the party's organising secretary in the Santal Parganas, making the party's first concerted effort to build its organisation in a region that had been a heartland of the JMM.[71] A close colleague of Babulal Marandi said of the party's intentions in promoting him that: 'The party felt they needed a tribal *pracharak* [worker] and saw Babulal Marandi as an appropriate candidate.' The party was already confident of the support of non-tribal 'outsiders' who knew 'that there was no alternative than the BJP for them'.[72] Marandi went on to defeat JMM leader Shibu Soren in the 1998 general elections, and subsequently became the first Chief Minister of Jharkhand in 2000.[73] Soren, had until this point been the most charismatic tribal politician, with a strong popular appeal, though he was starting to appear increasingly compromised.

The BJP sought to capitalise on the perceived corruption of key Jharkhand leaders, especially in the JMM. This mirrored the national rise of the BJP as a party with a reputation for cleanliness and discipline, in contrast to the increasing allegations of corruption surrounding Congress by the late 1980s, particularly with the Bofors case. The JMM had become closely associated with this narrative around Congress after the 1993 'cash for votes' case, in which Congress was alleged to have bought the support of four JMM MPs during a vote of confidence in Prime Minister Narasimha Rao. Many interviewees, including those with close ties to the JMM, pointed to the fact that JMM leaders showed an increasing concern for 'personal gain' from the late 1980s, especially after the creation of the Jharkhand Autonomous Area Council (JAAC) in 1994. Even though the autonomy and powers of the JAAC had been severely undermined by Chief Minister Lalu Prasad Yadav, one interviewee with a long association with the Jharkhand movement reported that 'After getting the council, the JMM wanted to divide the posts among themselves. Their aggression subsided and they became soft people.'[74] Devdas Apte said that the name of Vananchal had been adopted by the BJP in order to 'shed the legacy of Jharkhand', by which he meant that the cadre of most parties who had organised in the name of Jharkhand had become more interested in 'personal gain and looting'.[75]

After a 1996 case against Shibu Soren, senior JMM leaders, including Shailendra Mahato and Arjun Munda (who became the second Chief Minister of the new state after Babulal Marandi), left the party to join the BJP, disappointed with the growing corruption in the JMM and alienated by clashes with its leadership. The BJP's support for statehood was important in attracting defectors from the JMM. As Shailendra Mahato said, 'I thought at this time [when he left the JMM to join the BJP] the BJP will give a separate state.'[76] The BJP expanded into the space left by the unravelling JMM, and won an increasing share of the region's seats in state and national elections. A local newspaper editor commented, 'If the state had been formed in 1988, there would be no BJP in Jharkhand.'[77] Additionally, in the 1990s, the BJP became an increasingly national party and its commitment to create the state began to look more credible.

The traditional support base of the BJP among upper castes and non-tribals had been augmented with appeals to non-Christian tribals in the 1990s. The party's support for statehood helped to challenge notions of cultural or ethnic exclusivity associated with the demand. Some upper-caste villagers, for example, reported that they had begun to welcome the idea of statehood during Lalu Prasad Yadav's regime in Bihar, even though many remained wary about a state that they felt was being created primarily for *adivasis*. As one Rajput villager explained, 'I voted for the party which would give a new state as I was fed up of Lalu's atrocities. We just wished that his cruel name would be separate from our land.'[78]

Thus, the idea of statehood came to the centre of the political stage in Jharkhand as a lowest common denominator around which competing political elites and social movement activists coalesced. The agreement as to institutional form, however, barely concealed the conflicts between such groups. The idea of Jharkhand as a tribal homeland remained a strong popular memory but political convergence around statehood widened the social base of the demand. The process by which statehood for Jharkhand moved back to the centre of political competition exemplifies the notion that major instances of institutional change—in this case the creation of a new state—can be rooted in ambiguous compromises. Statehood became a subject for political agreement in the context of conflicts of interest and manoeuvres for position among social movement actors and political elites with connections to different socioeconomic constituencies. In this context, statehood was an institutional change to which almost all actors could agree despite more fundamental conflicts between them about the distribution of political and economic power. The next section will consider the parallel developments in Uttarakhand where interactions between social movements, political parties and the state also produced a more determined focus on statehood by the 1980s.

Situating the Uttarakhand Statehood Demand

The new state of Uttarakhand, meaning northern ('Uttar') region ('khand') is comprised of the Himalayan regions of Garhwal and Kumaon. It also encompasses the plains districts of Haridwar and Udham Singh Nagar. Garhwal and Kumaon take their names from the two medieval kingdoms in this area. They briefly came under the control of the Gurkhas in the late eighteenth century, but in 1815 were annexed by the East India Company. Kumaon and eastern Garhwal became a British district, known together as Kumaon division. Garhwal—or Tehri Garhwal—became a princely state.[79] After independence both regions became part of Uttar Pradesh. Physically the regions are contiguous but a lack of infrastructure links in the hills makes it difficult to travel directly between the two. As the map below shows, there are separate railway lines, for instance, running from the plains to the foothills in Garhwal and Kumaon, but not between the two sides. The hills are heavily forested, and the foothills run into high mountains close to the border with China (Tibet). Uttarakhand's water resources—the state is the source of both the Ganga and Yamuna rivers—have led to the development of major hydro-electric projects, such as the Tehri Dam. In the

1970s, the Chipko movement emerged with a powerful critique of modes of natural resource management in the hills and their impact on local communities.

Unlike Jharkhand, the demand for an Uttarakhand state was made by national rather than regional political parties in its earliest articulations. Demands were put forward by the veteran leader of the Communist Party of India P.C. Joshi in the 1950s, by the Janata Party from the late 1970s, and subsequently the BJP. In terms of its post-independence political history, a number of Congress politicians who were prominent on the national stage came from Uttarakhand, including the influential Chief Ministers of Uttar Pradesh G.B. Pant and N.D. Tiwari. At the outset, it is worth noting that Uttarakhand is considerably less populous than Jharkhand: it had a population of 8.4 million (or 5 per cent of Uttar Pradesh's total population) compared to Jharkhand's 26.9 million (25 per cent of Bihar's population) in the 2001 census. Thus, the political history of Uttarakhand is in some ways less complex than that of Jharkhand. While it has always been a distinctive geographical region, it had lower salience as a discrete political region on the national stage. As a region, Uttarakhand was more closely tied into national and state circuits of political power until the 1990s, compared to Jharkhand where one of the first non-Congress regional parties in India had taken shape (the Jharkhand Party). Yet it was also a site for social mobilisation from the 1970s that raised powerful critiques of the states' role in development and its management of natural resources. In Uttarakhand—like Jharkhand—we must also consider the evolution of a demand for statehood in the context of intersections between social movement activity and electoral politics.

This is a region with a powerful sacred geography in Hinduism, not least as the source of the Ganga and Yamuna rivers. Badrinath, in the high Himalayas near the Tibetan border, is one of the four major *dhāms* in India (which are situated at the four points of the compass). In addition, the four peaks of Badrinath, Yamunotri, Gangotri and Kedarnath form an increasingly popular pilgrimage circuit in their own right.[80] The Himalayas ('abode of snows') are also known as *devālaya* or 'abode of gods', and Mount Kailāsa is the dwelling place of Shiva.[81] These features made the area redolent with symbolism for the Hindu nationalist political project. But, as Diana Eck reminds us, such pilgrimage landscapes are also formative of regional identities in themselves and are not only

JHARKHAND AND UTTARAKHAND

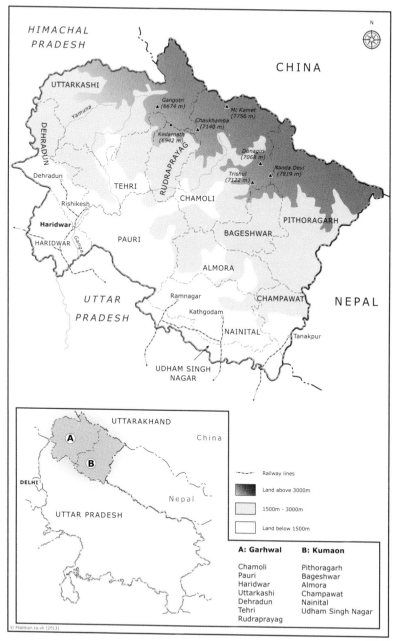

Map 7: Political and physical geography of Uttarakhand.

97

to be seen through a political lens.[82] Uttarakhand had an unusually large upper-caste population compared to other regions of India, and an OBC population of only a few per cent. Long-term traditions of Sanskritisation, whereby Khasa tribes were incorporated into Rajput and Brahmin castes, meant the hills have an unusually small population classified as OBCs.[83]

Chipko and Statehood

Beyond its hills, Uttarakhand's forested landscape has provided the backdrop for a politics of resistance. The Chipko movement began in Chamoli district in Garhwal in early 1973, after the Forest Department turned down an allocation of ash trees to make agricultural implements to Dasholi Gram Swarajya Sangh (DGSS), a cooperative set up to generate local employment by Chandi Prasad Bhatt. At the same time, 300 ash trees had been allocated as timber to a sports company from the plains called Symonds Company. Members of the DGSS began to protest by hugging trees to prevent them being felled by Symonds Company and the ensuing movement became known as Chipko (the Hindi verb *chipna* means 'to stick to').[84] A series of similar local agitations followed in other parts of Garhwal as the government pushed ahead with the auction of forest plots elsewhere. In 1974, protests also began in Kumaon. Protests that became grouped under the banner of Chipko continued over the course of the next ten years. Chipko found fame as an environmental movement that sought to conserve forests. It was often romanticised as an 'anti-development' or as an 'ecofeminist' protest, because of the prominent role of women in some of the protests.[85] There were shades, here, of the discourses connecting indigeneity, tribal rebellion and environmentalism that were prominent in Jharkhand. As Haripriya Rangan writes, Chipko was imbued with special symbolic importance giving it the status of a myth with a life independent of its context.[86] But within the region itself, readings of Chipko were less clear cut.

One reading of Chipko, offered by Ramachandra Guha, was as a series of local 'peasant protests' that reflected the moral political economy of peasant communities in the forests of the Uttarakhand Himalayas, which had been disturbed by the advent of commercial forestry. The movement, he suggests, sought 'to combat the growing social and ecological disintegration of hill society' by holding back commercial forestry. It should, Guha stressed, be read within the context of a longer history of regional movements that questioned the relationship between the state and the peasantry.[87] Mawdsley argues, however, that participation in the movement was often motivated as much by the concerns of people living in the hills for their sources of livelihood, as it was a rearguard action to preserve the cohesiveness of local peasant communities. Different groups, in more or less remote regions, had common concerns about the state's management of natural resources and the marginalisation of local communities, as well as the degradation of the environment that was so critical for livelihoods.[88] There are affinities between Chipko and the *jungle katao andolan* that took place at a similar time in Jharkhand, discussed earlier in this chapter: both movements contested the state's management of the forests and the promotion of commercial forestry.

The protests in different parts of the future state of Uttarakhand deployed some common tactics and contributed to a discourse about the political and moral economy of the hills and forests being distinct from the plains. As Mawdsley argues, the related protests in different areas made Chipko a 'social movement with regional implications'.[89] Mawdsley and Rangan both argue that people took part in the later statehood movement in 1994–95 for reasons essentially similar to those behind their earlier participation in Chipko—concerns over local livelihoods and the appropriateness of state policies for the distinctive economy of the hills and their residents.[90] In the 1970s, however, a demand for statehood did not find much purchase among activists within Chipko. Although Chipko may have contributed to new understandings of the region, those active in the various streams of the movement in its early years did not promote the idea of statehood per se. There was substantial diversity within the movement, moreover.

There were three major streams within the movement that became known as Chipko: one led by the 'Gandhian' Sunderlal Bahuguna in Garhwal, the second by Chandi Prasad Bhatt influenced by socialism, and a third by the Uttarakhand Sangarsh Vahini (USV) in Kumaon which was more Marxist in orientation.[91] None of these segments, despite their different ideological proclivities, found it useful to promote the goal of statehood. Indeed, the demand for statehood was for some time viewed with scepticism by those sympathetic to the movements. But a demand for a separate hill state had achieved some momentum elsewhere in the early 1970s. Students demanded universities for the hills (which the government subsequently established) and a Uttarakhand Rajya Sammelan (Uttarakhand state meeting) was convened in Almora district.[92] Most of those involved in Chipko, however, saw the movement as being opposed to the state, and were not primarily concerned with capturing state power.

It was in the late 1970s—with a Janata government at the Centre that was perceived generally to be sympathetic to regional movements, and with a Janata government in Uttar Pradesh—that more concerted voices were raised in favour of statehood. After the Janata Party formed governments in both Delhi and Uttar Pradesh from 1977–80, Janata Party MP Trepan Singh Negi led a campaign for statehood for the region and sought to reach out particularly to residents of Uttarakhand who were now living outside the hills.[93] Thus, as in Jharkhand, the coming to power of the Janata Party at both the state level and the centre, marked a new phase of interaction between social movements and electoral politics, a consequence of which was an emerging emphasis on statehood. A local newspaper editorial summarised the rationale behind the nascent demand:

The problem is that the majority of the state [Uttar Pradesh], moreover the country, are plains areas and when it comes to planning no close attention is given to the fact that the hills have special needs.[94]

In a bid to consolidate this kind of sentiment, and seeking to build a movement in the hills themselves rather than among Uttarakhandis resident outside the region, a new political party called the Uttarakhand Kranti Dal (Uttarakhand Revolutionary Group) was established in 1979 with the sole agenda of campaigning for statehood. Its primary base was in Kumaon initially, from where it won its first assembly seat in the 1980 assembly elections.

Many social movement activists at the time remained unconvinced that the creation of a new state would do anything to alter the nature of politics or the economic environment in the hills. After a degree of openness to the demand for statehood in the late 1970s, articles in the *Nainital Samachar*, a newspaper sympathetic to social movements in the region (especially the USV), began to waver about the idea of statehood. In 1979, Rajiv Shah wrote: 'by thinking about the idea of "our state"', he said, 'we build castles in the air in our hearts'.[95] Writers frequently sought to distance the social movements from the demand for statehood. Some highlighted the fact that the demand was generally only raised at election time and was being disproportionately backed by people who had left the hills to live in Delhi or Lucknow. 'These Delhiwalas think that they are the contractors of the votes and trees of this region', Narendra Rautela wrote.[96]

New State Regulation of Forests and Local Political Response

In Uttarakhand, the early 1980s signalled a reorientation of the attitude of the state towards social movements and their demands. As in Jharkhand, where Congress sought to co-opt the JMM,[97] the strategies pursued by Congress on its return to power at the centre in 1980 had implications for social movements in Uttarakhand, and indirectly on the development of demands for a new state. The Chipko movement had found increasing fame and recognition outside the region, represented as an environmental movement that wanted to preserve forests. One response by the central and state governments to Chipko and forestry movements elsewhere in India was to introduce new environmental regulations designed to prevent deforestation. These had the perverse effect of circumscribing other developmental activities in the region because they placed limits on what could be done in forested areas. Indira Gandhi's supposedly sympathetic response to Chipko, the new Forest Act of 1980, thus increased state control over the forests in the name of preventing deforestation. In 1981, in direct response to Chipko, a fifteen-year moratorium on felling trees at over 1000 feet was implemented. Indira Gandhi's response to Chipko, like her relationship with the JMM, had a somewhat similar impact on the social movements in both regions. The Chipko movement itself declined from this point—as the JMM's commitment to direct action around socioeconomic issues had.

The decline of Chipko was followed by a new wave of a different kind of social activism in the hills. The USV, with its base in Kumaon, launched an anti-alcohol movement in 1984. USV activists saw the spread of alcoholism as another consequence of the commercial penetration of the hills since the development of the road network in the 1960s. Protests were also initiated against the Tehri Dam in Garhwal, upon which construction had begun in 1978. Chipko's Gandhian leader Sunderlal Bahugana was especially associated with the anti-Tehri Dam movement, which has continued with varying degrees of vigour for several decades alongside the construction of the dam.[98] Another group, led by the UKD—a political party which employed movement-like tactics in this period—led a *jungle katao andolan*, a movement to cut down trees in 1988–9 as part of a protest against the perverse consequences of the new Forest Regulations. A participant in the *jungle katao andolan* emphasised to me that this was not an anti-environmental movement but one that sought to balance the basic needs of people for water, electricity, roads, schools etc. with the environment.[99]

There was also an intensification of activities linked directly to the statehood demand in this period. The UKD first contested elections in 1980 (again like the JMM) and won their first MLA in 1986 (Kashi Singh Airi in Didihat). In 1986 and 1987, the UKD led statehood rallies at the Kumaon and Garhwal Commissionaries. In September 1987, a twenty-four hour *bandh* and *chakka jam* (road block) were held and in November 1987, a statehood rally at Delhi Boat Club close to the parliament buildings in Delhi was attended by as many as 150,000 people.[100] In 1988, the Uttarakhand Sangarsh Vahini decided to also take up the campaign for statehood. They claimed to be fighting for more than simply statehood, distinguishing their claim from that of the UKD. An article in the *Nainital Samachar* announced: 'After a period of silence about the demand for a separate Uttarakhand state, the USV will itself lead a movement for a separate state.' The USV's vision was of a radically decentralised federal system in which all matters except foreign affairs, defence, communications, currency and railways would be devolved to the state level. Their slogan was 'Naye Bharat ke liye Naye Uttarakhand' (a new Uttarakhand for a new India). They began to link various strands of movement activity in the hills—such as the anti-liquor *andolan* and protests about new forest regulations—to the demand for statehood.[101] Thus, by the late 1980s, the idea of statehood had been taken up more widely among social movement activists.

Uttarakhand: A Sacred Territory for Hindu Nationalists

In the context of pro-statehood mobilisation by the UKD and other actors, local leaders of the BJP expressed their concern about the implications of the 1980 Forest Act for the region. Shoban Singh Jina, an elderly leader of the BJP, organised a meeting in Bhagtola in Almora district of the Kumaon hills in 1984 to discuss the 1980 Forest Act and Uttaranchal. Also present was Murli Manohar Joshi, a BJP politician of national stature whose family came from the region and who became one of the main cheerleaders for statehood in the national executive of the BJP.[102] At the meeting, Jina argued against the Forest Act and in favour of the need for a separate hill state.[103] The local leadership (including Shoban Singh Jina, Dr Murli Manohar Joshi, Shri Devendra Shastri, and Gobind Singh Bisht) passed resolutions on the need for statehood. They began to demand support from the national leadership of the party for the demand for a hill state as early as 1983.[104]

Another key proponent of the idea of statehood within the Sangh Parivar was the senior RSS *pracharak* Bhaurao Devras. The RSS believed that national security would be at risk in this border region without economic development. They were concerned about levels of youth unemployment and wanted to stem migration from the hills, which they saw as weakening India against its enemies.[105] Uttarakhand sits on the border with Nepal and China (Tibet). The region is a major recruiting and training ground for the Indian army—the military is one of the major local employers—and this contributes to the imagery of its contributions to the defence of the nation. As noted above, the region's sacred geography was a powerful inspiration for Hindu nationalists in Uttarakhand. These religious themes were not the preserve of Hindu nationalist politicians alone, but intersected with the symbolism employed by parts of the environmental movement in the region. As Mukul Sharma writes, for both groups, Hindu nationalists and environmentalists: 'The Himalayan region and Ganga are seen as symbols of a divine force, a thing of beauty and a point of contact with the infinite.'[106] Just as Uttar Pradesh's sacred geography had been employed to help preserve the state's unity in the 1950s, so the sacred geography of the Uttarakhand Himalayas became one source of legitimation behind the growing calls for the state's division made within the region from the 1980s onwards. But what was retained and common to most of the statehood movements that developed subsequently was a sense of Uttarakhand as being at the heart of the Indian 'nation'. This was not a putative regional nationalist movement but what Pradeep Kumar described as a 'centripetalist' movement.[107]

As in Jharkhand, the Hindu right saw the potential to link up with some of the activities of social movements in the region, as well as seeking to limit those parts of their activities that threatened their agenda. Dr Nityanand, an RSS worker and professor at DAV College in Dehra Dun, suggests that the RSS were also hoping to dampen the increasing agitations on the statehood question in the 1980s, which they felt had the potential to become disruptive.[108] In 1988, Bhaurao Devras suggested the formation of an apolitical organisation to raise awareness about the creation of a separate state in response to letters from RSS workers who said that they had attended local meetings and spoken in favour of statehood.[109] In the political field, the BJP national council also passed a resolution supporting statehood for what the party labelled 'Uttaranchal', as well as 'Vananchal' (the BJP's name for Jharkhand) in this period.[110] The BJP highlighted its commitment to statehood during the frequent elections of this period in 1989, 1991 and 1993. In 1991, the BJP won all four parliamentary seats in the hills districts. While at the helm of the Uttar Pradesh state government in 1991, the BJP introduced the first resolution supporting statehood for Uttarakhand in the state's legislative assembly.

Shifting Plains Politics and Mass Mobilisation in the Hills

The real moment at which a movement fused around the idea of state-hood came in 1994—later than in Jharkhand. The state government, a coalition Samajwadi Party-Bahujan Samaj Party administration led by Mulayam Singh Yadav, had announced a plan to implement a proposed 27 per cent reservation of places for OBCs in higher education institutions across Uttar Pradesh, including the hills with their unusually predominant upper caste, and tiny OBC, population. Students began to protest, complaining about the likely marginalisation of Uttarakhandis in local universities if the new quotas were introduced in the hills. Fairly soon, after the state government responded to the agitations by labelling them as reactionary 'anti-reservation' movements, these demonstrations spiralled into a mass regional campaign focused on a demand for statehood. The emergent statehood movement drew together a diverse coalition of social groups—including ex-servicemen, students and women's movements such as the Uttarakhand Mahila Manch—in months of protests, road blockades and disruption to local services in response to the provocations of the state government. The reason for Lucknow's provocation of the regional movement will be discussed in detail in chapter five when we look at the state level context. It is important to emphasise here that the protests of 1994–95 in Uttarakhand were genuinely mass-based and drew in new groups which had not been associated with the previous social movements, as well as an older generation of activists who had been involved with Chipko and other agitations. The protests remain a powerful memory in the region. Even people who were at school in 1994 remember the weeks of school closures entailed by the demonstrations.[111]

Nor were the protests simply a short-term response to the new reservations policy. It is difficult to see the mobilisation as a predominantly caste-based movement, although the post-Mandal climate in Uttar Pradesh served as the immediate trigger for mass mobilisation.[112] Rather, the demonstrations drew upon a much wider sense of marginality within the political economy of Uttar Pradesh. As Mawdsley argues, they reflected an increasing sense of the importance of capturing state power in order to influence and share in the shaping of development in the hills: 'The object of the Uttarakhand regional struggle was the *capture* not *rejection* of the state and thus state power.'[113] This focus on statehood was not the natural or inevitable conclusion to the movement(s) of the 1970s that had sought in some ways to keep the state, and statehood, at a distance. Rather the call for statehood arose within a broader political context and as a result of interaction between social movements, the state and new types of political party. In the latter case, the election—for the first time in 1989—of a party representing lower castes in UP, significantly altered the political landscape in Uttar Pradesh, as it had in Bihar too. As chapter five will show in more detail, changing political equations in the plains of Uttar Pradesh played an important role in galvanising pro-statehood sentiment in Uttarakhand, just as Lalu Prasad Yadav's election in Bihar altered strategies within Jharkhand. But this should not lead us to collapse the longer term history of the shaping of regional identity into a matrix that privileges the caste dimension to the mass movement for statehood in Uttarakhand. Post-Mandal politics provided the context and catalyst for the mass protests but they do not tell us everything about the content or substance of regional sentiment.

The statehood movement did not have one clear leadership—it contained multiple groups—although several umbrella organisations were formed. Students played an especially important role in the early months of the protests, and S.P. Sati, a student leader from Garhwal, was elected leader of the Uttarakhand Sanyukt Sangarsh Samiti (USSS, Uttarkhand United Struggle Committee) on 10 August 1994. Sati claimed to draw inspiration from the Communist Party of India (Marxist Liberation). He described the movement as having been conducted on many fronts—against 'liquor mafias, forest mafias, corruption' and against 'development at the cost of local people and the ecosystem'. Students, he said, had been fighting against 'old leaders' and had been unwilling to accept the UKD's leadership of the statehood movement.[114] As the protests continued, political parties tried to become more closely involved in directing the movement. Sati was replaced as leader of the USSS and on 29 August 1994, a meeting of all political parties (including Congress, BJP and the UKD) was held, in which all agreed to campaign for statehood in a non-partisan way and to join the campaign being led by the USSS.[115] Amid complaints that political parties were trying to steer the activities of the USSS, another student-led front was established in September called the Uttarakhand Chhatra Sangarsh Samiti (UCSS, Uttarakhand Students' Struggle Committee). On 2 September, at a major rally in Pauri, Garhwal the UCSS called a region-wide strike. As will be discussed in chapter five, Chief Minister Mulayam Singh Yadav responded by calling a pro-reservation *bandh* in Uttar Pradesh and sought to portray the Uttarakhand movement as a conservative backlash by defensive upper castes railing against reservations. As Pradeep Kumar argues, such insensitive handling of the demonstrations by the state government had achieved the sense of 'alienation' that was necessary for the consolidation of regional identity.[116]

It was from this point that the mass movement for statehood took off. The local media, especially Hindi-language newspapers such as *Amar Ujala* and *Dainik Jagran* played a central role in creating an appreciation of the regional spread of the movement, helping participants to identify with others involved in the struggle elsewhere in the hills. The secretary of the ex-servicemen's union—one of the organisations that had been involved in the regional movement—said: 'Our leader was the media. Every retired person sitting at home was excited to see their name in print. It encouraged them to come out to join the demonstrations.'[117] Unity between different actors within the regional movement was hard to maintain, reflecting the variety of motivations among different segments of the population for participating in the movement. The BJP and UKD increasingly organised their own activities, with rallies and *bandhs* continuing throughout 1994. Various talks were held at the central government level about Uttarakhand, but Prime Minister Narasimha Rao appealed to the state's leaders to find a negotiated solution to the conflict.[118] In early 1995, the Uttarakhand Sangarsh Samiti called for a boycott of scheduled *panchayat* and municipal elections. The Uttar Pradesh government decided to postpone the elections in the hills.[119] The intensity of public protest subsequently died down, and talks between activists and the central government took place in early 1996, especially about the idea of according Union Territory status to the region, which was favoured by some activists. However, soon afterwards, general elections were called and a new government elected in Delhi. The new Prime Minister Deve Gowda promised to grant statehood to Uttarakhand during his Republic Day address at the Red Fort in Delhi, but did not see this through.

Throughout the 1990s, the BJP consolidated their hold on parliamentary and state assembly seats in Uttarakhand. From one assembly seat of nineteen in 1989, they won fifteen in 1991. They dipped to ten seats in 1993 but by 1996 had won seventeen. They, rather than the regional party, the UKD, most expanded their electoral presence in the era of statehood agitations. This mirrored the BJP's expansion in Jharkhand during the 1990s. The party won all five parliamentary seats in Uttarakhand in 1991 and 1998, and three of five in 1994 (including the plains seat of Haridwar which was added to the two hill districts when the state was created). From the mid-1990s the Hindu right, and the Vishwa Hindu Parishad (VHP) in particular, also became more closely involved with the movement against the Tehri Dam. Sunderlal Bahugana was much criticised for his association with the VHP, especially after taking part in a VHP rally against the Tehri Dam in early 2000.[120] The concerted movement for statehood in Uttarakhand had emerged at the confluence of the politics of Mandal and Mandir, although it contained within it many diverse interests. In Uttarakhand too, then, an agreement among diverse actors about the need for statehood did not signify agreement as to the goals of statecraft in a new state.

Conclusion

In Uttarakhand a new state was not created in direct response to the periods of deepest mobilisation by social movements in the region, in this case in the mid-1990s. Nor was statehood the inevitable focus of the new phase of social movement mobilisation that began in the 1970s. Increasing emphasis on statehood arose out of change and competition within social movements, as well as interactions with electoral politics. In Jharkhand, radical leaders sought to sideline former colleagues perceived as having been co-opted by Congress, and argued that statehood had to be a priority as a first step to achieving other goals. In Uttarakhand, the USV sought to connect the idea of statehood with their ideological platforms in order not to lose ground to other political movements, especially the UKD. Political parties also took up demands for statehood. Much of this chapter has been concerned with the way in which the BJP pursued demands for 'Vananchal' and 'Uttaranchal' in a critical period of the party's expansion. Support for statehood intersected with, and stood alongside, the more aggressive promotion of a Hindu nationalist agenda from the late 1980s. This was one way in which the party set down regional roots.

By supporting demands for statehood, politicians (not only from the BJP) in both Jharkhand and Uttarakhand sought to achieve a variety of goals including the demobilisation of mass protests (some of which appeared threatening to their supporters), the undercutting of potential opponents in the electoral sphere as well as attempting to capitalise on the sense of moral community engendered by social movement activism, without necessarily taking on the full range of its claims. In the process, broad agreements among different actors evolved as to the form of political unit envisaged—a new state—but not as to the content of the political settlement that was to fill it. Furthermore, the more concentrated focus on statehood crowded out some of the ideological content of earlier social movements and reduced the extent to which statehood was seen as an institutional innovation that promised to alter fundamental aspects of the regions' political economies.

4

STATEHOOD WITHOUT A MOVEMENT

CHHATTISGARH

Despite some of Chhattisgarh's affinities with neighbouring Jharkhand in terms of its large *adivasi* population, its endowment with minerals and forests, and the nature of industrial development, the history of the statehood idea in these two regions is dissimilar. In Chhattisgarh there was no strong popular statehood movement, nor a strongly mobilised politics of indigeneity connected to the idea of a Chhattisgarh region. Indeed, the state's creation alongside Jharkhand and Uttarakhand is regarded by many in the region as something of a mystery. Although statehood for Chhattisgarh was proposed as early as 1948, it was competition in the 1990s between the two national parties vying for power in the region—Congress and the BJP—that brought the issue to the fore rather than pressure from social movements. Nevertheless, there are some common currents with developments in Jharkhand and Uttarakhand: the emergence of more competitive politics in the context of a decline in Congress Party dominance, the influence of Mandal, contentions over the trajectory of industrial development and the potential emergence of 'sons of the soil' politics.

At the outset of this chapter it is worth reflecting on the relationship between political regionalism and scholarly production. Very little has been written about the political and socioeconomic history of Chhattisgarh. This lacuna reflects the absence of strong political regionalism and we must be careful, when writing the history of regional politics after statehood was granted, not to bestow a significance or cohesiveness to the region as a political concept that it did not or does not possess. Regions are constructs anywhere, but the discussion of identity politics in Bastar later in this chapter, for instance, will problematise the notion of an essentially cohesive idea of Chhattisgarhi identity. Because of the smaller stock of scholarly material on Chhattisgarh and its political history, compared to Jharkhand or Uttarakhand, this chapter takes a somewhat longer view to situate the demand for statehood in its historical context.

Situating the Region and the Demand for Statehood

The state of Chhattisgarh is comprised of the rice-growing plains around Raipur and Bilaspur drained by the Mahanadi River, surrounded by hills and forests to the west, north and south. Like Jharkhand, agriculture is predominantly rain-fed. Chhattisgarh was known historically as the 'rice bowl' of Madhya Pradesh. The development of heavy industry began in the Chhattisgarh region after independence with the construction of a steel plant in Bhilai with Soviet assistance (production started in 1959), and the opening of the Bailadila mines which began exporting iron ore to Japan in 1966.

Chhattisgarh has considerable diversity in terms of its population, topography and administrative histories. While the plains districts today contain a mixed population, the geographically discrete regions of Bastar to the south and Surguja to the north retain majority tribal populations. The influence of tribal cultures contributes to a distinctive social structure, even in the plains areas where the assimilation of Gond tribals has taken place over centuries. Today, the Scheduled Tribe population of Chhattisgarh stands at 31.8 per cent: the highest concentration in any Indian state outside northeast India. Add to that the region's tiny upper caste population compared to other parts of the 'Hindi heartland' and a history of reformist movements among Scheduled Castes, particularly the Satnampanth and 'backward castes' such as the Kabirpanthis, and there are good reasons for seeing the region as idiosyncratic. Chhattisgarhi (a dialect of Hindi) is spoken in rural areas of the plains, while several tribal languages, Gondi most widely, are spoken elsewhere. Raipur and Bilaspur were part of the British-ruled Central Provinces and Berar.

CHHATTISGARH

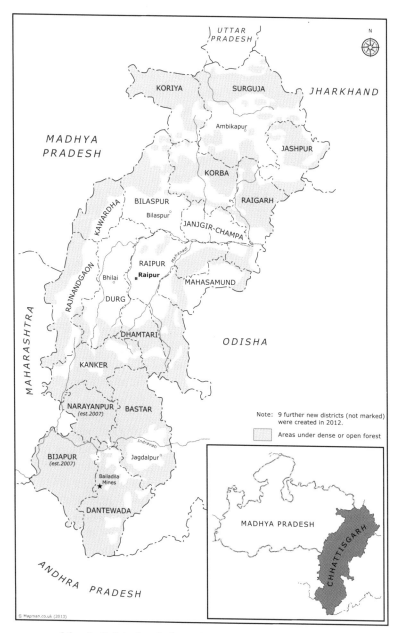

Map 8: Political and physical geography of Chhattisgarh.

Bastar was comprised of two feudatory states under the protection of the British, which were merged with Central Provinces and Berar in 1948. Surguja, to the north, also composed of formerly feudatory states under British protection, borders the Chotanagpur plateau of Jharkhand and was actually part of the 'Greater Jharkhand' demand. However there was little serious representation from Surguja to be part either of a new state of Jharkhand or in favour of a state of Chhattisgarh. Bastar was one of the larger princely states, and even after its merger (like Surguja) saw the strong influence of the former royal family. The name Chhattisgarh itself is said to derive from the political organisation of the kingdom of the Haihayas from the tenth century in the plains areas, which some suggest was organised around thirty-six ('chhattis' in Hindi) forts ('garh').[1]

Chhattisgarh is a major site for mineral production in India, accounting for 16 per cent of the country's reserves of coal, 19 per cent of its iron ore, 28 per cent of its diamonds, 11 per cent of its dolomite and 38 per cent of its tin ore.[2] The Bastar region alone accounts for about 10 per cent of India's reserves of iron ore, with major production taking place at the Bailadila iron ore mines located in Dantewada. The area also contains rich deposits of other valuable minerals. The largest part of Bastar's population is engaged in subsistence agriculture and in the collection of minor non-timber forest products such as tendu leaves (used in making *bidi* 'cigarettes') and sal seeds.[3] In Dantewada, the district with the lowest literacy rate in the whole of India according to the 2001 census (just 30.17 per cent), Maoists have been active since the 1980s. The People's War Group (PWG) have had a presence in Bastar raising demands around rights to land, livelihood, enforcement of wage payments and other local issues. From the mid-1990s, *sanghams* or local village organisations were established in many villages.[4] More recently, after the state's creation, the Andhra Pradesh state government's drive against PWG activity pushed many Maoists over the border into Chhattisgarh and made the Bastar area (including Dantewada) more central to Maoist activities in India. The Maoists claim their ultimate goal is the capture of state power in order to establish socialism in the area they call 'Dandakaranya Special Zone'.[5] From 2005, the conflict in Bastar took a new turn with the creation of a state-sponsored anti-Naxal militia, the *Salwa Judum* or 'purification hunt', and the intensification of efforts to exploit the area's rich natural resources.[6]

The other major tribal area of Chhattisgarh, Surguja, also contains substantial deposits of minerals. It has been at the epicentre of the efforts

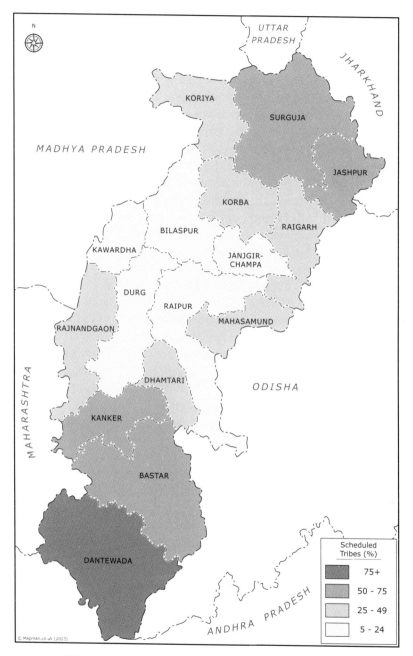

Map 9: Density of tribal population across Chhattisgarh.

by the Hindu right since independence to counter the influence of Christian missionaries through the establishment of schools and hospitals, as well as the more active propagation of Hinduism. It was in Jashpur, Surguja that the Vanvasi Kalyan Ashram was established in 1952, a Hindu nationalist organisation designed to reach out to tribal communities. The extraordinarily high identification of Scheduled Tribes in Chhattisgarh as Hindus in the census—94 per cent compared to 40 per cent in Jharkhand—reflects the extent to which Hinduism has become embedded in the social life of tribal regions,[7] which from the late 1980s have become electoral strongholds of the BJP. Although Chhattisgarh's 32 per cent *adivasi* population often leads to its description as a 'tribal' state alongside Jharkhand, the idea of statehood was not born in the predominantly tribal regions of Chhattisgarh.

The idea of statehood arose primarily in the plains areas. These areas have a smaller population of *adivasis* (as the map above illustrates) and a greater concentration of middle and lower castes categorised as OBCs: the largest *jatis* are Yadavs, Telis (Sahus), Kurmis and Malis (see table below). So-called 'Backward Classes' accounted for approximately 50 per cent of Chhattisgarh's population according to the 1931 census (the last to count caste). This is 10 per cent higher than the proportion of OBCs across Madhya Pradesh, and the OBC population is more concentrated in the plains areas of Chhattisgarh than elsewhere in the state. As Jonathan Parry points out, leaving aside Scheduled Caste Satnamis and Scheduled Tribes, at least 90 per cent of Chhattisgarh's population is included within the OBC category today.[8] The OBC category thus encompasses a vast range of socioeconomic classes. The Kurmis, for instance, who were some of the most vocal proponents of statehood for Chhattisgarh, are a dominant landowning group in many areas, although sidelined from political power historically. Chhattisgarh has a very small upper caste population in marked contrast to other parts of its parent state, and elsewhere in the Hindi heartland. In the 1931 census, Brahmins accounted for only 3.2 per cent of the population of the Chhattisgarh compared to between 12 and 21 per cent in other regions of Madhya Pradesh (see Table 4.1).

In the first few decades after independence, statehood for Chhattisgarh was an idea that circulated mainly among former Congress politicians who had joined the Socialist Party. They were especially concerned about agrarian issues and 'exploitation' within the region's industrial economy. The turning point in the demand for statehood, if any, came

CHHATTISGARH

Table 4.1: Distribution of castes in Madhya Pradesh, 1931 census.

Category	Madhya Pradesh	Vindhya Pradesh	Mahakoshal	Chhattisgarh	Madhya Pradesh
Upper castes	18.5	20.6	11.7	3.2	12.9
Brahmin	6.5	13.3	4.6	1.7	5.7
Rajput	9	4.5	5.6	0.9	5.3
Bania	2.2	2.1	1	0.5	1.4
Kayasth	0.7	0.7	0.5	0.1	0.5
Middle castes	0.87	0.34	2.96	0.17	1.11
Backward castes	37.3	42.25	39.29	50.13	40.67
Ahir (Yadav)	2.6	6	4.8	8.4	5.3
Dhimar	1.14	2.92	2.64	0.8	1.65
Gujar	2.9	0.04	1.1	0.02	1.23
Kachhi	3.25	6	–	–	1.9
Kumhar	1.6	1.7	0.9	0.8	1.2
Kurmi	1.6	4.7	2.6	2.9	2.6
Lodhi	2	2.7	4.4	0.9	2.25
Lohar	0.8	1.5	1.3	1	1.1
Mali	1	0.1	2.3	9.3	4.2
Nai	1.4	1.8	1.2	0.8	1.2
Teli	1.6	2.9	2.3	9.3	4.2
Scheduled Castes	16.7	14.7	11.9	12.5	14.05
Scheduled Tribes	13	14.5	25	31.7	21.62
Muslims	7	2.7	4.4	1.1	3.85

Source: Reproduced from a table in Christophe Jaffrelot (1996), *The Hindu Nationalist Movement*, p. 133.
NB.: Madhya Pradesh in the first column refers to the pre-1956 entity and in the final column to pre-2000.

in the 1980s after Madhya Pradesh's first non-Congress government had left office. From 1980 onwards both Congress and the BJP sought to expand their social base in Madhya Pradesh in order to respond to a changing electoral climate. Some new politicians in both parties from OBC castes promoted the idea of a Chhattisgarhi identity as a means of projecting an incipient 'sons of the soil' politics. This politics sought to draw attention to two things. Firstly, it highlighted the upper-caste stranglehold on political leadership in both the BJP and Congress. Secondly, it alluded to economic tensions between 'local' people and 'exploitative' outsiders. Fostering a form of regional political identity helped to open up room for a small class of new political elites who positioned themselves as 'sons of the soil'. But statehood for Chhattisgarh was never an idea with mass appeal.

Like other areas, Chhattisgarh also saw the emergence of a prominent new social movement in the 1970s, the Chhattisgarh Mines Shramik Sangh (CMSS), and its sister political wing the Chhattisgarh Mukti Morcha (CMM). The CMSS was predominantly a labour movement that sought to organise contract labourers in the Dalli-Rajhara iron ore mines which fed the Bhilai Steel Plant. In a similar way to the JMM, the CMM led by Shankar Guha Niyogi associated the idea of Chhattisgarh with a class of the exploited. Questions about displacement and the cornering of benefits of industrialisation by migrants arose in Chhattisgarh just as they had in Jharkhand. Yet despite the tensions between local Chhattisgarhis, especially *adivasis* employed as contract labourers and those seen as 'outsiders' who had come to Bhilai since the 1950s for employment in the steel plant and the surrounding township, the CMM—unlike its Jharkhandi counterpart—kept some distance from periodic demands for statehood. No strong ethno-regional movement emerged in Chhattisgarh.

Congress Factionalism, Social Change and Early Regional Demands

It was only with the linguistic reorganisation of states in 1956 that Chhattisgarh—the Hindi-speaking region of Central Provinces and Berar—was merged with other Hindi-speaking areas to form Madhya Pradesh. The Marathi-speaking Vidarbha region of Central Provinces and Berar was merged with present day Maharashtra. The notion of a distinct Chhattisgarhi cultural identity was first articulated during the nationalist movement against British rule when the region was part of Central Provinces and Berar. Chhattisgarhi Brahmins who were prominent locally in the freedom struggle such as Sunderlal Sharma, Thakur Pyarelal Singh and Hari Thakur, as well as a handful of Maharashtrian Brahmins resident in Chhattisgarh such as B.Y. Tamaskar and Madhavrao Sapre began to write and speak of a Chhattisgarhi identity, including its distinct language, during this period. All of these figures were interested in broader issues of 'social reform'. Sunderlal Sharma, a Hindu nationalist influenced by Dayanand Saraswati and the Arya Samaj, was known for his campaign against untouchability and in favour of temple entrance.[9] But it was in the course of political and economic competition among Congress politicians and local elites that the idea of Chhattisgarh first gained political traction.

As we have seen, the total percentage of Brahmins in Chhattisgarh was very small. Members of a number of non-Brahmin castes held prominent positions in social and economic life in Chhattisgarh, holding land and collecting revenue payments from tenant farmers as *malgujas* under local land settlements from the mid-nineteenth century, trading, having access to education and some also living in towns.[10] Although there was no history of anti-Brahmin political mobilisation in Chhattisgarh, an undercurrent of resentment was evident by the 1940s as a result of the domination of Congress politics by Ravishankar (R.S.) Shukla, whose family originated from outside Chhattisgarh. The division between supporters and opponents of the Shuklas formed the main line of factionalism within the Congress Party in Chhattisgarh in the first few decades after independence. This factionalism helped to generate the earliest calls for statehood.

R.S. Shukla, the first Chief Minister of the Central Provinces and Berar in 1946, was another of the region's 'freedom fighters'. He became the first Chief Minister of united Madhya Pradesh in 1956 until his death in December later that year. The Shuklas were Kanyakubja Brahmins, a label that denotes the region of Uttar Pradesh between Kanpur and Lucknow, from where many families migrated in the late nineteenth and early twentieth century, often in search of jobs in the administration and industry. Shukla's grandfather had moved to Rajnandgaon to work as a partner in the BNC Mills, one of the region's biggest and earliest industries, in the early twentieth century.[11] R.S. Shukla began to dominate Congress politics in the region from the 1930s. He was among a number of Hindi-speaking politicians who challenged the pre-eminence of Marathi politicians in the Congress Party of the old Central Provinces and Berar, as economic changes set back the cotton industry of Marathi-speaking Vidarbha and a growing non-Brahmin movement divided Marathi society.[12] R.S. Shukla increasingly overshadowed his Hindi-speaking rival, D.P. Mishra. Shukla's sons, Shyamacharan (S.C.) and Vidyacharan (V.C.), inherited and developed this position of dominance after R.S. Shukla's death in 1956. S.C. was Chief Minister of Madhya Pradesh in 1969–72, 1975–77 and 1989–90, and V.C. was an MP and Union Minister, including serving as Indira Gandhi's Information and Broadcasting Minister during the Emergency.

The other major group of Brahmins in the region are known as Saryu-pali Brahmins (from the eastern side of the Saryu river near Ayodhya), whose ancestors migrated to Chhattisgarh from the sixteenth and seventeenth century onwards as the predominantly Gond *adivasi*-inhabited plains were settled by Brahmins and cultivating castes from north India, and Telis and Chamars from Bihar and Baghelkhand (part of present-day Madhya Pradesh), followed by the Maratha conquest of the eighteenth century.[13] This older generation of Brahmin migrants became known as 'Chhattisgarhi Brahmins', while the Kanyakubja Brahmins later earned the political sobriquet 'non-Chhattisgarhi Brahmins' as they became the target of mild 'sons of the soil' type politics from the 1980s.

The domination of Kanyakubja Brahmins in local political and economic life prompted some of the early calls for Chhattisgarh to be made a separate state. In 1948, while R.S. Shukla was Chief Minister, B.Y. Tamaskar (an opponent of R.S. Shukla's who subsequently left Congress to join the Socialist Party) presented the first proposal for a separate state of Chhattisgarh at a Provincial Congress meeting held in Raipur, positing a separation of the Hindi-speaking districts from Marathi-speaking parts of the former British province. It coincided with stronger demands from Marathi Congress politicians in Vidarbha from 1939 onwards for a merger with other Marathi-speaking areas.[14] But, as an elderly Chhattisgarhi Brahmin from a large landowning family told me, 'no-one [in Chhattisgarh] had the guts to support it (even though they supported it privately) because they were fearful of R.S. Shukla. Everyone had their own interests, family affairs etc. and didn't want to anger R.S. Shukla. No one even seconded the proposal.' But he also stressed that the demand for statehood was weakly rooted: 'The educated people who demanded Chhattisgarh [in opposition to the domination of Kanyakubja Brahmins] did so to benefit themselves and to get ahead in the administration. They had no imagination or vision of a separate state.'[15]

A number of broad changes after independence changed social equations in Chhattisgarh, and introduced new forms of competition among political and economic elites as traditional landowning classes moved to urban areas and sought new forms of employment and political influence. The abolition of the *malguja* system of land administration, and subsequent Land Ceiling Act of 1959, especially affected Chhattisgarhi Brahmins, Kurmis and others who had been large landowners.[16] While many circumvented land ceilings legislation, broader social changes were under way which threatened the position of large landowners. After independence, many landowners began to rent their land to individual tenant farmers rather than manage the farming of their land themselves using local village labour. Kanyakubja Brahmins, by contrast, were not generally landowners or primarily reliant on earnings from landholdings. Chhattisgarhi Brahmin landlords who moved to urban areas such as Raipur often then found themselves in competition with Kanyakubja Brahmins for government jobs. Some objected that those in the administration were continuing to bring in 'outsiders' to fill positions in the administration. As a participant among a group of Chhattisgarhi Brahmins in Brahminpara, Raipur said during a focus group discussion about their life stories:

Right after independence, Kanyakubja Brahmins led the state. The result of this was that they imported people from Uttar Pradesh who were absorbed into government service. This led to unrest and people began to oppose Kanyakubja Brahmins. At one time, of fifteen MLAs, eleven would be Kanyakubja Brahmins. So gradually Kanyakubja Brahmins moved ahead and they are still dominant.[17]

At a similar time, a younger generation of Kurmis were becoming more politically assertive.[18] In 1946, the *Nau Yuvak Sangh* (New Youth Group) was established by young educated Kurmis to 'advance' Kurmi society. Kurmis are middle caste cultivators but are also recognised as OBCs in Chhattisgarh and Madhya Pradesh today. The *Nau Yuvak Sangh* secretary Purushottam Kaushik went on to become a Socialist Party MP after the Emergency in 1977, defeating V.C. Shukla in his Raipur constituency on a platform of statehood for Chhattisgarh. It was members of this group who first began to adopt the surname Chandraker (nowadays a common Kurmi surname) as they went to college for the first time. This was part of a growing group-consciousness among Kurmis. These young men, as a former member of the group recollected, were seeking something more than the traditional caste associations such as the Kurmi Mahasabha which focused on maintaining caste discipline and dispute resolution.[19] In 1948, Khubchand Baghel, another young, educated Kurmi, was elected chairman of the All India Kurmi Kshatriya Mahasabha at its annual session in Kanpur.[20] Baghel, who was briefly a member of the newly elected Vidhan Sabha in 1946 (having also submitted his resignation in this same year), became one of the foremost proponents of a separate Chhattisgarh, setting up the Chhattisgarh Mahasabha in 1956.

Praja Socialist Party and the Farmers of Chhattisgarh

In 1951, Khubchand Baghel, along with a group of 'pro-Chhattisgarh' leaders including Thakur Pyarelal Singh, B.Y. Tamaskar and Chedi Lal, left Congress. They joined the Kisan Mazdoor Praja Party (Farmer and Worker People's Party) established by Acharya Kripalani, which then merged with the Socialist Party of India to become the Praja Socialist Party. Two days after resigning from the Congress Party, Kripalani himself visited Raipur on 19 May 1951.[21] The Chhattisgarh Mahasabha subsequently set up by Baghel became associated with a number of struggles in the region, including movements demanding employment rights for locals at the newly established steel plant in Bhilai, campaigns for tribal land rights such as the Siawa Satyagraha in Dhamtari district and Lal Shamshah's land rights movement in Rajnandgaon. As Purushottam Kaushik (who also joined the Socialist Party but had never been in Congress) explained, the Chhattisgarh Mahasabha focused on uniting Chhattisgarhis against 'exploitation'.[22] Keyur Bhushan, joint secretary of the Chhattisgarh Mahasabha, outlined to me:

After independence, exploitation of tribals got worse. Contractors came to the area, mineral exploitation increased, rights to forest goods fell into the hands of contractors and forest officials. Movements started against these trends.[23]

Baghel also led farmers in a *dhan* (paddy*) satyagraha* during which 300 people were arrested calling for an increase in the price of paddy. This was a period in which farmers in Chhattisgarh were in a vulnerable position—the price of paddy had fallen, and the area was prone to drought.[24] Socialist politicians including Khubchand Baghel, B.Y. Tamaskar and later Purushottam Kaushik also periodically raised the idea of statehood for Chhattisgarh.[25]

Many of the politicians who joined the Praja Socialist Party (PSP) in Chhattisgarh were opposed to the close relationship between certain 'rice kings', who ran the rice mills and were powerful players in the rice trade, and the Congress leadership of the region.[26] The Socialist Party appealed primarily to landowning farmers and campaigned on issues such as irrigation, a fixed-rate for the sale of paddy, the implementation of land reform and land ceilings. As noted, the party also raised the idea of a separate Chhattisgarh state but not with a great degree of determination. The PSP had moderate electoral success, winning seven of approximately seventy assembly seats in present-day Chhattisgarh in

1962,[27] but only two in 1967. Nevertheless in the 1960s, the Socialists had more of a presence than the Jana Sangh in the plains areas of Chhattisgarh. At that time, the Jana Sangh performed better in other regions of Madhya Pradesh such as Vindhya Pradesh and Madhya Bharat.

It is noteworthy that in Chhattisgarh, Socialist politics was led by those groups who had often been dominant landowning groups under the British including Kurmis and 'Chhattisgarhi Brahmins' (between them these groups would have accounted for little more than 5 per cent of the population). According to Purushottam Kaushik, many of those in the Socialist Party were *malgujas* (the class who had collected revenue under the British) and the party spoke to the interests of farmers more than agricultural labourers. 'We weren't capitalists', he explained. 'We didn't want the country to develop at the cost of agriculture.' Nor was it a Communist Party, he stressed, dominated by labour or trade unions.[28] Indeed, another interviewee (a Congressman) described the main aim of the Socialist Party in Chhattisgarh as being to establish a compromise between agricultural labourers and *malgujas*.[29] Purushottam Kaushik noted that the Socialist Party floated the idea for statehood in Chhattisgarh, as in other parts of the country, on the grounds of addressing regional inequality. This articulation, he suggested, was subtly different from that of Khubchand Baghel, who was focused on Chhattisgarhi 'sentiment', the issue of exploitation and fighting for the self-respect of 'Chhattisgarhis' against an upper caste ruling class.

There was a relatively large middle peasantry in Chhattisgarh which helps to explain why the agrarian lobby attained some political importance and sought to mobilise outside Congress for greater influence. The rice-growing part of Madhya Pradesh including Chhattisgarh was unique among all the rice-growing regions of India for the fact that the largest part of the area under rice cultivation (64 per cent) was covered by holdings of over 4 hectares (10 acres).[30] Using figures from the 1961 census, it can be seen that these holdings of over four hectares were spread between approximately 24 per cent of the landholding population.[31] This contrasts with other rice-growing regions in north India where there was a more extreme concentration of landholdings. In eastern Uttar Pradesh, for example, the middle and rich peasantry (those with landholdings above 7.5 acres) comprised only 6.2 per cent of the cultivating population but controlled 36.9 per cent of the land in 1971. A politically assertive middle peasantry did not emerge in these circumstances.[32] The situation in Bihar was similar to eastern Uttar Pradesh. According to the 1970–71 Agricultural Census, medium sized landholders (10–25 acres) accounted for 7 per cent of households but 36 per cent of the land.[33] Yet despite the wider distribution of landholding in Chhattisgarh, the economic position of the middle and rich peasantry was none too secure there either. Most of the rice-growing region in Madhya Pradesh was unirrigated in 1961, which led to substantially lower yields than the average farm in states such as Andhra Pradesh and Tamil Nadu.[34] Agricultural modernisation had not progressed far in either Chhattisgarh or the rest of Madhya Pradesh. This region had not been a central beneficiary of the Green Revolution in the 1960s. Compared to other states in the 1990s, Madhya Pradesh still had a relatively small percentage of cropped land under improved seed varieties—40 per cent, compared to an all-India average of 59 per cent. It also had a slightly below average use of fertilisers and pesticide.[35] Furthermore, there has been a steady decline in the size of landholdings since the 1960s. According to figures calculated from the 1995–96 agricultural census, 45 per cent of the area farmed in Chhattisgarh was in holdings over 4 hectares—compared to 64 per cent in the 1961 census. These holdings accounted for just 7.4 per cent of the total number of landholdings. In 1995–96, 51.3 per cent of total operational holdings in Chhattisgarh were marginal holdings (under one hectare), covering 12.4 per cent of the total area.[36] This points to a deterioration in the position of many former medium and large landowners, and a substantial increase in the number of poor farmers.[37]

This was the agrarian context in which the PSP operated in Chhattisgarh. The party did not, however, become a serious alternative to the Congress in the region. It cannot be said either that there was broad popular support or any kind of mass mobilisation around the idea of statehood at this stage, even though the idea was mooted by some Socialist politicians. In 1967, in recognition that the movement against exploitation in Chhattisgarh was weakening, Khubchand Baghel established the Chhattisgarh Bhratr Sangh (Chhattisgarh Brotherhood Association) in a bid to 'rejuvenate' the movement.[38] However, he died in 1969, after having rejoined Congress (along with other Socialists), having also become a Rajya Sabha MP.

The return of Baghel and B.Y. Tamaskar to Congress conforms to Kothari's argument that opposition parties in this period functioned more as 'parties of pressure', maintaining links with factions within Congress rather than constituting a real electoral alternative to Congress.[39] Former Socialist MP Purushottam Kaushik described how Khubchand Baghel and B.Y. Tamaskar were persuaded to rejoin Congress:

Congress [had remained] very watchful [of the PSP] and tried to win them over. D.P. Mishra [Congress politician and long standing rival of the Shuklas] approached Tamaskar, the most intellectual of them all, and tried to convince him to come back to Congress. He said we'll form a government and get rid of this Shukla. So Tamaskar invites D.P. Mishra to lunch at his home in Durg and also invites Khubchand Baghel and Chedi Lal too. At the time, Khubchand Baghel used to consult me. He wanted me to come to the meeting but I said I was unwilling—I'd been fighting so long against the policies of Congress, I wasn't about to join the party. But he persuaded me to accompany him. Before the meeting we sat and talked. Tamaskar also tried to persuade me to join. I said to him, "We've been critical of the party in public meetings". But Tamaskar and others said to me: "Look, we're getting old. We want a rest—like bullocks rest in a cowshed (*kota*) when they get old. … So we're going to Congress, *aram karne ke liye* (to rest)" … I didn't think I needed to go to the *kota* at this time—I was young. But both Khubchand Baghel and Tamaskar joined and were nominated to Rajya Sabha.[40]

The periodic surfacing of the idea of statehood must be seen in this light. It was a device used by Socialist politicians to place pressure on Congress but not one that was pursued as a matter of conviction in its own right. The PSP gradually came to be overshadowed in Madhya Pradesh by the Jana Sangh, with which it allied across the state in 1967 and again in 1977. The Jana Sangh played the main role in the formation of the first non-Congress government in MP in 1967 and again in the post-Emergency Janata government of 1977. Yet it was the Socialist Party that had been the first to introduce the idea of statehood for Chhattisgarh and chalk out a possible constituency for the demand. The Socialists were also the first party in north India to actively try to increase the representation of lower castes in politics. In Chhattisgarh, the PSP refused tickets to some Brahmins for elections. Junior politicians from lower castes were also promoted early in their careers. Purushottam Kaushik, a Kurmi, for example, unexpectedly became a cabinet minister in the central government in 1977, after standing on a pro-statehood platform and defeating V.C. Shukla in the elections.

*The Chhattisgarh Mukti Morcha, the Industrial Workforce
and Chhattisgarhi 'Nationality'*

It was in and around the industrial sector of Bhilai that another definition of Chhattisgarhi identity came into sharp relief as a result of industrial development and the arrival of migrants to work in the steel
industry. The Chhattisgarh Mines Shramik Sangh (CMSS) was established in 1977 as a union for contract labourers in the Dalli Rajhara iron
ore mines which fed the Bhilai Steel Plant. Contract labourers, employed
informally, were more likely to come from the local area (typically *adivasis* or Scheduled Castes) than the mixed workforce on the public sector payroll in the mechanised mines. Led by Shankar Guha Niyogi, the
CMSS fought to extend the reach of trade unions to informal sector
mine workers, as a means of enforcing the statutory minimum wage and
minimum working standards for temporary, contract labourers. Ultimately Niyogi sought to hold the government to a promise to abolish
contract labour altogether in the mines. The CMSS also led a concerted
campaign against liquor consumption, which inspired the enmity of
local liquor traders. The Chhattisgarh Mukti Morcha (CMM) was
formed as a sister political wing. It also campaigned on broader issues
affecting *adivasis* in neighbouring areas such as malpractices in the
implementation of the food-for-work scheme and access rights to common land for landless labour.[41]

Niyogi posed a threat to the expanding industrial class in the region.
He was periodically arrested, but his stature was such among the tribal
population of Dalli-Rajhara and neighbouring areas that both Arjun
Singh and his some time ally, Jhumuklal Bhedia, as well as V.C. Shukla,
at various points, sought to align themselves with Niyogi in order to
capitalise on his support in the region.[42] This tactic bears some similarities to Congress attempts in Jharkhand to co-opt Shibu Soren and his
wing of the JMM, as examined in chapter three, except that, in this case,
Niyogi was not drawn into mainstream electoral politics. Bhedia fell out
with Niyogi after the CMSS fielded a candidate against him in the 1980
assembly elections, prompting Bhedia to form a rival union. In February
1981 Niyogi and Sahdev Sahu, president of the CMSS, were arrested
under the National Security Act and workers belonging to the union
were subject to repression.[43] Niyogi was murdered ten years later. In a
case later brought by the Central Bureau of Investigation, five local
industrialists were sentenced to imprisonment for life in 1997 for his

murder and the assassin given a death sentence. However, the acquittal of all but the hired killer, on the grounds of insufficient evidence, was upheld by the Supreme Court in a judgement in 2005.[44]

While Niyogi had been sympathetic to the idea of statehood for nationality groups, viewing the question through the framework of Soviet 'nationalities' policy, he did not make statehood for Chhattisgarh a major campaign platform, in contrast to the JMM, with whom he made common cause in other ways. He saw space to 'harness the forces generated by the loyalty to national identity in order to tackle the wider consequences of feudalism and colonialism'. He argued, however, that this had to be a struggle led by the peasantry and working classes to balance the existing interest of the 'Chhattisgarhi bourgeois and petty-bourgeois' in a new state. In a pamphlet entitled 'Chhattisgarh and National Question', he wrote:

The people want that the Chhattisgarh region should develop. It is by no means sure in the present political structure, that the creation of small states will automatically cure all the present ills. Nevertheless, when the vast majority of a nationality group feel that the creation of a smaller state on the basis of a distinct identity will enable them to participate actively in contributing to the national progress, and facilitate the appropriate and planned utilisation of the natural resources, and when they are ready jointly to work towards this goal, then the fulfilment of this demand becomes a democratic right of the people... Today, the Chhattisgarh bourgeois and petty bourgeois are becoming increasingly devoted to and enthusiastic about the idea of a Chhattisgarh state. Among the peasantry too, the idea that they should be granted a state of their own is becoming increasingly strong. Hence, it is the duty of the working class to interest itself actively in this question. Unless the campaign is guided in a definite direction and linked up with the question of the struggles for peoples' liberation it may be diverted into the wrong channels: militant Chhattisgarhism can harm this whole campaign.

In Chhattisgarh, in the near future, the struggle for the right of [the] national group to govern itself will proceed apace. This is because the enormous Chhattisgarhi population is dependent on agriculture, and the peasantry, especially all the Adivasi peasantry, are particularly oppressed and exploited. Because the land question is intimately connected with the national question and with this campaign, the peasantry will fight this battle with all their might...Hence, the working class will also join this battle, in their aid. The national bourgeoisie and the petty bourgeoisie, if for nothing else than because it is in their interest, will join the campaign or at least not oppose it.[45]

For Niyogi, *adivasis* were central to an incipient Chhattisgarhi nationality. But the CMM did not make the kind of transition from a notion of a 'political' Chhattisgarh to a 'territorial' Chhattisgarh that occurred with social movement activity in Jharkhand. Statehood did not become a central campaign platform for civil society organisations in Chhattisgarh.

Even though the CMM did not take leadership of a statehood campaign, the association of a Chhattisgarhi identity with local labouring classes was politically significant. As Parry argues, by the 1990s, the issue of 'sons of the soil' had developed, and, because of fierce competition for jobs, turned into a potentially 'explosive' issue in Bhilai. Since 'outsiders' have tended to dominate management positions in the local steel industry, and locals have been overrepresented among contract labourers, there is an apparent cultural division of labour. Parry notes that tensions between locals and outsiders were ultimately mitigated, to an extent, by the introduction of 'reservations' (affirmative action) for Other Backward Classes (OBCs) by the central government in 1990. The effect of reservations in Bhilai was to preserve a large proportion of jobs for the local population because the overwhelming majority of non-Scheduled Castes and non-Scheduled Tribes in the plains area of Chhattisgarh are classed as OBCs and the state list includes only those OBCs from Madhya Pradesh.[46] This gave locals an advantage over OBCs from other states who are not uniformly classified as OBCs in Madhya Pradesh. This may not have addressed the overrepresentation of Chhattisgarhis among contract labourers, but it possibly helped to ensure that the insider-outsider divide did not become a central political cleavage in Chhattisgarh.

'Tribal' Chhattisgarh, the Forest Economy and Hindu Nationalism

Thus far, our attention has largely been focused on the plains areas of Chhattisgarh around Raipur, Durg and Bilaspur where the concept of statehood was incubated. Tribal majority Bastar and Surguja to the south and north of the plains also form an important part of the landscape and political economy of Chhattisgarh. It is misleading to talk of an overarching *adivasi* identity in Chhattisgarh, or in Bastar or Surguja. There was little attempt to develop ethno-political mobilisation around a regional tribal identity across what is now Chhattisgarh, especially one linked to a demand for statehood within the federal system. This owes something to the non-congruity of the two majority tribal districts today and their different political economies.

Nevertheless, the development of an industrial economy—which began under the colonial state—did contribute to the shaping of a sense of a distinctive tribal identity in Bastar. As Archana Prasad shows, British industrial policy in Bastar's forests changed cultivation and hunting and gathering practices among Gond and Baiga tribes in Bastar, transforming them into labourers. In 1910, the first 'tribal revolt' was undertaken by the Marias in Bastar, with the slogan of 'Bastar for Bastaris', in protest at exploitation by lessees of the forest, Hindu *thekadars* (contractors) and the police.[47] An incipient tribal identity in Bastar did not, however, connect to a wider Chhattisgarhi identity.

For years after independence, the politics of Bastar and Surguja had been dominated by former princely families who mostly aligned themselves with Congress after 1947. However, the relationship between Congress and the former princes was by no means assured, as the case of Pravir Chandra Deo in Bastar attested. Pravir was installed as ruler of Bastar at the age of seven in 1936 after his mother's death. After independence, and Bastar's accession to Central Provinces and Berar, the state government seized Pravir's estate under Court of Wards on the ostensible grounds that he was not mentally fit to look after it at a time that a mining lease in Bastar had been granted to neighbouring Hyderabad state.[48] Pravir Chandra Deo, however, emerged as an unlikely figurehead of anti-government protests in a period of increasing commercial penetration of the forests of Bastar. In 1955, he established the Adivasi Kisan Mazdoor Sangh, campaigning for the return of his estate and taking up issues of concern to the local population. In 1957, Congress sought to capitalise on his popularity and he accepted a Congress ticket to contest the elections. Failing to get his estate back, he left Congress and set up a new group, the Adivasi Seva Dal. He eventually met his death in 1966, in a police-firing against protests that the group had been leading against paddy procurement. As Nandini Sundar writes, 'the people's grievances and Pravir's personal grievances [had come] to be symbols of Congress corruption and the government's support for certain groups at the expense of others.'[49]

Following the shooting, the Congress state government led by D.P. Mishra justified the lethal response to the protests on the grounds that Pravir Chandra Deo had wanted Bastar to secede from the rest of India, arguing that Bastar had been following the secessionist ambitions of Nagaland and Mizoram.[50] But Sundar argues plausibly that the internal political dynamic was more profound than any secessionist bid. She suggests that the episode with Pravir Chandra Deo had illustrated 'the loss of state legitimacy and the *adivasi* vision, however inchoate, of a different and more just polity'.[51]

If outright secessionist calls by Bastar have barely been in evidence, there have been periodic calls for the implementation of the Sixth Schedule. In 1995–96, a proposal to extend the Sixth Schedule to Bastar was made by the Madhya Pradesh Congress government, which would have provided for a greater degree of self-governance for local *adivasis* similar to that in the states of the northeast as compared to the existing Fifth Schedule provisions in scheduled areas. As Sundar writes, the debate about the Sixth Schedule in the mid-1990s brought the question of the 'indigenous, or of insiders versus outsiders…to a head'.[52] An anti-Sixth Schedule camp was led mainly by the BJP, with the support of a Congress faction led by Mahendra Karma. However instead of extending the Sixth Schedule, the central government brought in the Panchayat Extension to Scheduled Areas (PESA) Act in 1996, which gave special powers to *gram sabhas* in scheduled areas.

It was in these tribal-majority districts of Chhattisgarh that the Jana Sangh laid its strongest roots in the Chhattisgarh region of Madhya Pradesh from the 1960s onwards. The party expanded first in Surguja, and, in 1967, coinciding with the opening of the Bailadila mines, it also won the seat of Jagdalpur in Bastar for the first time. This constituency had seen considerable migration and demographic mixing over time, and—as in Jharkhand—the party appealed both to more recent migrants and *adivasis*.[53] A disproportionate number of the total seats won by the Jana Sangh (and then BJP) from the 1960s to the 1980s in Chhattisgarh were seats reserved for Scheduled Tribes (five of seven in 1967, seven of ten in 1972, five of six in 1980 and six of thirteen in 1985). But, as can be seen in table 4.2, it was in 1990 that the BJP made its most pronounced electoral breakthrough in these areas when it came to power across Madhya Pradesh. In these elections, the party won nine of twelve reserved seats in Surguja and eight of twelve in Bastar.

An important factor in the Jana Sangh's armoury (and later that of the BJP) in tribal Chhattisgarh, particularly in Surguja, was the work of the RSS and affiliated social work organisations. The Vanvasi Kalyan Ashram was established in Jashpur, Surguja in 1952, and along with other Sangh Parivar organisations, sought to check the spread of Christianity in the region by competing with the social work done by the churches.[54]

Hindu conservatism was represented in the local Congress Party too. In 1954, it was R.S. Shukla's Congress state government that established a Commission of enquiry under B.S. Niyogi, a former chairman of the Civil Service Commission, to study the activities of Christian missionaries in Surguja. The Commission's report effectively proposed the banning of all 'non-voluntary' conversions. The BJP later led 'reconversion' campaigns in a bid to attract Christian tribals 'back' to Hinduism. This rested on an attempt to incorporate animist tribal religious practice as part of the broader umbrella of Hinduism. Dilip Singh Judeo was one of the main BJP leaders associated with this effort.

Table 4.2: Electoral trends in seats reserved for Scheduled Tribes in Chhattisgarh, 1980–2003.

Party	1980	1985	1990	1993	1998	2003
Surguja						
INC	11	8	2	6	6	2
BJP	1	4	9	6	5	10
IND	0	0	1	0	1	0
Bastar						
INC	5	11	1	5	11	3
BJP	3	1	8	5	1	9
IND	2	0	1	0	0	0
Other	2	0	2	2	0	0
Other Reserved Seats						
INC	9	8	3	8	4	4
BJP	1	1	7	1	5	6
IND	0	1	0	0	0	0
Other	0	0	0	1	1	0
Total	34	34	34	34	34	34

Source: Calculated from Election Commission of India data (Surguja includes current Surguja and Jashpur districts; Bastar includes Kanker, Dantewada and Bastar—all seats in these districts are reserved for STs).

In Bastar and Surguja, the relationship between 'insiders' and 'outsiders' has been a sensitive one over time. These relations have contributed to the articulation of *adivasi* identities, though in themselves not strongly connected to an idea of Chhattisgarhi regionalism. As will be seen in the next section, Congress sought to exploit tensions between 'insiders' and 'outsiders' in order to isolate the BJP and set back their electoral expansion in Bastar and Surguja. In the 1990s, however, a consensus grew between both parties to highlight a demand for statehood for the broader region of Chhattisgarh. In subtle ways, political agreement in favour of statehood was geared towards defusing the potential for 'sons of the soil' tensions to become a more prominent focus for political mobilisation.

Congress and the Idea of Chhattisgarh

Until the 1980s, the main political party to promote the idea of statehood for Chhattisgarh had been the Praja Socialist Party. From 1980, however, the idea of statehood took a new turn. Pawan Diwan—a 'poet-sadhu' and figurehead of a cultural 'movement' in Chhattisgarh—established the Prthak Chhattisgarh Party (Separate Chhattisgarh Party) to contest the Lok Sabha elections. After Congress returned to power in 1980, the new Chief Minister Arjun Singh made concerted attempts of his own to promote a regional Chhattisgarhi identity.[55] He was motivated to a considerable degree by the desire to sideline the Shukla brothers, who had hitherto dominated the Congress party in Chhattisgarh and were also his major rivals within Congress. Singh pushed these goals by promoting an 'asli (real) Chhattisgarhi' leadership and highlighting the 'non-Chhattisgarhi' roots of the Shuklas. These moves should be understood against the backdrop of his concerted effort to change the social base of the Congress Party across Madhya Pradesh as a whole by appealing more to socially disadvantaged groups.

Arjun Singh made various symbolic overtures to famous 'Chhattisgarhi' individuals. He oversaw the construction of a 'Guru Ghasidas' (creator of the Satnampanth) university in Bilaspur, named a chair after Sunderlal Sharma (a Chhattisgarhi Brahmin) at Ravishanker University in Raipur, went to the village of Veer Narayan Singh (a tribal and 'martyr' of the 1857 uprising) and named a dam after him. Here Arjun Singh was borrowing the use of Veer Narayan Singh's story from the Chhattisgarh Mukti Morcha who had uncovered his story and used it to inspire people in the search for social justice.[56] These were fairly cynical attempts at co-option. As the People's Union for Democratic Rights wrote:

Many attempts were made to suppress the Veer Narayan Diwas on 19 December for a number of years. Then suddenly the state bestowed recognition to him. The peasant leader became a "freedom fighter". A great grandson was located and granted a pension.[57]

Arjun Singh often made reference to the 'great Chhattisgarhi', Khubchand Baghel, in his speeches and erected a number of statues of Chhattisgarhi figures across the region. He also negotiated the entrance of Pawan Diwan into the Congress Party.[58] He established a Chhattisgarh Vikas Pratikharan (Chhattisgarh Development Authority), which had few substantial powers, but helped to consolidate an idea of the region as being backward and in need of special assistance.[59] Singh also worked with new *adivasi* elites within Congress, such as Bhedia, who resented the domination of local politics by the Shukla brothers and felt that Chhattisgarh was being exploited by outsiders.[60]

In the 1980s and early 1990s, a new generation of OBC leaders in Chhattisgarh, to whom Arjun Singh extended his support, began to promote the idea of statehood. As Samuel Berthet also argues, OBCs were at the forefront of the promotion of a Chhattisgarhi identity.[61] These politicians included Vasudev Chandraker (Kurmi),[62] Chandulal Chandraker (Kurmi) and Bisahu Das Mahant[63] (Kabirpanthi OBC).[64] In Chhattisgarh the social background of Legislative Assembly members had changed with the election of larger numbers of OBC MLAs as part of the Janata government in 1977. A small further expansion of OBC representation took place in 1980, when at least seventeen OBC MLAs were elected in Chhattisgarh under the Congress banner. Between 1962 and 1980, the percentage of OBC MLAs in Chhattisgarh had increased from approximately 8.5 per cent to around 20 per cent—fairly similar to today, although still markedly below their proportion of the population.[65] This increase in OBC MLAs took place in Chhattisgarh ahead of the rest of Madhya Pradesh, reflecting the considerably larger OBC population in Chhattisgarh than the rest of the state. Arjun Singh gave a number of cabinet positions to OBC, SC and ST MLAs from Chhattisgarh in his government. Ahead of the 1985 Assembly elections, he also allotted a large share of the tickets across the state to OBCs, although there was only a small increase in the number elected. After the 1985 elections there was markedly more competition between the Congress and BJP (at least in the Chhattisgarh region of Madhya Pradesh) over the representation of the other backward classes. In 1985, all but two of the OBC MLAs were Congress. In 1990, eight of at least four-teen OBC MLAs from Chhattisgarh were BJP, two were Janata Dal and only four belonged to Congress.[66] Kurmis and Sahus are over-represented among elected representatives from OBC backgrounds.

These newer leaders within Congress made a case for the creation of a separate state based on factors such as Chhattisgarh's wealth of natural resources, the neglect of agricultural development and infrastructure, and the region's remoteness from Bhopal.[67] Chandulal Chandraker became one of the most vocal proponents of the statehood demand in Congress during his time as MP and national Congress spokesperson.[68] These politicians also highlighted the question of upper caste dominance of politics. As Digvijay Singh (who became Chief Minister of Madhya Pradesh in 1993) recollected, this generation of leaders were the first people to raise the issue of 'sons of the soil' in Chhattisgarh.[69] Charandas Mahant (son of Bisahu Das Mahant and a Congress politician today) confirmed this line of thinking, in saying that those Chief Ministers of Madhya Pradesh (such as S.C. Shukla) who had come from Chhattis-garh were not all really from Chhattisgarh. They came from old families who wanted to establish themselves in Delhi and across Madhya Pradesh. 'If we created a small state, their sphere of influence would reduce,' he said. 'Only those people from Chhattisgarh, who were born here, who have been here for 300–400 years wanted a separate state: outsiders didn't want it.'[70] An appeal to a Chhattisgarhi identity became something of a shorthand for identifying 'exploited classes', mirroring earlier articulations. As Pawan Diwan noted to me:

Lakhs of Chhattisgarhis have migrated from the region, but the landless shouldn't have to migrate to find work—they should be able to find work here. See how many outsiders have come here and become ministers, Chief Minis-ters. But Chhattisgarhis elsewhere are the labour class—they work hard and get nothing—everywhere they are exploited. And they don't contest elections elsewhere.[71]

The next chapter will discuss Arjun Singh's motives—as Chief Minis-ter of the whole of Madhya Pradesh—in promoting political regionalism in Chhattisgarh, while also introducing new affirmative action for OBCs (ahead of the implementation of the Mandal Commission recommenda-tions by the central government). But looking at politics within the Chhattisgarh region, competition between Congress and the increasingly assertive BJP over the representation of OBCs intensified over the course of the 1980s. This contest helped to explain both parties' emergent support for statehood.

Within Congress, Arjun Singh's efforts to build up new local leaders, who themselves began to discuss the idea of a separate state, constituted a direct challenge to the supremacy of the Shuklas. V.C. Shukla claimed that Arjun Singh was motivated by the intention of weakening their political base: 'Arjun Singh's entire or sole aim was to weaken our position in Chhattisgarh…Those that he promoted were not supporters of Chhattisgarh, but opponents of ours.'[72] Another Congress politician Bhupesh Baghel, a Kurmi, agreed that 'Arjun Singh did the basic work in building local leadership in order to weaken the Shuklas.'[73] The Shuklas remained at most lukewarm and sometimes outwardly hostile to the idea of statehood, viewing it primarily as a means of sidelining them.

A different picture of Arjun Singh's intentions emerges, however, in speaking to politicians from OBC castes in Chhattisgarh. Dr M.L. Yadu is a Yadav leader in Congress and was the chairman of the Chhattisgarh Asmita Pratikshan, an intellectual forum set up in 1995 to discuss the creation of a separate state. In an interview, he said animatedly that:

Arjun Singh gave politics to the OBCs (*Arjun Singh ne OBCs ko politics diya!*). Once in politics, no-one can send OBCs away or ignore them. And once Congress made these moves, then the BJP also started to think about involving OBCs more.[74]

Arjun Singh also played a role in supporting Ajit Jogi, who had been drawn into politics by Rajiv Gandhi and who became the first Chief Minister of the new state of Chhattisgarh in 2000. Jogi's background is disputed and has been the subject of an ongoing legal dispute. He claims to be an *adivasi* and has certificates stating that he is a Scheduled Tribe, but Jogi's 'true' identity has been questioned by those who claim that his family are *Satnamis* or local Scheduled Castes who converted to Christianity. The dispute a telling reflection of the fluidity of identity and its brush with state classificatory practices. While in power as Chief Minister from 2000 to 2003, Jogi projected a special affinity with both *adivasis* and *Satnamis*.

When he was in office between 1980 and 1985 Arjun Singh did not actually support the idea of statehood for Chhattisgarh, despite bolstering a sense of regional political community. But he paid increasing attention to the region, even contesting an assembly seat (Kharsiya) in Chhattisgarh after he returned as Chief Minister in 1988, worried about the erosion of Congress support in the region.[75] Later, while out of office in the early 1990s, he gave at least tacit support to the idea that Chhattisgarh should be made a separate state.[76] However this was not widely publicised and few people believed that statehood for Chhattisgarh was imminent or even likely. The following section focuses more closely on the reasons for the move to support statehood by local members of the BJP as well as Congress, with both parties adopting the demand in their manifestos for the 1993 state elections in Madhya Pradesh.

Political Regionalism and Democratic Deepening

The early 1990s were a time of intense competition between the BJP and Congress in Chhattisgarh. The BJP made its first electoral breakthrough in the 1990 state assembly elections, which brought it to power across Madhya Pradesh for the first time. They were subsequently defeated by Congress in the 1991 Lok Sabha elections, and again in the 1993 state elections which were held following the imposition of President's Rule in Madhya Pradesh in the context of post-Ayodhya violence. During these elections in 1993, for the first time, the local outfits of both Congress and the BJP offered their support for the creation of a separate state.

A number of interviewees associated with both parties stated simply that it was inter-party competition that led the parties to adopt a call for statehood during the 1993 election campaign. The idea of statehood, although promoted at a cultural level by people from diverse caste backgrounds including Chhattisgarhi Brahmins, was seen in political terms as a signal for the inclusion of non-upper caste and bania elites in the ruling class. Congress sought to make the question of the BJP's social base a major issue in the 1993 state elections. As a BJP Member of Parliament reported: 'In MP the BJP has been nicknamed the Bania Jain Party by the Congress (I) and other opposition groups and this name has stuck.'[77] Pawan Diwan, an early proponent of statehood, who had joined the Congress Party in 1980 on the suggestion of Chief Minister Arjun Singh, said that the demand for Chhattisgarh was formally added to the state Congress manifesto in 1993 'after the BJP was trying to capitalise on the issue'.[78] Keshav Singh Thakur, who had been a local BJP leader until around 1991 and then set up the Chhat-

Figure 4.1: Assembly seats won by Congress and BJP in Chhattisgarh 1980–2003.

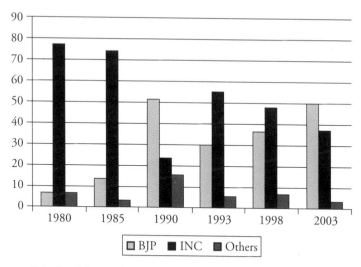

Source: Calculated from Electoral Commission of India data.

tisgarh Nirman Sarvadalli Manch (all party campaign for the creation of Chhattisgarh), confirmed this:

There was a process of 'constructive competition' between the BJP and Congress. The BJP thought if we don't support state creation then Congress will, and Congress thought, if we don't support state creation then BJP will. So both parties supported state creation.[79]

It is unlikely that the issue of statehood was an important vote winner for either party. The demand for statehood in Chhattisgarh lacked the kind of mass base, or public awareness, that was seen in either Jharkhand and Uttarakhand. The idea of statehood did, however, have significance at the intra-elite level in both Congress and the BJP, especially to aspiring leaders from backward classes, who favoured the promotion of a 'local' political leadership that would sideline the old Kanyakubja Brahmin elite in Congress and Banias, Thakurs and Maharashtrian Brahmins in the BJP.

During the 1993 elections—in a post-Mandal climate—Congress in Madhya Pradesh called for the implementation of the recommendations of the state backward classes commission established by Arjun Singh in the early 1980s.[80] In Chhattisgarh, Congress also drew particular attention to the decision by the BJP government (1990–92) to roll back the policy towards the mostly *adivasi* pickers of tendu leaves adopted by Arjun Singh's government in the late 1980s. This policy had attempted to eliminate traders or middlemen from the lucrative trade in Chhattisgarh by establishing cooperatives of tendu leaf pickers, but was rolled back by the short-lived BJP state government. The BJP government had also planned the inauguration of two new steel plants near Jagdalpur in Bastar which had become the subject of local protests against displacement.[81] During the 1993 elections, Congress drew attention to these economic policy changes under the BJP state government by pointing to the vested interests of party elites. They highlighted the personal interests of the BJP leader and former state president Lakhiram Agrawal, himself a *bania*, in the tendu leaf trade by adopting the slogan: '*Tendu tode adhe pet, munafa khaya Lakhi seth*' (the tendu leaves are plucked by the hungry, the profits are eaten by Lakhi seth).[82]

Such charges were taken seriously by members of the BJP, and some among those who pursued the statehood demand saw this as a way of changing the social profile of the BJP. Ramesh Bais has been the BJP MP for Raipur since 1989. He is a Kurmi and has held his seat since defeating V.C. Shukla in this year. He became Union Minister for Mines under the NDA government in Delhi in 1998. Bais was a key supporter of statehood within the BJP and it was clear that, for him, the Chhattisgarhi identity was associated with non-upper castes:

After the first elections [after state creation in 2003], people from the area are seeing the reason for which we created Chhattisgarh—so that the development of the state, the development of the original inhabitants (Chhattisgarh ki moolnivasi) who call themselves Chhattisgarhi would happen … After the formation of Chhattisgarh, the age of the Shuklas was over.

He argued that the BJP had lost two recent by-elections because 'people of the local area were not given importance' and instead the BJP was dominated by Agrawals, Banias, Sheths and Marwaris.[83]

Chandrashekhar Sahu, another local BJP leader, was one of the leaders of an internal statehood committee within the BJP. He agreed that the demand for Chhattisgarh within the BJP had gained strength at the same time as a conscious strategy of trying to attract backward castes away from Congress—through leaders like Ramesh Bais—in order to break Congress' strength in the region. 'The BJP was seen as a Bania or

traders party and this was a political liability', he said. 'People wouldn't
support such a party at the grassroots, so we wanted to change this.'
This, he noted, was part of the national strategy of 'social engineering',
the inclusion of more representatives of lower castes in the party appa-
ratus, forwarded by BJP national general secretary Govindacharya at the
time. He also said that the RSS was clear that Chhattisgarh should be
established because the region was being exploited, 'the true Chhattisgarhi "sons of the soil" were being exploited by an outside exploiter
class.'[84] Thus, as in Jharkhand, the (limited) foray into social engineering
by the BJP coincided with their embrace of political regionalism.

Like Congress, support for statehood was a move made initially by
local BJP leaders rather than being a decision taken or endorsed by the
national leadership. Indeed, it should be stressed, that many local politicians—from both parties—did not expect their national leadership, let
alone central government, to take up the call for statehood. Within the
BJP, the first formal discussion of the statehood idea was at the National
Executive Meeting in Gandhinagar in 1991, where a political resolution
on Chhattisgarh failed. After the party's poor showing in the 1993
assembly elections—it lost over 100 seats and 5 per cent of the popular
vote across Madhya Pradesh—and in the 1996 Lok Sabha elections, the
BJP worried increasingly about its social profile and indiscipline among
party workers. As Jaffrelot notes, it also worried about the rise of the
Bahujan Samaj Party (BSP) across Madhya Pradesh and appointed a
Janadhar Badhao Samiti (Committee for Broadening the Base).[85] This
committee, headed by Babulal Gaur, recommended a more forthright
promotion of lower castes within the party and spoke of a need to influence 'our leaders from the high castes…to welcome the feelings of equality'.[86] Thus the idea of creating a new state in Chhattisgarh found
support among politicians from OBC castes in both BJP and Congress,
in the context of wider concerns to deepen the social roots of both
national parties across Madhya Pradesh.

Following the Congress victory in state elections in 1993, bringing
Digvijay Singh to power, a resolution in favour of statehood for Chhattisgarh was passed with little fanfare in the Madhya Pradesh Legislative
Assembly in 1994. Yet, the state government did little to push the issue
further at the national level. The BJP began to seize the initiative on
Chhattisgarh more aggressively from 1995. This followed the death of
the main Congress proponent of Chhattisgarh, Chandulal Chandraker,

national party spokesman and former president of the Chhattisgarh Rajya Nirman Manch (Chhattisgarh State Creation Committee, CRNM)—an all party outfit set up in the early 1990s. After this, the BJP started to dominate the CRNM, and also established a Chhattisgarh Nirman Samiti (Chhattisgarh Creation Committee) within the BJP convened by Lakhiram Agrawal (former Madhya Pradesh BJP state president) and Chandrashekhar Sahu.[87] It was in this period that the demand for Chhattisgarh was first approved by the BJP's National Executive after a hostile debate at its meeting in Bhopal, and then included in the BJP's general election manifesto in 1996.

By 1998, the BJP latched on to the idea of statehood as a potential vote winner. When Atal Bihari Vajpayee visited Raipur ahead of the parliamentary elections in 1998, the MP Ramesh Bais advised him that the BJP would be helped to win if they promised to create Chhattisgarh, alongside Jharkhand and Uttarakhand.[88] Vajpayee pledged at an election rally that if the people gave the BJP all eleven seats, the BJP would give them Chhattisgarh. They won seven in the end.

Blurring Insider-Outsider Divisions: Not Going the 'Orissa Route'

As has been shown, appeals to a Chhattisgarhi identity had been used by various politicians as a means to identify a general class of the exploited or marginalised. This meaning did not become the basis for region-wide political mobilisation of the economically and socially marginalised. Instead, the promotion of the idea of Chhattisgarh by political parties appeared to be a means of, symbolically at least, tying dominant social and economic interests to the wider local population and seeking to avoid the mobilisation of either class- or identity-based groups in the region. Indeed, a fear about the potential for insider-outsider conflicts seems to have encouraged some local business-people and traders to support the idea of statehood.

A conversation at the Raipur Development Authority with the BJP-affiliated vice chairman and several colleagues brought to light some of the sensitivities around the possible association of a Chhattisgarhi identity with 'anti-outsider' sentiment or the potential for politicians to mobilise around such an identity. They were initially at pains to stress that all parties supported statehood and no-one was opposed, asserting that Chhattisgarh does not have any anti-outsider sentiment and that this played no role in the demand for statehood. Anyone who settles in the region, they averred, is accepted as a Chhattisgarhi after a few years. State creation, they suggested, had been a boon for business because of infrastructural development such as the improved rail and air connections to the new state capital. But they slowly went on to acknowledge that things had become 'bad' with a rise of 'casteism' under Ajit Jogi, the first Chief Minister of the new state, who had been 'worse for business' than the subsequent BJP government. Under Jogi, there was a fear that Chhattisgarh 'might go the Orissa route [referring to anti-Marwari violence in Orissa some years previously] but people realised they didn't want to create a second Orissa and so voted Jogi out'.[89]

Strikingly, once the BJP came behind the demand for Chhattisgarh fully, the attempt to link the demand for state creation with an expansion of the party's social base was downplayed. As has been suggested, the demand had originally been associated with some OBC leaders, but upper caste leaders who had previously been reticent became more active in also backing the demand. In some ways, support for Chhattisgarh's statehood was a way for the BJP to adapt to a post-Mandal environment without having to rock the boat too much. The BJP's official rationale for statehood highlighted the question of 'regional neglect' and the potential for greater exploitation of the region's natural resources, rather than any particular social constituency for statehood. As Lakhiram Agrawal, a Bania and senior BJP leader in Madhya Pradesh said, 'Bhagwan [God] gave everything [forests, minerals, rivers etc.] to Chhattisgarh, but it wasn't being used by Madhya Pradesh.' Agrawal confessed to having previously seen himself as a leader of Madhya Pradesh (rather than only Chhattisgarh), but subsequently adopted the view that 'Chhattisgarh could only develop when it was a separate state.'[90] The BJP tied the debate about Chhattisgarh into a national debate about the advantages of small states for development, rather than linking it to social issues. Given that Congress was in power in Madhya Pradesh for most of the period in which the demand was raised, the charge of regional neglect was harder for Congress to make.

After the BJP came to power at the Centre in 1998 and signalled its intention to go ahead with its plans to create new states, even V.C. Shukla added his voice to those demanding a new state. He had been gradually marginalised in Chhattisgarhi politics from 1980 onwards. As we have seen, he had interpreted Arjun Singh's promotion of a Chhattisgarhi identity and statehood as a direct bid to undermine him. In 1987, he was expelled from Congress as a result of his conflict with Rajiv Gandhi and joined V.P. Singh's anti-Rajiv campaign after the Bofors scandal. He subsequently returned to Congress but was again defeated in the Lok Sabha elections by Ramesh Bais in 1996. In 1999 Digvijay Singh persuaded him to withdraw from the election contest in favour of a Sahu (OBC) candidate.[91] V.C. Shukla himself says that he decided to support the campaign for statehood only once there was a credible commitment by the Centre to support the move.[92] This can be seen as a rational manoeuvre by Shukla to try to protect his position in a future state. It is also a testament to how shallow popular participation in the statehood demand had been before 1999–2000 that a number of the villagers interviewed during focus group discussions in several districts of Chhattisgarh associated the demand for statehood above all with V.C. Shukla and said that the only pro-statehood rallies they had taken part in were those organised by V.C. himself.[93]

Conclusion

In Chhattisgarh, unlike Jharkhand and Uttarakhand, statehood was granted to a region in which public clamour for a change in state borders had been historically extremely limited. This chapter has presented an in-depth account of the political origins of the idea of statehood in the Chhattisgarh region. It has delineated the competing ideologies and political motives that inspired a number of actors to float the idea of statehood, or to appeal to a Chhattisgarh identity over time. For the Chhattisgarh Mukti Morcha and some Socialist politicians this was an identity that was to be understood in class terms as a means of critiquing patterns of exploitation within the industrial economy. But from the earliest calls for a separate state, the demand has as often been raised by politicians, often Kurmis, resentful of the dominance of Congress politics in the region by a very narrow elite and one family in particular. A Chhattisgarhi identity has been used to denote a large, inchoate set of social groups falling into SC, ST and OBC categories who are seen as 'local' by contrast with the 'outsiders' who occupy upper echelons of both Congress and the BJP. Yet, the question of who is included as a Chhattisgarhi within such definitions is almost studiedly vague. Indeed, the effect of convergence in favour of statehood by the late 1990s was to weaken the strong association of any particular social group(s) with the claim to statehood. The consolidation of the idea of statehood took place in a period of political transition, in which party competition had opened up with the rotation of power between Congress and the BJP, and in which the Shuklas appeared increasingly sidelined. These patterns intersected with developments across the rest of Madhya Pradesh. Together, they opened up the borders of the state as features of the political landscape that could be subject to change.

Party convergence in favour of statehood for Chhattisgarh arose from competition between Congress and the BJP locally. The turning point in the trajectory of the statehood demand, if any, can be seen during the regime of Arjun Singh in the 1980s. Singh fostered a Chhattisgarhi identity as a bid to co-opt lower caste elites in Congress, neutralise the appeal of the Socialists and sideline his rivals in Congress. Changes in state level politics across the Hindi heartland, and after 1990 the implementation of the Mandal Commission recommendations, made the political incorporation of lower castes a more pressing challenge for Chief Ministers.

The next chapter will show that the responses to such dilemmas by Chief Ministers and other state-level politicians started to open up new sub-state regional political arenas, and shaped a context in which the division of Hindi-speaking states became more conceivable from the perspectives of state capitals, too.

5

THE VIEW FROM THE STATE CAPITALS

This chapter shifts its gaze upwards to the state level to consider the question of state creation from the vantage point of the state capital. It looks at why politicians from the same state but based outside the region for which statehood was demanded also began to promote or give life to the idea of changing state boundaries as one response to changing forms of politics in Hindi-speaking states. In particular, I will show that the political mobilisation of lower and middle castes from the late 1960s onwards and the gradual challenge to upper caste dominance of state-level politics helped to bring the question of state division to the centre of the political arenas of Bihar, Madhya Pradesh and Uttar Pradesh, not just within the regions demanding statehood. In each case, a state-wide leader brought the borders of their state into political play from 1980 onwards as they tried to hold together cross-state political alliances. As I have outlined, state borders are a form of institution that develop stickiness over time. In order to explain when and why states might be subdivided, it is critical to understand how a degree of flexibility as to the boundaries of a state opens up at the centre of the political arena, not simply within a region seeking statehood.

In Madhya Pradesh, Arjun Singh, the Congress Chief Minister of Madhya Pradesh for much of the 1980s, promoted a Chhattisgarhi regional identity at the same time as he fostered an OBC leadership in the region. It was his successor as Chief Minister Digvijay Singh who was in power when the state assembly passed a resolution supporting statehood in 1994. In Uttar Pradesh, Mulayam Singh Yadav, the Sama-jwadi Party Chief Minister from 1989–91 and 1993–95 (and after Uttarakhand's creation between 2003–7), actively provoked a regional movement in Uttarakhand which he portrayed as an upper caste reaction to his social justice agenda elsewhere in Uttar Pradesh. In Bihar, Chief Minister Lalu Prasad Yadav, while opposed to the bifurcation of his state, also helped to draw the statehood issue into the centre of the state-level political arena by arguing in the late 1990s that his political opponents were motivated by a conspiracy to divide the state. We can see each of these leaders as 'political entrepreneurs'. As Wyatt argues:

Political entrepreneurs help define the profound disagreements, or cleavages, in political opinion which become the object of competition between political parties. Social divisions provide raw materials that political entrepreneurs use to construct narratives of political conflict that work to their advantage.[1]

The discussion in this chapter will show how the response, and contribution, of these political entrepreneurs to the transformation of state-level political arenas in Hindi-speaking states provided crucial traction for the idea of statehood.

By the 1990s, a politics of seeking social justice through caste-based electoral mobilisation had been firmly established in north India through the ascendancy of the Janata Dal (and its later offshoots) in Bihar, the Samajwadi Party and Bahujan Samaj Party in Uttar Pradesh, and with the brief spell of the National Front government in Delhi from 1989–91, which implemented the Mandal Commission recommendations for new 'reservations' or affirmative action policies for 'Other Backward Classes' (OBCs). These new political configurations gave rise—indirectly—to new ways of thinking about the boundaries of Hindi speaking states. As the existing boundaries of Hindi-speaking states came to be challenged not only within potential breakaway regions but at the heart of state political arenas, territorial restructuring looked increasingly plausible in this meta-region. New approaches to envisioning the territory of existing states, including the possibility of creating new states, emerged as one form of tactical response to the increasing challenge of projecting political power across large, diverse states. That this could happen suggested that earlier legitimations of state borders in north India had been weakened. These had derived strength from a sacred geography in the case of Uttar Pradesh and were underpinned both by upper caste political dominance and a desire among the national political leadership to limit state reorganisation to a linguistic principle.

The 'Missing Middle': Importance of the State Level in Explaining State Creation

According to Article 3 of the Indian Constitution, as we have seen, states must be consulted on the question of a revision of their borders but they have no right of veto. If the power to create new states therefore lies with the central government, why do the actions of state leaders matter? In the first place, the BJP only pushed ahead with state creation where the state legislative assembly had previously passed legislation in favour of statehood for a region. Home Minister L.K. Advani himself had stressed that—despite the BJP's manifesto commitments to create states in certain regions (including Delhi and Vidarbha as well as Chhattisgarh, Jharkhand and Uttarakhand) and existing constitutional rights to do otherwise—the government would not create states without the approval of the state government concerned. This is consistent with the historical approach of the central government, generally, to move ahead with state creation only where there was a good deal of agreement on both sides of a state to be divided.[2] Thus it becomes important to explain why state assemblies in Bihar, Madhya Pradesh and Uttar Pradesh approved resolutions supporting the division of their states, and why this did not happen in other states. Structural and political changes that were taking place across the large states of north India—especially the decline of upper caste political dominance—acted as the broad canvas against which decisions about new borders were made. They help to explain why it was in the Hindi belt, and not in linguistic states in south or west India, that new states were created in 2000.

That some Chief Ministers were willing to engage in politics that brought the borders of their states into question appears somewhat paradoxical. The large size of the Hindi-speaking states, and their parliamentary contingents, had helped to bolster their prominence in national political life. The potential breakaway regions of these states were, furthermore, well-endowed with natural resources. Electricity generated in Chhattisgarh was responsible for much of Madhya Pradesh's power supply and Uttarakhand's hydropower was important for Uttar Pradesh.

The Chief Ministers were gambling with seats, natural resources and revenues. This much had been clear to leaders of Bihar who had remained steadfastly opposed to the demand for Jharkhand for decades. It was the politicisation of caste and the challenge to upper caste dominance within Hindi speaking states which had the most significant impact on the political discourse about state size and political regionalism. Claims for social justice for lower castes and better access to political power were not typically made on a territorial basis. But in pursuing—and responding to—the politics of caste based empowerment, state leaders and their political opponents helped to give space to the demands for the bifurcation of Bihar, Madhya Pradesh and Uttar Pradesh. A new willingness, however casual, to play politics with borders even from within state capitals helped to open up the existing boundaries of states to question from an increasing range of actors.

Ultimately the legislative assemblies of all three states passed resolutions approving the division of their states—in Uttar Pradesh for the first time in 1991, in Madhya Pradesh in 1994 and in Bihar in 1997 (although this was subsequently rescinded). The passage of such resolutions did not always reflect a firm commitment or intention on the part of respective state leaderships to push the central government to take action to create states. As I have argued elsewhere, the politics of statehood has often been carried out with a conspicuous absence of serious intent.[3] State leaders felt that they could act with a certain degree of impunity when promoting—tacitly or explicitly—statehood demands because the Centre had historically been so reluctant to create new states, especially in places where language was not the major issue. Politicians of many hues have encouraged or at the least paid lip service to calls for statehood that they never expected to see the light of day (and did not intend to fight for at higher levels of the federal system). They have offered support to statehood demands to serve shorter term political objectives such as sidelining political competitors, co-opting potential opponents or cobbling together a fragile legislative majority. Nevertheless, the possibility that such resolutions could be passed with minimal complaint reflects an increasing willingness among political elites to countenance changes to state boundaries, at least at a rhetorical level. State borders were now subject to question from both sides of these states. This helps to explain why it was in these regions that new states could be created, and not in linguistic states in south or west

India, where borders were not subject to question on both sides of a state to be divided. Employing the metaphor of borders as a form of institution, we can see that from the 1980s onwards the territorial expanse of the states of Bihar, Madhya Pradesh and Uttar Pradesh began to appear less firmly institutionalised as social and political change provided new reasons for political elites to treat state borders as potentially being subject to change.

Regional Identities in Hindi-Versus Non-Hindi-Speaking States

In the first three decades after independence, state-based regional identities were arguably less important in many Hindi-speaking parts of India than elsewhere because states were better seen as sub-divisions of a larger national identity. As Kymlicka points out, multi-ethnic or multi-national federal systems tend to be comprised of a mixture of 'nationality-based' and 'regional-based' units.[4] 'Regional-based' units can be seen as divisions of a larger national group and typically have a closer association with the federal centre. They are more willing to relinquish powers to the central government than 'nationality-based units', home to distinct ethnic or national groups which are likely instead to seek greater powers from the centre. Together the regional units comprise what Brendan O'Leary calls the *staatsvolk* or members of the numerically dominant community in a federation.[5] For some time in India the *staatsvolk* could be thought of as the Hindi-speaking population of north India.

Political identities in predominantly Hindu, Hindi-speaking north India were less tied up with state boundaries than those in states which were dominated by a non-Hindi language or a religion other than Hinduism. It is also the case that the affective ties of language that, as Mitchell has described, had come to be experienced as natural in the early part of the twentieth century in southern India—and which were fused with emotional intensity in the case of the movement for statehood in Andhra Pradesh—were absent as ingredients for the formation of regional political community in northern India, at least within individual states.[6] The Hindi language movement after independence, incubated particularly within Uttar Pradesh but also in other Hindi-speaking states, had its sights on the promotion of Hindi across India as a national language.[7] But this was the objective of political elites within 'regional' rather than 'nationality-based' federal units. The defence of the integrity of the existing borders of Uttar Pradesh made by senior politicians in the 1950s including Chief Minister and subsequent Home Minister G.B. Pant (as described in chapter two) was based on the centrality of Uttar Pradesh to the integrity of India as a whole.

The reason that the idea of creating new states in north India became a subject for greater political debate was that the *staatsvolk* itself fractured. As Adeney points out, the rise of parties representing lower castes and Dalits such as the Bahujan Samaj Party (BSP), Janata Dal (JD) and Samajwadi Party suggested a weakening of the idea of a *staatsvolk* premised on Hindi-speaking north India as the dominant political community in India.[8] This was also reflected in the relative decline of north Indian politicians at the helm of power in New Delhi: since 1991, just one among India's five prime ministers was elected from a constituency in Uttar Pradesh, compared to seven of the eight that came before this date.[9] This study suggests that it was the challenge to upper caste dominance—and especially the entrenchment of 'Other Backward Classes' as a category for political mobilisation—that began to create reasons for politicians who had not earlier been involved with demands for statehood to question the existing large borders of some north Indian states in light of the geographically uneven spread of lower and middle caste *jatis*. These processes also brought to life new ways of conceiving of the sacred geography of a state such as Uttar Pradesh that problematised earlier legitimations of its extant borders. The emergence of lower caste and Dalit parties in north Indian states in the 1980s and 1990s represented the erosion of a *staatsvolk* based loosely on a community of Hindi speakers but bolstered by upper caste dominance. It coincided with, and contributed to, a broader decentralisation of political and economic power to the state-level across India.

The Changing Character of State Politics in the Hindi Heartland

The patterns of political competition across Indian states have been shaped by the way in which lower castes and classes have been incorporated into different party systems and state institutions.[10] This incorporation took place in the wake of the erosion of Congress ascendancy and the challenges to upper caste dominance of politics in north India. Congress suffered heavier electoral defeats across the Hindi heartland than any other region of the country in the 1977 general elections held after the Emergency. The Janata Party government was, as Jaffrelot argues, 'a milestone in the quest for power of the lower castes and the *kisan* [farmer]'.[11] All but three MPs in the Hindi belt belonged to the Janata Party. While many of these MPs were former Jana Sangh politicians, they were joined by Charan Singh's Bharatiya Lok Dal and the Socialist Party, votaries respectively of agrarian interests and reservation policies for lower castes.

The first systematic attempt to mobilise lower castes as a discrete part of society in north India was made by the Socialist leader Rammanohar Lohia. From the late 1950s, Lohia—leader of the Samyukta Socialist Party until his death in 1967—advocated affirmative action for lower castes in the administration and elections. Lohia sought to use caste-based political mobilisation to create a large interest-based coalition of multiple groups all 'sharing common and disadvantaged social-structural locations'.[12] In 1959, the party adopted a call for 60 per cent reservations for backward sections of society (including Scheduled Castes, Scheduled Tribes, OBCs and women). The mobilisation of agrarian classes intersected with, but did not exactly overlap with, the emergence of what Jaffrelot calls a 'quota politics'—a programme of using reservations in government jobs and education as a means of politicising lower castes.[13] The categories of owner cultivator and OBC are not identical. But in practice, many proponents of farmers' politics and those seeking to build political coalitions on the basis of backward caste identities both tended to see these two programmes as interrelated. Land reforms, including the abolition of intermediaries and of tenancy, helped some OBC caste groups such as Kurmis, Koeris and Yadavs in Bihar, and Yadavs, Kurmis, Lodhis, Gujars and Koeris in Uttar Pradesh, to become owner-cultivators. The effects of the new politics of quotas were therefore felt in combination with the new agrarian politics, although tensions existed between the two agendas because many middle peasants were intermediate castes—such as Jats in Uttar Pradesh—who were not recognised as OBCs.

The consolidation of horizontal caste categories is commonly referred to as substantialisation (after Louis Dumont) or the ethnicisation of caste, as it implies a shift from caste hierarchy towards competition between more horizontally conceived caste groupings.[14] To varying degrees, processes of substantialisation had been taking place across

India since the 1950s and earlier, as education and communications spread, land reforms and agrarian change altered socioeconomic relations, and urbanisation created new spaces of interaction. But, in states such as Bihar and Uttar Pradesh, it was the politicisation of caste by socialists, the Janata Dal and its successors that did the most to drive the deepening of horizontal identities and challenge prevailing structures of upper caste dominance of social relations and administration. The implementation of the Mandal Commission recommendations and political activism around 'OBC' identities were central to the consolidation of horizontal caste categories by these parties. In parallel, the Bahujan Samaj Party—established in 1994—developed alternative strategies for appealing to 'oppressed' groups, but with a primary interest in mobilising Dalits to seize political power. The new forms of caste based empowerment through politics and control of the state helped to constitute new political subjectivities or what Michelutti describes as the 'vernacularisation' of democracy as it became embedded in new social settings and idioms.[15]

The culmination of a bid to create a political coalition around the OBC category came with the implementation of the recommendations of the Mandal Commission (set up by the Janata Party Government of 1977–79) in 1990 by V.P. Singh's Janata Dal-led government in New Delhi. The Janata Dal brought together Socialists and the successors to Charan Singh's Lok Dal. Most states had implemented their own commissions to consider the needs of the 'backward classes' before this, although they fared differently in implementing their various recommendations.[16] The most decisive increase in overall OBC participation (judged by turnout) had also already occurred by 1971. As Yadav shows, there was no significant increase in OBC electoral turnout between 1971 and 1998. What changed was the effectiveness and greater concentration of OBC votes, with the coming to power of new parties in north India.[17] In 1989, a Janata Dal government came to power in Uttar Pradesh and Mulayam Singh Yadav was selected as Chief Minister. He initially presented himself as a leader who would attempt to marry 'kisan politics' and 'quota politics'. However, he increasingly focused on lower caste politics more exclusively, splitting with Ajit Singh (Charan Singh's son, representative of Jat farmers and leader of a faction within the JD) to form the Samajwadi (Socialist) Party in November 1992.[18] In 1990, another Yadav politician, Lalu Prasad Yadav, came to power as JD Chief

Minister of Bihar. In Madhya Pradesh, by contrast, state leadership since 1990 has alternated between Congress and the BJP.[19] Both parties have been cognisant of incorporating lower castes, although change has been more gradual than in Uttar Pradesh or Bihar.

The political mobilisation of lower castes under the OBC banner, in addition to the emergence of owner-cultivators as an important political force, changed state-level political arenas in north India. Although the Congress vote recovered somewhat in 1980, the proportion of seats and votes won by Congress was considerably lower than in 1967 and 1971.[20] Furthermore, although the Congress (I) did return to power across the Hindi heartland in 1980, as Lloyd Rudolph and Susanne Hoeber Rudolph show, it failed to re-establish its supposedly special relationship with minorities including Scheduled Castes and Muslims. The three years of Janata government at the Centre, and in some states, had also seen moves towards the implementation of affirmative action measures for 'backward classes'. As the Rudolphs argued, the Congress Party could not afford to see the 1980 elections, in which they returned to power at the Centre and in many states, including Madhya Pradesh, as a 'restoration'.[21] Where the Congress Party failed to react to slowly changing patterns of political assertion and social dominance, it did not tend to survive in power into the 1990s. As Hasan argues it was Congress' failure to mount any mobilisation in response to mass movements in Uttar Pradesh of Dalits and OBCs, as well as the middle and rich peasantry, that led to its decline in Uttar Pradesh.[22]

Within this new political context, Chief Ministers faced a challenge in forging durable state-wide social coalitions to underpin new political formations. There was substantial regional variation in the geographical spread of different caste groups within large states such as Bihar, Madhya Pradesh and Uttar Pradesh. The political geographic context was such that the spatial distribution of neither particular owner-cultivator groups nor OBC communities corresponded neatly with state boundaries. The OBC castes found in north India are spatially disaggregated and closely tied to localised patterns of land ownership and agricultural production. Yadavs, for example, constituted the most numerous caste group in most of the northern districts of Bihar but not in the southern districts (that became Jharkhand). They also formed the largest caste group in much of eastern Uttar Pradesh, but not in western or central Uttar Pradesh, the southern plains or in the hills of Uttarakhand.[23] Only approximately 2 per cent of the entire population of Uttarakhand belonged to any community categorised officially as OBC. Brass's study of the politicisation of the peasantry in Uttar Pradesh highlights the emergence of different structures of power within different regions of Uttar Pradesh and their effect in producing distinct regional patterns of party competition within the state.[24] In Madhya Pradesh, as Jaffrelot shows, no group among the OBCs, apart from the Yadavs, accounted for more than 5 per cent of the state's population. In addition, no caste was spread evenly across the state: this fragmentation of lower castes 'stunted feelings of solidarity among them.'[25] Furthermore, the emotional and political integration of the regions that had been merged to form Madhya Pradesh in 1956 had proceeded slowly.[26]

Beyond spatial disaggregation, the OBCs are far from representing a united social or economic category, with persistent claims that certain groups among them have cornered the benefits of reservations. Yadavs, in particular, have been at the helm of the promotion of an OBC political category in Bihar and Uttar Pradesh and have been some of its main beneficiaries. 'Instead of developing horizontal solidarities,' Jaffrelot notes, 'they [lower castes in the north] are engaged in competition based on the criterion of status.'[27] This increased the difficulties of crafting stable, state-wide political coalitions based on lower caste political identities and, as I will show below, created new reasons for borders to be questioned. Both Mulayam Singh Yadav and Lalu Prasad Yadav sought to promote broad coalitions for social justice that pitted lower castes against upper castes. The promotion or provocation of regional identities was simply one among many symbolic tools used in an attempt to hold together such unwieldy political coalitions. The politicisation of regional identities was relatively marginal to the larger politics of social justice, but consequential in the history of state creation.

Madhya Pradesh: Regional Dimensions of Factional Conflict and Social Change

In the one state of the Hindi heartland in which Congress continued to dominate politics in the 1990s—Madhya Pradesh—its leadership from the 1980s onwards proactively sought to co-opt the support of backward castes. The party did this from a low base. In 1984, Madhya Pradesh had a smaller proportion of MPs from lower castes than most states in

India.[28] Congress maintained its preeminence in the absence of a rival regional party representing lower or intermediate castes. This was a state whose politics had long been dominated by a narrow range of social interests drawn from a handful of prosperous families, many of which were the former rulers of princely states. As a result of the nature of its birth, as an amalgamation of Hindi-speaking regions hived off from the non-Hindi speaking states, there was no dominant state-wide political class, and factionalism in the state's Congress Party was among the most notorious in the country.[29]

Arjun Singh (Chief Minister 1980–85; 1988–89) was born into the Rajput princely family of Rewa in the Vindhya Pradesh region of Madhya Pradesh. Upon taking over as Chief Minister, he faced two major challenges. Firstly, if the Congress Party was to survive, he needed to adapt to the new political landscape that had come to fruition in the three years of Janata rule. Secondly, as described in the previous chapter, he needed to keep his main factional rivals at bay, including the Shukla brothers in Chhattisgarh. In the context of regionally differentiated socioeconomic change across Madhya Pradesh and in the absence of any dominant state-wide OBC community, the promotion of a regional Chhattisgarhi identity helped him address both these challenges.

Arjun Singh encouraged the politicisation of a sub-state regional identity in Chhattisgarh as a means of recognising the growing assertiveness of lower and middle castes in that region, particularly Kurmis who combined their status as OBCs with a history of landownership. He sought to pit this new generation of politicians against the existing urban, upper caste regional leadership of Congress. As the previous chapter demonstrated, Chhattisgarh had a much smaller upper caste population than elsewhere in Madhya Pradesh and had also increased its share of OBC political representatives before other regions of the state. The promotion of a mild 'sons of the soil' politics linked to a statehood demand had the added appeal of helping Arjun Singh to sideline his key factional rivals within the Congress Party who were the targets of such politics.

When Arjun Singh became Chief Minister in 1980 he sought to consolidate Congress' relationship with SCs and STs as well as building alliances with members of groups classified as Other Backward Classes. As Shaibal Gupta notes, '[Arjun Singh's] efforts assume importance because of the fact that [they] preceded the self-initiated upsurge of the backward castes in Indian politics.' Although the Madhya Pradesh government had not faced pressure from below for OBC representation in the 1980s and 1990s, 'the state thought it prudent to initiate measures for empowering the poor and marginalised.'[30] In 1981, Arjun Singh established the Mahajan Commission to undertake a survey of the OBC population in the state and make recommendations to the government about their needs.[31] Digvijay Singh, an MLA at the time, worked with Arjun Singh to set up the Mahajan Commission. He said in retrospect that it had made good electoral sense to foster OBC leadership: 'After all democracy is a game of numbers…therefore we did try to co-opt leaders [of OBCs] in the Congress Party.'[32] Arjun Singh also introduced policies to give land rights to slum dwellers and to improve the rights of rickshaw pullers. The state government implemented two of the minor recommendations of the Mahajan Commission which in 1983 reported a need for quotas for OBCs in technical colleges and for the introduction of scholarships for higher studies, but these decisions were challenged by the High Court which issued a stay order.[33]

Arjun Singh's deference to a sense of Chhattisgarhi identity, outlined in the previous chapter, was designed in part to reach out to upwardly mobile groups of farmers, including landowning Kurmi OBCs, to whom the Socialists had also appealed with their call for statehood. In the early 1980s, Arjun Singh sought to appeal to farmers across Madhya Pradesh, as farmers' movements in various parts of India had increased awareness of the significance of farmers as an important political constituency. Arjun Singh sought to fan the resentment of owner-cultivator farmers in Chhattisgarh against the domination of politics and administration in the region by 'non-Chhattisgarhi Brahmins' such as the Shukla brothers—his factional rivals. He also tried to undercut the appeal to their interests by the Socialist Party. Addressing a meeting near Raipur soon after taking over as Chief Minister, Arjun Singh said:

There were people all around Raipur who were taking the name of farmers and raising the demand for a separate Chhattisgarh and misleading people. Of these there was one person—Purushottam Kaushik—who is today running an *andolan* [movement] in the name of Chhattisgarh…[but] when Kaushik was a central minister he didn't raise the demand for Chhattisgarh once.[34]

Arjun Singh's promotion of a Chhattisgarhi regional identity was a classic Congress bid to co-opt potential opponents, but it was also linked to other policies designed to appeal to lower castes. At this point, it should be emphasised, Singh was promoting a regional identity but was not in favour of statehood for Chhattisgarh.

Individuals among the OBC leadership fostered by Arjun Singh in Chhattisgarh in the 1980s went on to become some of the main spokespeople for statehood. It should be emphasised again that there is little evidence of the success, if any, of such appeals to the wider public. A deep-rooted movement for statehood never took off. Rather, the evidence is suggestive both of manoeuvrings confined to relatively few individuals, and of the building of alliances by Arjun Singh with loyal local leaders, who were unlikely to challenge his authority because they were partly dependent on him for their position. Nevertheless, Arjun Singh's actions helped to propel the idea of statehood, even if this remained confined to a small political elite. It was arguably his politics that laid the groundwork for the creation of Chhattisgarh itself. Madhya Pradesh's next Congress Chief Minister, Digvijay Singh, was much less proactive on the question of Chhattisgarh, although he did preside over the passage of a resolution supporting statehood in the Legislative Assembly.

In the early 1990s, the statehood demand was made vocally by Congress national spokesperson and Durg MP Chandulal Chandraker, Chair of the Chhattisgarh Rajya Nirman Manch, and by Ajit Jogi. Arjun Singh, by now out of office, had also begun to speak openly in favour of statehood for Chhattisgarh by 1993, and possibly before. It is notable that this coincided with the first organisational elections in the party, which had intensified factional conflict, and with the state elections of 1993. It would have been difficult for Digvijay Singh to have opposed the demand for statehood in this context; he could be said to have been something of an empty vessel in the politics of statehood, neither actively supporting nor opposing. On 17 March 1994, a few months after Congress returned to power, the Madhya Pradesh legislative assembly passed a cross-party resolution in favour of the creation of a separate state. Senior individuals within both parties continued to oppose, or drag their feet about, the idea of state creation. Nevertheless, the Vidhan Sabha resolution, together with election manifesto commitments, ultimately reduced the room for manoeuvre for their national parties and initiated a pattern of competition between BJP and Congress on the issue, which eventually made it more difficult for either party to oppose state creation.

In 1994, few people actually expected that the state would be created, nor did they see this as a pivotal moment. During the debate in the legislative assembly on the resolution, and several times afterwards, Chief Minister Digvijay Singh said that the creation of a separate state would only be taken up if the central government formed a second States Reorganisation Commission.[35] He also said that if the 'demand for Chhattisgarh is relevant,' then the claims to statehood of other regions in Madhya Pradesh such as Vindhya Pradesh and Bundelkhand should also be considered.[36] In an interview in April 2007, he acknowledged that there probably was some truth to the claim that he had not taken the idea of statehood too seriously because, he said, there was no 'mass movement'. His tolerance of the demand appeared to be largely pragmatic. Asked whether he thought a consensus was developing more broadly in favour of smaller states, he said: 'No. If you have decentralisation and empowerment of the people then the issue of large versus small states is negated.'[37] Digvijay Singh was more interested in other forms of decentralisation through *panchayats*, as well as pursuing an aggressive agenda of Dalit empowerment. In a major institutional reform under Digvijay Singh, Madhya Pradesh became one of only a handful of Indian states to devolve substantial amounts of responsibility to the *panchayats* or local councils under new Panchayati Raj legislation.[38] He could afford to be fairly confident that the Narasimha Rao government at the Centre would not support the creation of a new state—especially because Rao feared encouraging a separate movement for statehood in his home region of Telangana—and therefore there was little danger in acquiescing to the demand for statehood.

Thus, in Madhya Pradesh, sub-state political regionalism gained traction in the 1980s in the context of attempts by the Congress Chief Minister to reach out to a younger generation of OBC politicians and agrarian interests, and to sideline his factional rivals in Chhattisgarh. The resolution of the legislative assembly approving the potential bifurcation of Madhya Pradesh did not reflect strong sentiment in favour of breaking up the state. But the fact that this could be discussed relatively casually emphasised that the territorial shape of Madhya Pradesh was open to question across the state.

Uttar Pradesh: Consolidating a Lower Caste Political Community via Regional Mobilisation

In Uttar Pradesh, a mixture of Congress and upper-caste political dominance had ensured the maintenance of the state's borders against challenge in the 1950s and 1960s, as illustrated in chapter two. By the early 1990s, the scenario had changed markedly: several Chief Ministers of Uttar Pradesh oversaw the passage of resolutions in the state assembly supporting the creation of a new hill state. The first resolution for a state of 'Uttaranchal' was made under the BJP government of Kalyan Singh in 1991. Ultimately, however, it was Mulayam Singh Yadav who as Chief Minister did most to precipitate the bifurcation of his state. He was Chief Minister three times, between 1989–91, 1993–95 and 2003–07. In 1991, Mulayam Singh Yadav had argued that the division of the state was not in the interests of the people.[39] But in January 1994, his government appointed the Kaushik Committee to study the grievances of people in the hills. The Committee recommended in April 1994 that a new state of Uttarakhand be formed from eight districts (Uttarkashi, Dehradun, Tehri Garhwal, Chamoli, Pauri Garhwal, Pithoragarh, Almora and Nainital), with its capital in Gairsain—a central place accessible from all points in the hills. How can we account for Mulayam Singh Yadav's volte-face with regards to the demand for a hill state in Uttarakhand? As seen in chapter four, the deepest popular mobilisation around statehood in Uttarakhand came in 1994–95, at a crucial juncture in the history of lower caste political mobilisation in Uttar Pradesh. This section will show how and why he provoked regional mobilisation in Uttarakhand as part of an attempt to hold together a political coalition in the plains of his state.

Mulayam Singh Yadav is a socialist politician and former wrestler whose political formation was shaped by the ideas of both Lohia and Charan Singh.[40] While in power, he developed a political platform grounded in appeals for social justice for lower castes. As a Yadav, he was motivated strongly by a commitment to the empowerment of his fellow caste members, but also claimed to seek social justice for all lower castes or OBCs. In addition he projected lower caste political mobilisation as a counterweight to the communal politics of the BJP. Muslims were an important constituency of the electoral coalitions built by both Mulayam Singh Yadav and Laloo Prasad Yadav in neighbouring Bihar. In December 1993, a Samajwadi Party-Bahujan Samaj Party coalition government (SP-BSP) came to power, led by Mulayam Singh Yadav. For the first time, the State Assembly of Uttar Pradesh was dominated by OBCs, Dalits and Muslims.[41] The SP-BSP ministry of 1993–95 came at a critical point in the wake of 'Mandalisation', pitched against a resurgent Hindu nationalism on the national stage following the demolition of the Babri Masjid in Ayodhya. However, the attempt to forge a united political front between OBCs and Dalits soon came under strain.

The coalition government pointed up some of the contradictions of the nature of lower caste political empowerment thus far. The mobilisation of OBCs as a potential united front had been galvanised by the implementation of the Mandal Commission in 1990. This provoked counter-mobilisation by the non-beneficiaries of new reservations, especially upper castes, helping to consolidate the political resonance of the formerly bureaucratic OBC label. But transformation in the state administration had not kept pace: while there was an increase in the number of SCs and Muslims in the higher ranks of the state bureaucracy, especially from 1993–5 as the quota for SCs was filled, the growth in the number of OBCs was insignificant.[42] As Hasan argues, political mobilisation of lower castes had not heralded—or been precipitated by—a radical structural transformation in Uttar Pradesh's society or economy. While the political power of OBCs and Dalits had increased, it had not laid the foundations for a class-based politics. This made for a shaky foundation upon which to build a stable political coalition, especially given substantial economic differentiation among OBCs. Furthermore, inequalities within the OBC category and the consolidation of a privileged, so-called 'creamy layer', were exploited by other parties, including the BJP, who reached out to Kurmis and Lodhis in central Uttar Pradesh, for instance.[43]

The political empowerment of OBCs did not easily lead to affinity with Dalits either. The socioeconomic position of Scheduled Castes was different: they were more likely to work as agricultural labourers than non-SC castes.[44] They had been earlier 'beneficiaries' of reservations in government employment, education and politics from the time of independence. By mid-1994, there were serious tensions between Mulayam Singh Yadav's Samajwadi Party and Kanshi Ram's BSP.[45] It was at this point that the agitation in Uttarakhand began and Mulayam Singh Yadav seized an ostensible opportunity to bolster a lower caste political coalition in which strains were clearly showing.

In early 1994, the state government had decided to move ahead with the implementation of a Mandal Commission recommendation that 27 per cent of government jobs, seats in *panchayats* and places in medical, engineering and management colleges across Uttar Pradesh be reserved for OBCs. The state government's decision to include Uttarakhand in this provision, despite its OBC population of only a few per cent, sparked a series of protests by students in the hills, who feared they would be sidelined by the arrival of more students from the plains to fill the new quotas in higher education institutions. Mulayam Singh Yadav, however, fuelled a deeper mass mobilisation in Uttarakhand by making a number of provocative statements in which he sought to paint the protests in Uttarakhand as anti-reservation and led by 'chauvinist upper castes'. These seemed to be designed as a means of bolstering his own lower caste coalition in the rest of Uttar Pradesh. It is unlikely that the Uttar Pradesh state government had deliberately provoked the ire of Uttarakhandis by extending reservations in this way. As a former top bureaucrat in Uttar Pradesh said in an interview, confirming the fears of many who had argued for statehood for the hill region on the basis of regional neglect, 'Uttarakhand just didn't figure too much in mainline politics in Uttar Pradesh'.[46] But it was after a provocative response by the state government to the protests, as discussed in chapter three, that the demonstrations in the hills were transformed into a fully-fledged movement focusing on the demand for statehood.

Mulayam Singh Yadav made a series of deliberately controversial statements in response to the anti-reservation demonstrations in Uttarakhand in July and August 1994. In August 1994, he was reported to have directed the Vice Chancellors of Kumaon and Garhwal Universities to admit OBC students from the plains if they could not fill the new quotas locally.[47] He then warned that the protests in Uttarakhand might result in an 'anti-hill' backlash in the plains.[48] In September 1994, the SP and BSP called a pro-reservation *bandh* in Uttar Pradesh in which three people were reported killed and over 200 injured in clashes between pro- and anti-reservationists. From this point, it appeared that the state government was deliberately attempting to intensify the protests for its political gain. Yadav made the minimal concession of offering a new 2 per cent quota for the hills and a 10 per cent quota for poor upper-castes, but remained committed to the 27 per cent quota for OBCs in Uttarakhand.[49] Nevertheless, Mulayam Singh Yadav repeatedly also argued that statehood was the only solution to the problems of the hills.[50] In October, protestors marching from Uttarakhand to Delhi were fired on by police at Muzaffarnagar, an event that pushed the Uttarakhand issue to the forefront of national politics. A number of people died and several accusations of rape were made by female protesters. From this point on, the agitation for statehood intensified markedly.

Once the protests had started, Mulayam Singh Yadav encouraged them. In doing so, his reasons were similar to those of Arjun Singh in boosting the emergence of a regional identity in Chhattisgarh: to hold together a fragile political coalition and to sideline his political rivals. He attempted to cement the fraying political coalition of lower castes outside the hills by portraying the protesters in the hills as chauvinistic upper castes and reigniting the reservations issue which had been so prominent in his first period as Chief Minister in 1989–91, the time of the implementation of the Mandal Commission recommendations. His response also made life more difficult for his opponents. The BJP's support for statehood allowed Yadav to associate the party with what he described as 'anti-reservation' protests in Uttarakhand, thereby seeking to stymie the party's attempts to reach out to OBCs elsewhere in Uttar Pradesh. Moreover, Mulayam Singh Yadav saw a chance to increase the disarray of the Congress Party in Uttar Pradesh (and nationally) by exploiting existing divisions between its Uttar Pradesh state president, three-time former Chief Minister ND Tiwari, who hailed from the Uttarakhand hills, and the Prime Minister Narasimha Rao.

Yadav's tactics placed Congress in a compromised position, especially because it was providing support to the Mulayam Singh Yadav-led state government from the outside. On one hand, Congress had been haemorrhaging upper caste support to the BJP for some time as many upper castes turned to Hindu nationalism and the campaign for a Ram Mandir. The Congress therefore did not want to lose further ground among upper castes by appearing to oppose the demand for a hill state, which was being painted as an upper caste issue, and which the BJP were supporting. Against this backdrop, N.D. Tiwari—a Brahmin—was reappointed as Uttar Pradesh Congress Committee (UPCC) president in August 1994, replacing the backward caste Mahabir Prasad, with a bid to rejuvenate the party organisation.[51] Tiwari called for Congress to withdraw the support it was giving to the Yadav government from outside because of its failure to deal appropriately with the protests in Uttarakhand. But Prime Minister Narasimha Rao and Congress leaders at the Centre simply urged the Chief Minister to negotiate with the protesters. The tensions between Tiwari and the Prime Minister were sufficiently serious, and the protests in Uttarakhand sufficiently disruptive, that the affair repeatedly appeared on the front pages of national newspapers. Mulayam Singh Yadav's aim, wrote columnist Manoj Joshi, was on the one hand to use the Uttarakhand agitation to marginalise N.D. Tiwari and transform him into a 'minor hill politician' and, on the other, to regain the momentum he had lost while in coalition government with the BSP.[52] Congress MP Harikesh Bahadur summed up the predicament of the party: 'Mulayam Singh is running the government with the help of the Congress, yet he is blackmailing us. If we withdraw support, he will say we are anti-reservation; if we don't, he grows stronger at our expense.'[53]

Thus, in Uttar Pradesh, the question of statehood acquired political urgency in the context of a struggle for political supremacy in the plains of Uttar Pradesh. The fact that the territorial borders of Uttar Pradesh became a major subject for debate in the course of political contestation around responses to Mandal, reflected how much had changed since the staunch opposition to Uttar Pradesh's division in the 1950s on the basis of its sacred geography. As an astute newspaper columnist observed in 1994: 'Today Ram and Krishna themselves have become divisive elements with Ram purloined by the BJP and Mulayam Singh Yadav claiming to be *yaduvanshi* and a member of OBC Krishna clan.'[54]

Bihar: Lalu Prasad Yadav and the Embodiment of Regional Politics

In Bihar, as in the other states of the Hindi heartland, the return of Congress to power in 1980 was less an affirmation of the social relationships that had hitherto underpinned the party's political dominance than a reflection of the fragmentation of the opposition. The brief spell of Janata government led by Karpoori Thakur had challenged the upper caste grip on power but fell apart under the weight of its own contradictions and in the absence of a politically organised coalition of lower castes.[55] The 1980s, with the return of Jagannath Mishra as Congress Chief Minister, were a period of instability and considerable violence in Bihar. As Frankel notes:

The Forward Castes could no longer rely on Brahmanical ideology to preserve their position as the dominant class. Rather, they clung to power through corruption and coercion. But no other ideology or social class was in a position to fill the authority vacuum created…Bihar edged towards social chaos as politics degenerated into a naked struggle for power between opposing lathis.[56]

In 1990, politics in Bihar saw a profound shift epitomised by the ascendancy of Lalu Prasad Yadav, who became the Janata Dal (JD) Chief Minister in 1990. This took place months after the election of the JD-led National Front at the national level in 1989 and the election of Mulayam Singh Yadav in Uttar Pradesh. Lalu Prasad Yadav also had a background in socialist politics, and saw Karpoori Thakur as his mentor.[57]

The state and politics in Bihar have been deeply shaped by the historical dominance of local, landed upper caste Brahmin, Bhumihar, Kayasth and Rajput elites. As a number of authors point out, the politics of lower caste political empowerment in Bihar involved an involution of the state as a new generation of lower caste political leaders sought to weaken a bureaucracy that had been in the grip of upper castes.[58] Lalu's reputation as a populist backward caste leader, fighting against upper caste dominance, went hand in hand with corruption and the continued criminalisation of the state, although this time in the hands of lower castes. This was vividly symbolised in Lalu's imprisonment in 1997 on charges of involvement in a major corruption case involving the Animal Husbandry Department, known as the Fodder Scam, and the coronation of his politically inexperienced wife, Rabri Devi, as Chief Minister in his place. Lalu split the Janata Dal to form the Rashtriya Janata Dal (RJD) after former party colleagues withdrew their support over the Fodder Scam. Control of the state was used in pursuit of a politics of social justice and lower caste empowerment. This was a deeply personal politics in which, as Jeffrey Witsoe notes, 'for many people Lalu came to personify the state.'[59] The effects of this style of rule on the functioning of the state have been well explored elsewhere, but Lalu's embodiment of a crusade for social justice also became important for the continuing territorial integrity of Bihar.

Under Lalu—and his successors—a form of political regionalism emerged in Bihar that has pitted the state against the central government. The creation of Jharkhand became a major pawn in the battle between the NDA central government and the Bihar state government. In the later 1990s, bitter tensions developed between the RJD state government and the BJP-led central government. The NDA coalition in Delhi included a major opponent of Lalu Prasad Yadav—the Samata

Party,[60] formed by Nitish Kumar (a Kurmi politician and later Chief Minister) and George Fernandes, which had split from the JD led by the Chief Minister, and formed an alliance with the BJP.

When Lalu's wife, Rabri Devi, took over as Chief Minister in 1997 at the helm of the smaller RJD she introduced a resolution supporting the creation of Jharkhand in the state assembly. The Bihar government's support for statehood was a matter of pure political expediency and not a sign of a genuine political conversion to the desirability, or even acceptability, of creating Jharkhand. The resolution was passed in order to secure the support of MLAs from the southern districts of Bihar, that would become the future Jharkhand state, in a vote of no confidence. Lalu was strongly opposed to the creation of Jharkhand, famously exclaiming, 'Jharkhand over my dead body.' He had overseen the creation of a Jharkhand Autonomous Area Council (JAAC) in 1994 but done little to seriously empower it. Ever since the Fodder Scam broke, Lalu had sought more decisively to portray himself as a champion of Bihar's unity and pit himself against a separate Jharkhand.[61] This can be seen as something of a response to the gradual fracturing of Lalu's coalition of lower castes. In addition to his alleged involvement in the Fodder Scam, there was increasing political competition within north Bihar as the lower caste coalition that Lalu Prasad Yadav had tried to construct looked increasingly frayed. In 1994, Nitish Kumar had left the Janata Dal to form the Samata Party in protest at the sidelining of non-Yadav castes. As in Uttar Pradesh, this political competition between caste groups was concentrated in the region outside the districts for which statehood was demanded. The demography of Chotanagpur and Santal Parganas in south Bihar was quite different from north Bihar, and the RJD (as well as the Samata Party) had a weaker base in the districts which went on to become Jharkhand.

Thus in Bihar, as in Madhya Pradesh and Uttar Pradesh, the weak correspondence between state boundaries and caste demography in the context of new political formations helped to bring into question the territorial reach of state boundaries within the parent state, too. Even though the state assembly's vote on statehood for Jharkhand in 1997 represented little more than a tactical concession on the part of the RJD, bifurcation was an idea that gained traction gradually in north Bihar. Therefore, this can be seen as something of a turning point in Bihar's politics vis-à-vis Jharkhand. As Brishim Patel, a Janata Dal (U) minister in Nitish Kumar's government after 2005, said: 'Jharkhand was born in 1997 after the first resolution was passed. After this initiative, even though Lalu thought he could go back on it, this wasn't possible because the momentum was already there.'[62] After the election of the NDA central government, the Jharkhand issue was manipulated by both Lalu and the central government.

During the 1998 election campaign, some of Bihar's opposition parties argued that President's Rule should be applied because of a deterioration in the law and order situation. George Fernandes' Samata Party (a member of the NDA) pledged to push for the introduction of President's Rule in Bihar if elected. Lalu increasingly argued that the BJP's support for the creation of Jharkhand and the central government's attempt to remove the RJD government by applying President's Rule were connected. He accused the central government of a 'conspiracy' to divide Bihar. In September 1998, as the central government prepared to forward the proposed legislation to divide Bihar, Madhya Pradesh and Uttar Pradesh to the relevant state assemblies, he repeated the refrain that Jharkhand could only be created over his dead body. His chosen language was telling: he was connecting a physical threat to his own person (represented in his imprisonment on corruption charges which he portrayed as part of an upper caste conspiracy) with the threat to suspend the state government, all portrayed as a challenge to the unity of Bihar. The Governor of Bihar, Sundar Singh Bhandari—a partisan appointee with an RSS background—had also recommended that the central government take action against the government of Bihar saying the situation was 'ripe' for President's Rule. Lalu responded by declaring that the RJD would lead a mass movement to stop the 'Sangh Parivar's conspiracy to divide Bihar'.[63] He portrayed the threat of President's Rule as a covert means of dividing Bihar, and on 15 September the Bihar cabinet withdrew the earlier resolution it had adopted in favour of creating Jharkhand.[64] On 21 September, the Bihar Assembly rejected the Bihar Reorganisation Bill. The following day, the Union Cabinet formally recommended the imposition of President's Rule in Bihar (although this was rejected by the President). [65]

Bihar's state borders had thus become part of a political tussle between Lalu Prasad Yadav in Bihar, who claimed to embody the state's unity, and the BJP-led central government. At the same time, however, BJP politicians in north Bihar began to make a more positive case for the benefits that would accrue to the region if it were separated from Jharkhand. This was the first time that any politicians in north Bihar had actively supported the division of the northern districts from the resource-rich, revenue-generating districts of south Bihar. Sushil Kumar Modi, a senior BJP politician in north Bihar who went on to become Deputy Chief Minister in Nitish Kumar's government from 2005, and Saryu Roy, a north Bihari who became the BJP's first general secretary for the Jharkhand state unit after 2000, said that by the late 1990s they had begun to argue that separation from Jharkhand would help north Bihar. They argued that separation from Jharkhand would spur industrialisation in north Bihar. Sushil Kumar Modi said that he had sought to counter one of Lalu's arguments that if Jharkhand were created all that would be left was 'sand', by arguing that when Bihar was united no industries or investment came to north Bihar: all investment was going to south Bihar, and 'because they were earning money from South Bihar, politicians didn't care about North Bihar.'[66] In a similar vein, Saryu Roy said:

If you are an industrialist, you will build a factory in Chennai or Bangalore, or in Chotanagpur or Santal Parganas itself, rather than North Bihar because of its poor infrastructure…If Bihar was separate, it would have separate budgetary support from the government for industrial development. Separation of Jharkhand would be a boon in disguise for industrial and agricultural development.[67]

Thus, in Bihar, as in Uttar Pradesh and Madhya Pradesh, the advent of a new era of state politics had opened up new ways of conceiving the territorial organisation of the Hindi heartland. The state government in Bihar opposed the state's bifurcation more vociferously than their counterparts in UP and Uttar Pradesh and Madhya Pradesh, but state boundaries had become a major issue at the heart of the state's political arena.

Conclusion

Bihar, Madhya Pradesh and Uttar Pradesh are each a congery of multiple regions with diverse patterns of topography, political economy and political history. These states did not have the strong founding myths of states in other parts of the country, or the foundations for regional identities grounded in language. The coming to power of new parties that mobilised around an agenda of social justice for lower castes—and the attempt in Madhya Pradesh to respond to a social justice agenda under the auspices of a Congress government—changed the logic of state politics. Despite the non-territorial nature of claims for social justice and improved lower caste political representation, the politics of caste-based empowerment threw up new reasons to question the territorial organisation of Hindi-speaking states. One thing that all the cases discussed in this chapter have in common is that the manipulation of statehood demands by Chief Ministers and their political opponents represented a rhetorical rather than a substantive response to the question of how to project and build political power over space. It contributed neither to the building of transformative party organisations capable of addressing the long-term needs of the poor nor to the fostering of new regional identities. Instead, these political entrepreneurs manipulated statehood demands to serve short term political goals. It is perhaps an unpalatable truth that these short-term machinations—in response to a deeper shift in the constellation of social and political power—helped significantly to determine the success of these particular statehood demands by ensuring that they found a good degree of acceptance within their 'parent' states. By 1997, each of the state assemblies had passed a resolution that accepted, in principle, the division of their states. It was the changing logic of state politics in Bihar, Madhya Pradesh and Uttar Pradesh in the 1980s and 1990s that ensured it was from these states—and not elsewhere—that new states were created in 2000. The next chapter turns to look at the short term political dynamics that determined the decision by the federal government to create Chhattisgarh, Jharkhand and Uttarakhand.

6

FEDERAL POLITICS AND THE CREATION
OF NEW STATES

Within three weeks of each other in the autumn of 2000, the three new states came into being. Chhattisgarh was formed on 1 November, Uttaranchal (as it was then called) on 8 November, and Jharkhand saw its foundation day on 15 November. Bills to create the three states had first been tabled in the Lok Sabha in December 1998, several months after the BJP-led National Democratic Alliance had taken office. The legislation fell with the government in April 1999, but was reintroduced in the NDA's next term and received presidential assent in August 2000. It was significant that the states were created under a BJP-led government. As Ajit Jogi, the first Congress Chief Minister of Chhattisgarh, in office from 2000 to 2003, admitted: 'To be honest, if Congress had been ruling then we would never have got the state. Congress didn't want to open floodgates: there were around 50 other demands for statehood.'[1]

This chapter focuses on the national logic that complemented developments at the regional and state levels. We have already seen (in chapters two to four) how the BJP's own internal party thinking about state creation changed over time from outright hostility in the 1960s to support for particular statehood demands by the late 1980s. In this chapter, I recount the story from when the BJP formed its first central government in May 1998 and set in motion the process of creating the new states. It will become apparent that political opportunism and alliance calculations played a significant role in the short term in pushing forward the agenda of states reorganisation in 2000 and in ensuring that the states were actually created. Even though the BJP had offered its support to various statehood demands, there was nothing to say that it would treat these as a priority once it reached office. However, it was the longer term developments explored in earlier chapters at state and sub-state levels that were critical in determining where states were created and where they were not in 2000. The second half of this chapter will therefore look at the 'negative' cases—places such as Vidarbha and Telangana that did not achieve statehood in 2000.

Developments at the national and subnational levels evolve according to distinct temporal logics. The actual introduction of legislation to effect state creation at the national level is a short term process, in contrast to slower-moving processes of change at the subnational level that we have analysed in earlier chapters. The existence of a time delay between the periods of most intense grassroots mobilisation and the eventual creation of the states reflects the way in which demands for statehood get picked up through a federal filter and lodged on the national agenda in ways that are not always closely tied in to regional political timetables. To use Paul Pierson's analogy, this is more like an earthquake than a tornado—'a quick outcome but a very slow-moving, long-term causal process'.[2]

National Coalition Government and Federal Restructuring

When it became clear that the BJP had reached the limits of electoral expansion based on Hindu nationalism alone, the formation of alliances with regional partners became an increasingly important strategy for the party. In 1996, the BJP won its largest number of seats yet, but failed to find the allies necessary to form a national government. This paved the way for the relatively short-lived United Front governments of Deve Gowda and then I.K. Gujral. Ahead of the Lok Sabha elections in 1998, the BJP sought to strike alliances with regional parties outside of its strongholds. As Heath has shown, the alliances the BJP formed before the 1998 elections helped the party to expand its social support base.[3]

Strategies of alliance formation influenced the shape that the territorial restructuring of India's federal system eventually took in 2000. In order to form the first National Democratic Alliance of 1998, the BJP was forced to drop some of the more controversial aspects of its own programme (such as the abolition of Article 370 governing Jammu and Kashmir's relation with the Union government, the construction of the Ram Mandir and the introduction of a uniform civil code) in accordance with the preferences of its allies. Among the other things it abandoned was the commitment to create the state of Vidarbha because of its alliance with the Shiv Sena in Maharashtra. The demand for Telangana had not been on the official party programme since the early 1970s. Thus the government's reliance on the support of the main regional party of Andhra Pradesh, the Telugu Desam Party, did not require a fresh concession. The opposition towards state bifurcation by regional parties in Maharashtra and Andhra Pradesh reflected the fact that state politics in south and west India had not been transformed since 1980 in any way that might have brought state boundaries into contention across the political class, as had occurred within Bihar, Madhya Pradesh and Uttar Pradesh. I will look at this in more detail towards the end of the chapter.

The demands for Chhattisgarh, Jharkhand, Uttarakhand and, at that stage, full statehood for Delhi, stayed on the agenda. Soon after the NDA took office in May 1998, Home Minister L.K. Advani announced that a cabinet sub-committee had been established to report on the creation of Chhattisgarh, Jharkhand and Uttarakhand, and that a decision had been taken to push ahead with granting full statehood to Delhi.[4] The BJP claimed that in creating these states it was simply responding to regional demands that had already been supported by the relevant state assembly. As Advani explained subsequently:

We, this government, have made a criterion that if a region wants to become a separate state and there is opposition in the rest of the state, then there is no common agreement. But if the rest of the state agrees—as in Bihar, Madhya Pradesh and Uttar Pradesh the Vidhan Sabha passed resolutions—only then will we mention the issue.[5]

He also said: 'Administrative and economic viability, besides the overwhelming aspirations of the people of the region for the creation of the new states were the only criteria for introduction of the Bills.'[6] National BJP party officials and bureaucrats interviewed during fieldwork repeatedly emphasised that the central government had only acted to create states where there was already agreement in favour of a state within the state concerned.

There was no constitutional requirement to act only after the assent of the state government concerned. The assertion that the government was only acting on the instructions of state assemblies served two purposes. Firstly, it suggested that state creation was a decentralised process and one that was not driven by the short term political interests of the BJP. Secondly, the construction gave a veneer of political cover to the BJP. It gave them a clear reason not to push ahead with their earlier pledges on Telangana and Vidarbha in the face of opposition from allies. In no state other than Bihar, Madhya Pradesh and Uttar Pradesh had a state assembly approved a resolution advocating bifurcation. In each of these states the state assembly had passed one or more resolutions supporting statehood before the NDA government had taken office. Although Bihar's legislative assembly went on to reject the proposed legislation to create Jharkhand, in 1998 Bihar was ruled by an opposition party—not a NDA ally—thus, the BJP pushed ahead anyway. The BJP's formulation that it was acting on the basis of state assembly approval undeniably masked the extent to which political opportunism played a role in the short term in proceeding with the project of state reorganisation.

Table 5.1: Lok Sabha election results 1998–2004.

	1998	1999	2004
NDA	278	300	189
(of which BJP)	182	182	138
Congress + allies	171	137	221
Left Parties	41	43	62
BSP	5	14	19
SP+	20	26	39
Others	28	23	13
Total	543	543	543

It has been suggested that one reason for the BJP's short term motivation to create the states was that new states might offer a handful of safe seats for the BJP in the context of the small parliamentary majorities of the NDA government. Since 1989, no national party had won an outright majority. This meant that small numbers of seats were critical to the formation of governments at the Centre as well as to the ability of those governments to enact legislation in parliament. For this reason Mawdsley suggests that the BJP faced an electoral incentive to support state creation in order to secure more parliamentary seats.[7] In 1998, when the states reorganisation bills were first tabled, the NDA had only six seats over a majority in the Lok Sabha (see the Table 5.1). Their vulnerability was demonstrated when the withdrawal of one of their regional allies led to the collapse of the government in April 1999, the original states reorganisation bills expiring along with it.

The three states between them contained thirty new seats.[8] Yet the BJP was already winning a large share of the seats in the proposed new states by the late 1990s (as shown in Table 5.2). They could not therefore expect much of an additional dividend after state creation, although they might hope to consolidate their existing position. By pushing ahead with state creation, the BJP ran other risks, such as the potential loss of support from alliance partners such as the Akali Dal (eight seats) who were unhappy about the inclusion of Udham Singh Nagar, an area in which many Punjabi Sikhs had settled as agriculturalists after partition, in Uttarakhand. The idea that the states were created because it was in the BJP's electoral interests is thus not entirely supported by the parliamentary arithmetic. But the motivation to shore up its own position in the regions that were to become states, as well as potentially be in a position to form a greater number of state governments, was without doubt an attraction for the party.

Table 5.2: Lok Sabha seats won by BJP in each region 1998–2004.

	Total seats	1998	1999	2004
Chhattisgarh	11	7	8	10
Jharkhand	14	12	11	1
Uttarakhand	5	5	4	3

Source: Calculated from ECI data.

The one short term factor that dominated the debate about state creation in the NDA's first term, as discussed in the previous chapter, was the conflict between the central government and the state government in Bihar. The three states reorganisation bills were tabled in the Lok Sabha on 23 December 1998, amid protests from both the RJD and Samajwadi Party (the latter was unhappy at the proposed inclusion of Haridwar in Uttarakhand). An increasingly fractious NDA government and an emboldened opposition prevented any further action on the statehood bills. The Bihar question, indeed, became a touchstone issue for the ability of the government to command the confidence of parliament more broadly. In February 1999, the cabinet had finally secured presidential agreement for its second attempt to impose President's Rule in Bihar, following the alleged massacre of eleven Dalits in Jehanabad by the Ranvir Sena, a private landlord army. The move to impose President's Rule was supported by Congress, but a number of the BJP's regional coalition partners such as the Akali Dal and TDP were uneasy about the principle of suspending the state government in this manner. In March, the government was forced to pull back from applying President's Rule because although it had managed to get the support of the Lok Sabha, it knew it would lose a vote on the issue in the Rajya Sabha. In April, the central government was dissolved after the Tamil politician Jayalalithaa withdrew her party's support. Jayalalithaa left on grounds unrelated to Bihar or state creation, but the consequences of her departure demonstrated the fragile majority of the first Vajpayee government.

The Importance of Contingent Events

The legislation to create all three states was eventually passed in July-August 2000 after the NDA was returned to power with a more secure majority. Several things had changed by then, reflecting the importance of contingency in the endgame of state creation. In the first place, fresh elections had been held in Bihar in February 2000. The RJD had been reelected, supported by Congress this time, on the condition that progress would be made towards the creation of Jharkhand (Congress by this time was allied with the JMM in Jharkhand). The new electoral arithmetic in Bihar also helped to make state creation a more attractive option for the RJD. The latter's seat share had fallen, although they had done better than expected and remained the single largest party. In undivided Bihar after the 2000 elections, the RJD had 124 MLAs and with its allies, a total of 163 MLAs—an exact majority. But in a divided Bihar the RJD would have 115 MLAs, just seven short of a majority by itself in a new house of 243 seats (see table below). In April 2000, the

Bihar Legislative Assembly ratified the new Bihar Reorganisation Bill, including an amendment to name the state Jharkhand, instead of Vananchal. Even so, many MPs from north Bihar (including from the RJD, JD (U) and Samata Party) voted against the legislation when it reached the Lok Sabha.

The fact that the NDA had failed to form a government after the February 2000 state elections in Bihar may also have been significant. A BJP worker in Jharkhand confessed, for example, that he and some party colleagues had worked against the wishes of the central BJP leadership in order to undermine the formation of a coalition government by Nitish Kumar in Bihar after state elections. They did so because if Kumar had managed to put together a coalition, he would have been reliant on the support of BJP legislators from Jharkhand in the legislative assembly and therefore would have been unlikely to agree to the creation of the state.[9] Ultimately, Congress' support was also necessary to get the bills ratified by the Rajya Sabha, so the shift in their position was important. By mid-2000, Congress had begun to encourage its state units to launch agitations for the 'speedy creation' of the states. It accused the NDA of dragging its feet, especially after the government failed to table the legislation during the Budget session of Parliament. Congress thereby hoped to deprive the BJP of some of the credit for state creation.

Table 5.3: Bihar state assembly election results in 2000.

	Total seats	RJD	BJP	Samata	Congress	JD(U)	JMM	Others	Ind.
Jharkhand	81	9	32	5	11	3	12	8	2
All Bihar	324	124	66	34	24	21	12	23	20

Source: Figures calculated from ECI.

Contentious issues remained once the legislation had been approved in principle. The need for a compensation package for north Bihar for losing Jharkhand was pushed heavily by the Samata Party and JD (U). The state government of Uttar Pradesh opposed the inclusion of Haridwar in Uttaranchal. The state assembly of Orissa passed a motion calling for the 'remerger' of the districts of Seraikella and Kharsawan from Jharkhand into Orissa. There were also disagreements over the proposed division of assets and responsibilities between the new units and their parent states, especially the power-generating capacity of Chhattisgarh, and the hydroelectric plants in Uttarakhand which had previously generated approximately 40 per cent of of Uttar Pradesh's electricity and over which the Uttar Pradesh government wanted to retain control. The manner in which these issues were resolved reflected the centralised process of decision-making about state creation in the final instance. As one senior civil servant who was closely involved in the negotiations said, the consultation of state governments was ultimately done in a light-hearted manner, and on all important decisions it was the will of the centre that would finally prevail.[10] The central government did not honour all amendments passed by state governments, and parliament was not obliged to pass bills back to state assemblies for approval after changes had been made. There was more controversy about the exact content of the Uttar Pradesh Reorganisation Bill than any other. Finally, the plains districts of Haridwar and Udham Singh Nagar were both added to the hill districts of Uttarakhand, against opposition from the state government and from within Udham Singh Nagar, where a campaign by Sikh farmers in the *terai* area, supported by the Akali Dal and Samajwadi Party, demanded they remain in Uttar Pradesh. The main rationale given for the inclusion of these plains areas was to make the new state 'economically viable', particularly to promote agriculture and industrial development in the new state.

Legislation to create all three states eventually received presidential assent on 28 August 2000, and the states were created across three weeks in November. No fresh elections were held to the new state assemblies. In Jharkhand, a BJP-led government, led by Babulal Marandi, took over. In Uttaranchal (as it was named at the point of its creation), a BJP government led by Nityanand Swami, was formed—and the region's nineteen assembly seats divided into seventy. In Chhattisgarh, Congress formed a government led by Ajit Jogi. The question of granting full statehood to Delhi was not pursued to fruition, in light of difficulties in agreeing the territory and jurisdictions of the Delhi state government vis-à-vis the National Capital Territory under control of the Home Ministry. Neither Telangana nor Vidarbha were discussed seriously at the cabinet level. The creation of new states at this particular point in time was, then, a somewhat opportunistic process—reflecting the short-term political priorities of coalition partners in Delhi, as in the case of Bihar especially. But in all three cases, the only reason that these demands had reached the national agenda was that political momentum had built around them within changing regional political arenas. In none, however, was mobilisation in favour of statehood at a peak of mobilisation, requiring concessions from the central government in 2000. Rather, the semi-independent logic of the national political regime dictated when the states would come into being.

Why were no other states created in 2000?

In this last section, I will consider why states were not created by the central government in other parts of India at this time. I will first briefly look at the case of Rajasthan—the only large state in north India that did not undergo any serious debate about bifurcation. I will then go on to look at the cases of Vidarbha and Telangana, which inspired much more substantial debate, and consider why these demands did not gain traction in 2000.

The only large state in Hindi-speaking north India which was not bifurcated in 2000 is Rajasthan. Rajasthan also happens not to have seen any demand or movement for statehood within its borders. In Bihar, Uttar Pradesh and Madhya Pradesh, it was the challenge to upper caste dominance of politics and the political mobilisation of lower castes that made it more difficult for state leaders to project power across states. This helped demands for statehood become part of the currency of politics at the state-level, as political entrepreneurs stoked or provoked regional movements in order to help them consolidate cross-state political coalitions in conditions in which there were no lower or intermediate castes with a geographical spread that reached across their states. By contrast, in Rajasthan, the existence of two competing state-wide identities—centred on Jats and Rajputs—reduced the salience of sub-state regional movements, despite the existence of regional inequality. Jats are present across most of Rajasthan, although with regional variation in terms of their concentration. Historically, they have dominated the Congress Party organisation in the state. The BJP has exploited what Rob Jenkins describes as Rajput Hindutva, in order to counter the consolidation of Jat political power across Rajasthan by celebrating the 'Rajput ethic' as a vision of a stable and more just social order. The BJP has fostered distrust of the politically dominant Jats as a means of encouraging solidarity among Rajputs, as well as reaching out to other non-Jat communities.[11] In this context, political regionalism has not been a major feature of Rajasthani politics.

In the non-Hindi belt states of Maharashtra and Andhra Pradesh, non-Brahmin castes have also constituted the dominant castes in state politics since the creation of these linguistic states—the Maratha-Kunbis in Maharashtra, and Reddys/Kammas in Andhra. The regional, non-Congress parties or alliances that have come to power in these states in the 1980s and 1990s have drawn on regional identities grounded in language and culture as an alternative pole for state-wide political mobilisation of a kind not so readily available to north Indian leaders. Whilst it is important not to overstate the extent to which common socioeconomic interests hold together the different groups that have been attracted, at various points, to regional parties such as the TDP and Shiv Sena, the reference to a frame of regional identity has been important in their electoral strategies and helps to explain their hostility to an agenda of state bifurcation.

Vidarbha and Telangana: Inhospitable Politics and Countervailing State Identities

In Maharashtra, the long-term dominance of the Congress Party in electoral politics resting on a Maratha-Kunbi social formation,[12] pushed the opposition to Congress into regional pockets, causing them also to focus on mobilising disparate non-Maratha groups, particularly OBCs and Dalits. It was an alliance between the BJP and a regional party—the Shiv Sena—which heralded the most cohesive challenge to Congress. In 1995, a BJP-Shiv Sena coalition government was elected. This was the first non-Congress government to complete a full term in the history of the state. The Shiv Sena, which appealed to a Marathi chauvinist regional identity, was staunchly opposed to the idea of dividing the state. Although the BJP had flirted with support for statehood in Vidarbha, it quietly placed the issue on the back-burner after the combine came to power.

The idea of creating a separate Marathi-speaking Vidarbha in the east of present-day Maharashtra dates back to before independence, when the region was part of the multilingual Central Provinces and Berar. But since independence, and the subsequent merger with other Marathi-speaking districts that eventually became the state of Maharashtra in 1960, the demand for statehood has been raised on the grounds of regional economic inequality. The rights of the merging Marathi-speaking regions to equitable development were supposedly assured under Article 371 (2) which provided for development boards for Vidarbha and Marathwada. Vidarbha is home to three quarters of Maharashtra's forests, two-thirds of its minerals and has a power surplus, but the major industrial growth has taken place around Mumbai-Thane-Pune.[13]

The trajectory of the BJP's support for statehood for Vidarbha has some similarities with the activities of its local leaders in Chhattisgarh, Jharkhand and Uttarakhand. In their 1991 manifesto, the BJP referred to the region's 'acute sense of neglect' and promised to create a Regional Development Council (while promising statehood for Uttaranchal, Vananchal and Delhi). It was in 1996 that the demand for statehood in Vidarbha found a place in the party election manifesto, alongside that for Chhattisgarh. Despite the alliance with the Shiv Sena, the demand appeared in the BJP's 1996 and 1998 Lok Sabha manifestos, but was dropped from the 1999 document.[14] The difference, in this case, between Maharashtra and the states in the Hindi heartland, is that in the former the BJP had created an alliance with the Shiv Sena in 1989, a regionalist party that was engaged in a political project which, from the mid-1980s, was based on an aggressive communal populism intertwined with Marathi pride, and the 'sons of the soil' mobilisation it had encouraged in Mumbai from the mid-1960s.[15] The Shiv Sena's opposition to bifurcating Maharashtra was the main reason why the BJP did not pursue the idea after it came to power at the Centre from 1998.

The fact that statehood for Vidarbha remains an ongoing demand makes it possible to see how local politicians frequently support the idea of statehood for short term reasons, without necessarily expecting a new state to see the light of day, and that they can shift their position over time. The apparently fickle nature of political support for Vidarbha's statehood was reflected in off the record comments by a senior BJP politician in Nagpur in November 2008 who said that he pays lip service to the demand in public statements because it is party policy, but feels it would be better for the region to remain part of Maharashtra because of the economic opportunities offered through being connected with Mumbai.[16] In 1996, another high ranking BJP organiser is quoted by Thomas Blom Hansen, again off the record, as saying that the BJP was relaxed about the attempt of local Congress leaders to hijack the issue of statehood because the creation of a separate state would benefit the BJP more than Congress, leaving the BJP dominant in Vidarbha and the Shiv Sena dominant in western Maharashtra, the coast and Marathwada.[17] It is likely that one would have come across similar sentiments of non-committal among local politicians before statehood was granted in Chhattisgarh, another state without a serious mass movement.

Nationalist Congress Party leader Sharad Pawar—a master political strategist and former Chief Minister of Maharashtra—also subsequently hinted that he might support the creation of Vidarbha despite his typical reputation for being strongly opposed to the division of Maharashtra.[18] His mooting of the idea was read as a move to put his 'allies' in the Congress Party under pressure because it is dissident congressmen in Vidarbha who had been raising the demand for statehood. It is perhaps also a useful issue to keep alive in a bid to stoke tensions in the BJP-Shiv Sena alliance. This is another reflection of how statehood is drawn into short term political manoeuvres which have a logic that is independent from broader questions about the desirability of creating more, smaler states.

Statehood fitted in to the BJP's aim to carve out a distinctive regional base in Vidarbha while in opposition to Congress, but the political imperatives for pursuing this goal through to its conclusion (bifurcation) were few—especially after the BJP-Shiv Sena alliance won the state elections in 1995.[19] The Shiv Sena's pan-Maharashtrian political platform strongly contradicted the idea of bifurcation. By contrast, there was no regional party or political combine in Bihar, Madhya Pradesh or Uttar Pradesh that both appealed to voters across the state and won seats in the potentially seceding region. Furthermore, as a poor region of a rich state, the incentives for actually separating from Maharashtra are fewer in Vidarbha than in the resource-rich regions of otherwise poor states that became states in 2000.[20]

In the case of Telangana, too, the ascendancy of a regional party with an electoral appeal based on linguistic regionalism lessened the likelihood that the state would or could be bifurcated in 2000. The most straightforward answer to the question of why the BJP did not pursue the creation of Telangana once it came to power at the helm of the NDA government was that the central government was reliant on the support—from outside—of MPs from the Telugu Desam Party (TDP) led by Chandrababu Naidu, which was opposed to the division of Andhra Pradesh. It should also be noted that the creation of Telangana was absent from the BJP's general election manifestos in the 1990s once the party began to provide official backing to individual statehood demands elsewhere. This is striking because it was the emergence of a demand for statehood for Telangana in the late 1960s that had encouraged the Jana Sangh to start to embrace abstract arguments in favour of states reorganisation. But in the 1980s and 1990s, the Telangana demand had little momentum within the region and the BJP more generally was in a weak position across Andhra Pradesh.

Telangana had been incorporated with Coastal Andhra and Rayala-seema to form the new state of Andhra Pradesh in 1956. Earlier, it had comprised the Telugu-speaking region of the domains of the Nizam of Hyderabad. Although Telangana was included in Andhra Pradesh on the grounds of its common language, the region had not played a central role in the agitation for an Andhra state in the early 1950s. As Mitchell notes, residents of Telangana have always 'been most ambivalent about being part of a state defined in relation to Telugu'.[21] To allay the fears about the potential for Telangana to be 'swamped' by the more prosperous regions of Andhra Pradesh (where the earlier emergence of commercial agriculture had driven greater prosperity),[22] a gentleman's agreement was signed by representatives of Andhra and Telangana in 1956. This set out commitments to divide government expenditure proportionately between regions, improve educational facilities in the Telangana region, protect the status of Urdu, ensure that recruitment to the state public services takes place on the basis of the population of both regions, control the sale of agricultural land in Telangana, and to establish a regional council to oversee the 'all-round' development of the region. Yet, after the merger, the provisions of this agreement were not strictly upheld, and subsequent rules to protect the appointment of locals to government jobs were widely flouted.

A 1969 agitation for Telangana statehood was led by students, teachers and non-gazetted government officers. Government officials resented the entrance of 'non-*mulkis*' (those from outside the former Hyderabad state), who were often better educated (and lower paid) than *mulki* officials, into positions in Telangana and demanded the repatriation of officers from coastal Andhra. Students and teachers also highlighted a sense of grievance about wider educational disadvantage in the Telangana region, compared to other parts of Andhra. In the countryside, further grievances arose among local landed communities, who complained about the migration of farmers from coastal Andhra into the Telangana region, where they were able to cheaply buy and develop land.[23] The Jai Telangana agitation lasted from December 1968 to November 1969, after which central government concessions, together with splits within the movement itself, contributed to its deceleration. But in 1972, the state saw another brief movement for separate statehood, this time led by coastal Andhras aggrieved by the Supreme Court and state government's upholding of the so-called *mulki* rules, favouring the employment of locals in public employment in Telangana.

By the 1980s and 1990s, however, the demand for bifurcating Andhra Pradesh had weakened. This reflected the transition in regional politics with the rise of the Telugu Desam Party (TDP). The TDP, led by N.T. Rama Rao, was formed in March 1982 and came to power in January 1983. Central to its platform was a declaration of Telugu pride, a call for greater state autonomy, opposition to Congress manipulation of Andhra politics and to the paltry condition of the faction-ridden state party.[24] The TDP was the first party to successfully unite broad-based opposition to Congress across Andhra into a viable electoral platform, catalysed by the charismatic personality of NTR in the early 1980s. The strength of the TDP's appeal to a regional cultural and linguistic identity, particularly to those who resented the political dominance of Reddys in Congress locally,[25] helped to sideline the question of statehood for Telangana in the 1980s and 1990s. Again, Andhra Pradesh stood in contrast to states of the Hindi heartland in which borders became politicised in the course of the transformations from an era of Congress Party dominance. In Andhra, by contrast (and similarly to Maharashtra), the TDP gave succour to a state-wide identity as part of its anti-Congress politics.

The BJP itself had a weak electoral base in Andhra Pradesh in this era, as in other southern states. The only region of the state in which it won a handful of seats in this period was the Telangana region. Political competition was dominated by Congress and the TDP throughout the 1980s and 1990s. When the BJP did substantially increase the number of seats it contested in 1994 (as shown in Table 5.4), it still did not succeed in making inroads by winning seats. The party did not even contest seats in most of the rest of the state. In 1997, the BJP's state executive passed a resolution supporting statehood for Telangana and, in the 1998 elections, local BJP politicians took a pro-statehood stance, however, the demand for Telangana found no place in its national election manifesto.

Thus when the BJP came to power in 1998 and moved ahead with creating new states in Chhattisgarh, Jharkhand and Uttarakhand, it had not laid the kind of groundwork in Andhra Pradesh as it had in these regions. This helps explain why the demand for Telangana was not high up the BJP's agenda. Its reliance on TDP support in parliament meant that the BJP did not push further with this particular, intermittent, demand for statehood.

Table 5.4: Party Competition in Telangana: state assembly elections, 1985–1999.

Year	TDP		Congress		BJP		Left Parties		Other/Independents	
	Won	Cont.	Won	Cont.	Won	Cont.	Won	Cont.	Won	Cont.
1985	59	74	14	107	8	9	15	19	11	624
1989	19	73	58	105	5	10	12	21	13	490
1994	69	82	6	107	3	104	21	22	8	731
1999	50	91	42	107	8	15	2	42	5	511

Source: Political Parties and Elections in Indian States: 1990–2003 (Statistical Supplement, *Journal of Indian School of Political Economy*, XV:1&2, January-June 2003).
Key: Cont=seats contested.

The politics of statehood debates in Andhra Pradesh and Maharashtra underlines the fact that the story of state creation in 2000 had deep roots within the specific political changes underway in Hindi heartland states in the 1980s and 1990s with the mobilisation of lower castes. The correspondence of the borders of Andhra Pradesh and Maharashtra with linguistic communities of Telugu and Marathi speakers made it less likely that state division would become a subject around which political consensus would emerge, because the existence of strong regional parties drawing on state-wide, linguistic identities allowed them to build pan-state electoral coalitions. Furthermore, both states contain a mega-city—Hyderabad and Mumbai—making their potential bifurcation more contentious.

Other Constitutional Reforms: A Grander Programme?

Did state creation fit alongside a broader vision for constitutional or federal reform? Soon after the NDA came back to power in 1999, they appointed a National Commission to Review the Working of the Constitution. This gave a fresh airing to the idea of establishing a presidential system of government, an idea that the BJP had toyed with at various points of its history. But the commission was little more than a talking shop, and no significant constitutional changes emerged under the NDA. One question of federal practice did arise, related to the distribution of parliamentary seats between states. The NDA government passed the Constitution (Eighty-fourth Amendment) Act 2001, which extended the freeze on redistributing seats between states on the basis of population until 2026. In India, democratic 'malapportionment' has arisen because of a constitutional amendment first passed during the Emergency which froze the number of seats per state according to their share of the population in the 1971 census.

The term malapportionment indicates the extent to which states are over- or under-represented in legislatures in relation to their population size. Extreme malapportionment is at odds with the democratic principle of 'one person, one vote'. As Snyder and Samuels write, 'In a malapportioned system, all citizens can enjoy a free and equal opportunity to *formulate* and *signify* their preferences yet nevertheless lack the opportunity to have their preferences *weighed* equally.'[26] The 1976 constitutional amendment had stated that the freeze on seat distribution would last until 2000. The NDA decided to continue the freeze. Strikingly— though probably only a matter of coincidence—the statement of objects and reasons prefacing the subsequent constitutional amendment on this issue was written on exactly the day that Uttaranchal was born. The preface explained that the amendment was intended 'as a motivational measure to enable the State Government to pursue the agenda for population stabilisation'.[27] This continued the (questionable) logic of the original amendment in 1976, which sought to maintain incentives for the northern states to bring down population growth and not penalise southern states, which had made more progress in this regard, by reducing their seats.

The consequence of the freeze on the reassignment of seats was that the northern states continued to be underrepresented on the basis of population size, and southern seats overrepresented.[28] It is not at all clear that the debate about creating new states was connected publicly to the question of freezing the redistribution of seats according to population.[29] But the coincidence of timing cannot be entirely ignored. The creation of Chhattisgarh, Jharkhand and Uttarakhand entailed the creation of less severely under-represented states than their parent states (because of the somewhat lower population densities of these regions) and worsened the representation of their parent states which are already under-represented compared to other states.[30] Practically, this has meant that the vote of a citizen in a new state during a general election counts for marginally more than that of a citizen in its parent state. By entrenching the disadvantage faced by certain regions of north India, the freeze on seat distribution had the effect of artificially restricting the number of seats that regional, lower caste parties—such as the BSP, SP and RJD (all opponents of the BJP)—with their base in the underrepresented areas (especially in the remaining parts of Uttar Pradesh and Bihar after state creation), could win in parliament.

Conclusion

This chapter has shown that the actual creation of the three states in 2000 responded to short term logics of alliance politics at the national level. The decisions to push ahead with state creation in Bihar, Madhya Pradesh and Uttar Pradesh, and not in Maharashtra or Andhra Pradesh, reflect the nature of state politics in these regions, together with the alliances which the BJP had entered with regional parties. The BJP created states in regions of the Hindi heartland in which it had done well electorally in the 1990s. These regions were peripheral to the main centres of lower caste political mobilisation in Bihar and Uttar Pradesh. The BJP had already made electoral progress in each of the regions by the late 1990s and thus did not stand to gain many more seats in parliament as a result of state creation, though it did gain the possibility of being able to form state governments in more places. In the long term, it was the BJP's gradual conversion to a regionalist policy from the 1970s onwards that was critical in helping to link a host of political changes at the subnational level to the eventual territorial reorganisation of India's federalism.

7

AFTER 2000

FURTHER REORGANISATION?

Whether India's internal borders will, or should, be revised again has remained an open question. Critics of state creation often fear that it will create a 'pandora's box' of further demands. This final chapter will consider the story of federal reorganisation as it stands after 2000, focusing on the resurgent demand for Telangana and the debate about Uttar Pradesh's reorganisation which have both been asserted with greater intensity since 2000, but not necessarily because of 2000.

Over a decade after the creation of Chhattisgarh, Jharkhand and Uttarakhand, many other demands for statehood are periodically raised. These include Bodoland (in Assam), Coorg (in Karnataka), Vidarbha (in Maharashtra), Greater Cooch Behar and Gorkhaland (in West Bengal), Bhojpur and Mithila (in Bihar), Saurashtra (in Gujarat), Harit Pradesh, Bundelkhand and Poorvanchal (in Uttar Pradesh), and Telangana (in Andhra Pradesh). Strikingly, some of the most active 'movements' for statehood in recent years have been seen in 'linguistic' states: the movement for Telangana in Andhra Pradesh, and that for Gorkhaland in West Bengal. The idea of 'trifurcating' Uttar Pradesh has received attention since Mayawati declared her support for the idea during her time as Chief Minister of the state. The potential for reorganising state boundaries goes beyond those regions with active—or 'paper'—demands, however. Rasheeduddin Khan, for example, proposed a redrawing of the federal map along the lines of fifty-eight 'socio-cultural regions'.[1]

185

The story told in *Remapping India* would suggest that the fate of any of these demands rests on the intersection of conditions at the sub-state, state and federal levels. In Telangana, the potential for state-wide agreement about a redrawing of state boundaries, in recent years, has been undermined by the early intervention of the central government, as well as by the contentious position of the state capital, Hyderabad, within a putative Telangana state. In Uttar Pradesh, the renewal of a debate about restructuring the state's boundaries owes much to the alternative imaginings of the state's sacred geography by the BSP while in power. In this chapter, as a coda to the main discussion of the book, I sketch the contours of these two prominent debates about the potential for further states reorganisation.

Resurgence of the Demand for Telangana

While the demand for Telangana had been a relative non-issue when Chhattisgarh, Jharkhand and Uttarakhand were created, new life was breathed into the idea of statehood in this region during the 2000s. The renewed momentum behind the demand in this period (the last time it was seriously mobilised was in the late 1960s) owes much to the sudden emergence of a leadership vacuum at the heart of state politics. In office from 1996–2004, TDP Chief Minister Chandrababu Naidu had developed a centralised style of political and economic management that was continued by his successor, the Congress Chief Minister Y.S. Rajasekhara Reddy.[2] The strategy employed by both Naidu and Y.S. Rajasekhara Reddy involved keeping a tight rein on dissent and power challenges within their respective parties, as well as employing complex populist strategies to maintain grassroots support while overseeing programmes of economic reform. It is no coincidence that the Telangana demand took a more dramatic turn during the political vacuum that emerged after Y.S. Rajasekhara Reddy death in a helicopter accident in September 2009.

While statehood had been back on the political agenda since the early 2000s, events in Telangana came to a head in late 2009. The leader of the regional pro-Telangana party K. Chandrashekhar Rao had launched a hunger strike for statehood on November 29 2009. After footage appeared that purported to show K. Chandrashekhar Rao breaking his fast by accepting a glass of fruit juice, he was pushed to maintain his fast by angry student protestors at Osmania University in Hyderabad, and

Kakatiya University in Warangal district. As K. Chandrashekhar Rao's condition deteriorated, and protests in Telangana intensified under the spotlight of persistent TV coverage, Home Minister P. Chidambaram issued a statement on 9 December 2009 that the 'process of creating Telangana will be initiated'. This apparent statement of intent by the central government to create Telangana sent shockwaves through local political circles. Chidambaram's statement stood in stark contrast to the more usual, non-committal responses of the central government to demands for statehood.[3] The statement provoked opposition to state creation from other regions of Andhra Pradesh of an intensity that apparently took the central government and Congress Party leadership by surprise. Local political observers suggest that, had Y.S. Rajasekhara Reddy been alive the situation may not have developed in this fashion, but in the political vacuum that followed his death, the central government became directly involved in a debate about state creation. This central government involvement, in the absence of any effective agreement among actors at the state level in favour of statehood, distinguished the debate about Telangana from 2009 onwards from the process of state creation witnessed in the states created in 2000. In these earlier cases, central government involvement came long after strong popular demands for statehood.

The re-emergence of a popular constituency in favour of statehood for Telangana reflected perceptions that economic development in and around Hyderabad since the mid-1990s has been exclusionary. A powerful sense that the new economy has been dominated by caste and kinship networks originating in coastal Andhra and Rayalaseema, linked closely to international migratory and capital flows, and that urban-oriented growth strategies have neglected the fate of a struggling countryside, gave a new lease of life to earlier framings of the Telangana demand which drew on the need to protect the jobs and land of 'local', *mulki*, communities from outside competition.

The renewed agitation that began in late 2009 in Telangana built upon many of the themes seen in the late 1960s and early 1970s, but in the context of more recent trajectories of economic growth driven by IT sector expansion and the growth of real estate markets in the 2000s. Statehood claimants complained that development in Hyderabad has favoured those from outside the Telangana region, and that the region has been subject to a form of internal colonialism, in which rural areas have long been discriminated against, especially in the provision of irrigation. The Srikrishna Committee, commissioned by the central government to report on the case for statehood for Telangana after the December protests, reported that one point of view expressed to the committee was that patterns of investment in and around Hyderabad under the TDP and Congress governments of Andhra Pradesh since 1982 had not favoured the local population:

During this period, large areas of resourceful land, including *wakf* lands in and around Hyderabad, were acquired at much cheaper prices for and by "outsiders" (persons not belonging to Telangana region) at a great advantage to them ignoring the interest of the locals. Although the industrial and economic developmental base that was created by these "outsiders", using these lands, contributed to general economic and industrial growth and incidental employment benefits, the higher end dividends in terms of incomes and jobs and other similar avenues in these attractive efforts were taken away again by the "outsiders", leaving the locals with lower-end jobs and less attractive opportunities.[4]

During the 2000s, the idea of statehood for Telangana became a pawn in electoral competition in Andhra Pradesh. Political parties in opposition at the state level made opportunistic use of the Telangana issue as they sought to put pressure on the state leadership. The Telangana Rashtri Samiti (TRS) had been formed in 2001 by K. Chandrashekhar Rao, a former TDP cabinet minister, piqued at his apparent demotion by Chandrababu Naidu from a cabinet post to deputy speaker of the legislative assembly. At a similar time, the Congress, led by Y.S. Rajasekhara Reddy, began to use the Telangana issue to put pressure on the TDP government during *panchayat* elections in 2001. Congress MLAs from the region formed a Telangana Congress Legislator's Forum, and called on the Congress leadership to support the idea of statehood. In the Lok Sabha elections in 2004, Congress formed an alliance with the TRS. The subsequent Common Minimum Programme of the Congress-led United Progressive Alliance central government promised that the government would 'consider the demand for the formation of a Telangana state at an appropriate time after due consultations and consensus'. Furthermore, K. Chandreshekhar Rao was made a minister in the central government. These moves by Congress were overseen by Y.S. Rajasekhara Reddy, and interviewees in 2011 expressed a degree of scepticism as to their true motives. Most saw the alliance with the TRS as a bid to encourage opposition unity against the TDP during the 2004 state and national elections. Some Congress politicians within Telangana are critical of Y.S. Rajasekhara

Reddy for not being serious about Telangana, and of politicians from the region for 'selling out'.[5] The TRS withdrew its support to the UPA in 2006, arguing that the central government had made no progress in tackling the question of Telangana. Yet the TRS seemed unable to capture the imagination of the public as an electoral force. Repeated by-elections held in 2006, 2007 and 2008, following the resignation of TRS legislators, saw the party's position deteriorate. The TRS, as Srinivasulu and Satyanarayana argue, was held at arm's length by social and cultural organisations, who looked down upon the party's reliance on lobbying and electoral politics as well as the inability of the party's leadership, dominated by an upper caste elite of Vellamas and Reddys, to articulate a deeper sociocultural vision of Telangana.[6] Ahead of the 2009 elections, it was the TDP who entered an alliance with the TRS against Congress.

These short-term manoeuvres bear a resemblance to state-level political dynamics and the often apparently casual politicisation of state boundaries seen in Bihar, Madhya Pradesh and Uttar Pradesh before their bifurcation. Yet, the central government's direct intervention in the debate about Telangana in December 2009, suggesting that it would act on the demand for statehood, hardened positions on the ground in Andhra Pradesh. In all the '2000 states', the central government's reluctance to respond to demands for statehood from one part of a state largely meant that debates about state creation remained quarantined within state borders. The low expectations that the central government would intervene to create a state (and the centralised constitutional procedure for creating a state) had the effect of reducing the incentives for political parties to mobilise opposition to state creation. In Andhra Pradesh, the involvement of the central government—especially before the tabling of a resolution on statehood in the state assembly—raised the stakes. The intervention of the central government and Congress party leadership was made more likely as a result of the infighting within the local Congress Party that emerged after Y.S. Rajasekhara Reddy's death, especially as his son Jagan Mohan Reddy broke away to form his own 'Y.S. Rajasekhara Reddy Congress Party'. Disarray within the state Congress party drew the national Congress leadership into the debate over Telangana.

There are two further reasons why consensus has been less likely to emerge in favour of bifurcation across Andhra Pradesh, compared to demands within the Hindi heartland in recent decades. The first is the existence of a stronger state-wide identity, drawing on a shared language as highlighted in the previous chapter. It might be noted, however, that language has not been central to the anti-Telangana protests within Coastal Andhra and Rayalaseema. Furthermore, pro-Telangana activists have used the differences between the Telugu dialect spoken in Telangana and that spoken elsewhere, as well as alleged discrimination towards the Telangana dialect in Telugu films and popular culture as a justification for separation, challenging the logic that Telugu unites the people of Andhra Pradesh.[7] Arguably more important today, then, are cross state kinship and economic networks among the political and business elite, underpinned by the status of Hyderabad. Hyderabad's location within the potentially 'seceding' region constitutes the second reason why the idea of bifurcation is problematic for the regions of Coastal Andhra and Rayalaseema. The Srikrishna Committee reported having received submissions that outlined fears of losing an engine of growth, as well as a sentiment that Hyderabad was no longer merely a 'Telangana city' but a national metropolis.

One explanation for the opposition to the formation of Telangana by those from outside the region with economic interests in the state capital is their concern for the security of their investments should the state come into being with a new political leadership. It is often assumed by activists and journalists within Telangana that such concerns arise from fears around the insecurity of property rights in a situation where deals over land acquisition have not been wholly transparent, or where property is *benami* (literally, 'without name', i.e. the title is not in the name of the true beneficial owner). Some real estate players in Hyderabad also cultivate overt links to politicians from other regions of Andhra Pradesh.[8] Nevertheless, opposition to the creation of Telangana from coastal Andhra on the grounds of economic interests in Hyderabad was not an inevitable state of affairs. In the mid-2000s, after Congress allied with the TRS and came back to power in Andhra Pradesh, there were reports of considerable land speculation in the area between Guntur and Vijayawada, where it was assumed the new capital of Andhra Pradesh would be located if Telangana were formed. Furthermore, before 2009, few political actors were actively campaigning against Telangana.

AFTER 2000: FURTHER REORGANISATION?

Business and the Telangana Demand

The attitude of businesses in Hyderabad itself towards the idea of statehood appears to range from apprehension to active support. The giant nets completely shrouding the GVK One mall in Banjara Hills when I visited Hyderabad days after the publication of the Srikrishna Committee report in January 2011 were a visible sign of the kinds of protests for which some businesses in the city were preparing. The report had recommended the continuation of a United Andhra with some constitutional and statutory protection for the Telangana region, as being the most workable option. Though protests in Hyderabad in late 2009 and early 2010 had proved to be a serious disruption to economic activity, the publication of the findings and recommendations of the Srikrishna report were not followed by major demonstrations, *bandhs*, attacks on businesses or visible disruption to daily life in the state capital.

A week after the Srikrishna report was published, I was invited to attend a 'Telangana Round Table' hosted by the Telangana Development Forum, a group set up by non-resident Indian (NRI) businessmen from the region. The round table at a hotel in Hyderabad brought together senior industrialists, politicians from all major parties and academics to discuss the way forward for the statehood demand. The only sign of the heated protests that have accompanied the Telangana demand was an unexpected, but well choreographed *Gandhigiri* protest by members of the Telangana Non-Gazetted Officers Association (TNGO)—followed by TV cameras—who stormed into the quiet conference room to offer flowers to TDP MLA Janardhan Reddy, seeking assurance of his support for Telangana. The general sentiment of almost all present was an acceptance of the idea of state creation. The attitudes towards state creation offered the industrialists who were present varied from emotional commitment to the Telangana cause, arising from their involvement as students in the 1969 protests (a retiree and former NRI quipped that he had 'lost a year in 1969'), to a sense that smaller states promoted faster growth. Some highlighted approvingly the experience of rapid economic growth by newer states like Chhattisgarh. More generally, they expressed their concerns for how to shape a pro-business regime in a new state and ensure that pro-Telangana agitations did not threaten industrial interests. The MLAs and MPs present were keen, in turn, to reassure industrialists that their investments in Hyderabad would be protected. One

Congress MLA, however, made the suggestion that those from outside the region should describe themselves as 'Telanganaites'—'if you identify yourself with the local guys,' he said, 'the problems will be over'. This sentiment mirrored some of the views of business people in Chhattisgarh towards state creation, discussed in chapter four, and reflected a similar attempt to distance a regional identity from exclusive association with 'sons of the soil'.

At the sub-state level in Telangana, there is a greater degree of agreement in favour of statehood compared to that found across the state. Representatives of all major political parties in Telangana, with the exception of the CPI (M) and the Majlis-Ittehadul Muslimeen (MIM) in Hyderabad, have offered support for statehood. The demand receives broad social support, and while it is often directed against Kammas from Coastal Andhra and Reddys from Ralayalaseema, it is not associated with any particular social group within Telangana. The TRS itself is led by an upper caste Vellama, although K. Chandrashekhar Rao has said that the first Chief Minister of a future Telangana state should be a Dalit.

Lastly, at the national level, it is not clear whether conditions support the creation of Telangana. All parties, especially Congress, are worried about the potential electoral backlash in a residual Andhra state. Regional allies of both the Congress and BJP in other states will be wary about the signal sent by the first division of a linguistic state. In recent years, no national or aspiring national party with a commitment to the creation of Telangana has risen to a position of power in the central government. Conditions are, therefore, rather different than those which faced the BJP-led NDA government when it created Chhattisgarh, Jharkhand and Uttarakhand. It might be remembered, however, that none of those states was created in close proximity to intense pro-statehood agitations, so the longer term future of the Telangana demand may look different. It remains to be seen whether federal coalition politics evolves in ways that promote the creation of Telangana.

* * *

AFTER 2000: FURTHER REORGANISATION?

The BSP and the Trifurcation of Uttar Pradesh

The idea that Uttar Pradesh should be divided into multiple states is not new. But it is a notion that lay relatively dormant for the four decades following the debates of the 1950s when the States Reorganisation Commission held its deliberations. The separation of Uttarakhand in 2000 did not give rise to any further serious debate about the viability or desirability of the plains of Uttar Pradesh, home to 16.5 per cent of India's population,[9] continuing as one unit. Nevertheless, after 2007 when the Bahujan Samaj Party (BSP) won the first outright electoral majority in the state since 1989, the suggestion that Uttar Pradesh should be reorganised into as many as four states received high profile, if low key, lip service from the BSP as well as senior politicians from other parties in different regions of the state.[10] There has been no popular mobilisation around the state's division. But the willingness of politicians from multiple political parties to bring the borders of Uttar Pradesh into question reflects the transformation of the party system in the context of the erosion of Congress Party dominance, and the sidelining of conceptions of a sacred geography that claimed the necessity of a united Uttar Pradesh. In 2012, however, a new state government led by the Samajwadi Party was elected, who argued against the state's 'trifurcation' during the state elections, thus the immediate future of the debates about Uttar Pradesh's reorganisation is, at the time of writing, uncertain.

The BSP and Uttar Pradesh's Symbolic Geography

The BSP presented the need to reorganise Uttar Pradesh as a question of development. Mayawati stated in December 2009 that: 'I was always in favour of smaller states as they are much simpler to govern'.[11] In an interview, the state BSP president Swami Prasad Maurya suggested that their thinking was influenced by Ambedkar's views on the desirability of smaller states, and noted that since they had been in government, the BSP had divided large districts within Uttar Pradesh such as Meerut into multiple districts.[12] But asked whether he thought the division of Uttar Pradesh would ever really happen, Swami Prasad Maurya replied: 'It can happen one day—when Mayawati will be Prime Minister!' He had already offered the observation that this is

193

currently a 'theoretical' demand only, and that the BSP were not trying to create an agitation around it. Furthermore, he said, the reorganisation of Uttar Pradesh would not be a big issue at election time. Such replies underscored the symbolic nature of the BSP's interest in the reorganisation of Uttar Pradesh.

Reorganising Uttar Pradesh was not a major party priority, although it ended up receiving a little more attention during state elections in 2012 than Swami Prasad Maurya had predicted. BSP thinking on the issue appeared to be connected to a broader attempt to recast the sacred geography of Uttar Pradesh to advance a symbolic agenda of social justice, in line with longer traditions of Dalit political mobilisation.[13] In illustration of this fact, after my interview with the BSP president ended, we began to discuss how Lucknow had changed physically since I had last visited seven years earlier. Swami Prasad Maurya ran through each of the new monuments constructed by Mayawati since coming to power to honour 'heroes of the downtrodden' including Kanshi Ram, Ambedkar, and Buddha. He emphasised that this physical reshaping of the city of Lucknow was linked to what Mayawati has sought to do for Buddhist sites throughout Uttar Pradesh. I left the meeting with a glossy promotional guide to Uttar Pradesh Buddhist Tourism in hand. Entitled 'Towards an Equalitarian Society', this coffee table book sets out BSP intentions to recast Uttar Pradesh as the 'Land of Lord Buddha', and make the state a key destination for Buddhist pilgrims. It notes the attempts to promote a Buddhist circuit linking the sites of Sarnath, Shravasti, Sankisa, Kaushambi, Kushinagar and Kapilvastu. Four new districts were created within this circuit in 1997 and given names associated with Buddha (and eleven other districts were created elsewhere). One of the new districts, Gautam Buddha Nagar involved the amalgamation of Noida, Greater Noida and Dadari districts which border Delhi. It is the site of India's new Formula One racing circuit: the Buddh International Circuit. The book also reproduces a more recent letter from Mayawati to Railway Minister Lalu Prasad Yadav in 2006, petitioning for the creation of a circular rail network to link these Buddhist sites. Although this promotional book does not mention the idea of reorganising Uttar Pradesh into multiple states, it—and the discussion that preceded the gift—provided a sense of how the BSP's thoughts on reorganisation fit with their broader thinking about the sacred geography of Uttar Pradesh. These images offer a vision of Uttar Pradesh that is diametrically opposed to G.B. Pant's assertion in 1955 that: 'No power on earth can cut up the land of Rama and Krishna, of Ganga and Yamuna.' They also clearly draw a line under the more recent politicisation of parts of the state's sacred geography by Hindu nationalists focused on Ayodhya.

* * *

The BSP's thinking about state reorganisation reflects the extent to which potential changes to the boundaries of Uttar Pradesh have become part of the discourse of state politics following the decline of Congress dominance. The BSP are not the only party to have brought Uttar Pradesh's borders into question. The demand for a separate state in western Uttar Pradesh is associated in particular with Ajit Singh, the leader of the Rashtriya Lok Dal and son of Choudhury Charan Singh. This western region covers the regions of Rohilkhand, Upper Doab and Lower Doab, with Meerut and Agra as its major cities. Ajit Singh has raised the demand with some persistence, forming a number of local pro-statehood outfits since the 1996 Lok Sabha elections, in which he lost his seat to the BJP candidate. In June 2000, he formed the Harit Pradesh Nirman Samiti (Green State Creation Committee), providing the latest appellation for the proposed state. As Jagpal Singh argues, Ajit Singh's pursuit of statehood is best understood through the lens of political expediency. During an era of coalition politics in Uttar Pradesh from the mid-1990s until the BSP's outright victory in 2007, the statehood demand provided a convenient bargaining chip for Ajit Singh to negotiate terms of entry for his party, the Rashtriya Lok Dal, into various regional (and national) coalitions, although he was often seen as doing little to further the demand while in power.[14] The demand is also seen as an attempt to carve out space for renewed Jat influence in Uttar Pradesh, since Jats are more concentrated in the western districts. The tenor of the statehood demand in this relatively more prosperous region tends to be anti-redistributive, founded on slogans such as 'Paschimi Uttar Pradesh ki kamai ko poorvi Uttar Pradesh walein khatein hai' (western Uttar Pradesh toils, while eastern Uttar Pradesh eats).[15] Western Uttar Pradesh boasts the highest levels of agricultural productivity in the state, and, as the site of almost half of Uttar Pradesh's industries, is also its most diversified economy.[16] The demand also draws on the familiar complaints about Uttar Pradesh's size and distances to its capital city, Lucknow, as well as the region's distinct geography and cultural heritage. While there has been scant popular mobilisation in favour of statehood, the demand has intertwined with calls by lawyers since the late 1970s for a separate bench of the high court in Meerut in western Uttar Pradesh. As this has not been successful, lawyers in Meerut have increasingly turned their attention to the demand for statehood.[17]

After the formation of the state government by the BSP in 2007, it is the Bundelkhand region, however, that provided momentum to the reorganisation debate. Uttar Pradesh's Bundelkhand districts appear on a map as a protrusion into Madhya Pradesh. Historically, the region of Bundelkhand drew in six districts that today fall under Madhya Pradesh, as well as the seven districts in Uttar Pradesh. Bundelkhand is a hilly region, geographically distinct from the Gangetic parts of Uttar Pradesh, with a low population density and with Jhansi its largest town. Bundelkhand is officially designated as a 'backward region' of Uttar Pradesh, along with eastern Uttar Pradesh (or 'Purvanchal'). Agriculture is the primary economic activity, but the region also contains deposits of minerals such as limestone, granite and sand. In the 1980s and 1990s, Bundelkhand had the highest rate of poverty in the state.[18] Between 2004 and 2008, drought-like conditions drew attention to conditions of severe agrarian distress and distress-induced migration in the region.[19] Raja Bundela, a film actor and director who contested the 2004 Lok Sabha elections for the Congress party, has been spearheading a statehood demand for the region.

Congress made a strategic decision to focus on Bundelkhand in its bid to revive its fortunes in Uttar Pradesh. It was in the context of intensifying competition between Congress and the BSP that the question of reorganising Uttar Pradesh more generally found political voice since 2007. In early 2008, a Congress MLA from Jhansi (who subsequently was elected to parliament and became a union minister in 2009) tabled a resolution in support of statehood for Bundelkhand in the legislative assembly.[20] A week before a visit to Jhansi by Rahul Gandhi in January 2008, state Congress president Rita Bahuguna reported that the state leadership had met Prime Minister Manmohan Singh to seek 'reconstitution of the second State Reorganisation Commission for considering our demand for a separate Bundelkhand State.'[21] The day before Rahul Gandhi's visit, Mayawati used the occasion of her birthday celebrations to reiterate her own party's support for 'trifurcation', but insisted that the initiative on state creation must be taken by the central government. From this point, the debate between Congress and BSP took on a circular shape with the BSP calling on the central government to act, and Congress calling on the BSP to send the central government a state assembly resolution supporting the division of Uttar Pradesh. Shortly before the 2012 state elections, the Uttar Pradesh state assembly eventually passed a voice resolution in favour of the state's division into four.

By contrast to the tussle over Bundelkhand, discussions about statehood for the eastern region, often known as 'Purvanchal', have been more muted. The main individual to have taken up the mantle of statehood for this region is a former Samajwadi Party politician, Amar Singh, who is seeking a new political home. The idea of Purvanchal has received support from former and serving Chief Ministers of the neighbouring state of Bihar, Lalu Prasad Yadav and Nitish Kumar.[22] Congress Union Rural Development Minister Jairam Ramesh has also stated that for Purvanchal's sake, Uttar Pradesh should be divided so as to resolve the 'administrative nightmare arising from its size and population'.[23] As with the other demands within Uttar Pradesh, that made for Purvanchal has been pushed more strongly since the central government's intervention in Telangana in December 2009, but none of these regions has witnessed the kind of popular mobilisation in favour of statehood that was seen in Telangana in 2009.

At the state level, the BSP's willingness to question Uttar Pradesh's borders was due to the weakened relevance of the kind of justifications for unity made in the 1950s for Dalit politicians. The BSP also highlighted the administrative challenges of governing such a large state. The BSP's support is also suggestive of the incentives faced by some Chief Ministers to sponsor statehood demands as part of a strategy, ironically, of holding together state-wide electoral coalitions. Electoral competition looks different across regions of Uttar Pradesh. By drawing attention to the idea of trifurcation, the BSP could attempt to accommodate different patterns of electoral contestation in each region of Uttar Pradesh by seeking to neutralise challenges made on a 'regional' basis. It is unclear how debates about the state's reorganisation will develop under the new Samajwadi Party state government, which came to power in 2012 opposed to the state's 'trifurcation'.

In a national context, the BSP's treatment of state creation had some parallels with the BJP's approach in the 1970s and 1980s, at a time when the BJP was also an aspirant national party. Mayawati's positioning on the statehood issue may reflect party thinking about how it should project itself as a national party. Dividing Uttar Pradesh would give the BSP the potential to come to power in more than one state, allowing it to present itself as more of a national than regional party. It may also be noted that the BSP has offered its support to other ongoing demands for statehood such as Telangana and Vidarbha, as part of its attempts to expand the reach of the party beyond Uttar Pradesh and neighbouring states.

The scope for further reorganisation of state boundaries anywhere in India will rest on the emergence of favourable conditions in both state and federal politics, as this book has demonstrated. State borders remain sticky features of the political landscape that are not easily, lightly or rapidly reorganised. Yet the continued willingness to debate state boundaries whether for symbolic, political, economic or administrative reasons means that the potential further remapping of India's federal geography is likely to remain on the agenda for the foreseeable future.

8

CONCLUSION

The account of state creation offered in this book contrasts with other theories and popular understandings of state creation which have tended to emphasise the intentional agency of actors at a particular level of the federal system seeking short-term electoral, economic or representational gains—either on the part of historically marginalised communities or of dominant socioeconomic interests. The stress on an element of unintentionality, or ambiguity, in my analysis underlines the fact that the act of state creation was the contingent result of multiple processes within India's federal system. The shifts in position of multiple actors for a variety of reasons within the regions that demanded statehood, their parent state capitals and New Delhi were a vital part of the complex dance that laid the foundations for a change in state boundaries. They helped to create a situation in which the idea of changing state boundaries shifted from being potentially threatening to an almost routinised part of political discourse.

The approach taken in the book has disavowed a deterministic model of path-dependent change or a focus on 'critical junctures', episodes which establish certain directions of change and close off others.[1] These are prominent devices used by historical institutionalists, but in a multi-level political system, it can be problematic to identify such junctures or points of departure along new paths. This is because change at one level of the federal system will not necessarily provoke a reaction at another level in a linear or predictable fashion. In the case of state creation, the central government will not necessarily intervene to create a new state where a resolution has been passed by the relevant state assembly or where there is a wide measure of agreement/acquiescence within the region concerned, though these factors are important conditions once a central government is seized by the question of creating new states. *Remapping India* has offered a dynamic causal account which pays attention to relationships between levels of the federal system, and to the conjunction of political processes unfolding according to different yet often overlapping timetables, that influence each other while also retaining a degree of autonomy from each other. As such, the analysis reinforces Orren and Skowronek's vision of a disorderly politics made up of multiple orders, each with their own logic and temporal underpinning that 'abrade against each other and, in the process, drive further change'.[2] The study has highlighted, in particular, the significance of challenges to upper caste political dominance and to the electoral hegemony of the Congress Party in north and central India, in conjunction with the rise of Hindu nationalist politics from 1980 onwards, as shifts which helped to unsettle the fixity of state borders in this region but not ones that unleashed pre-determined pathways to the creation of new states.

Remapping India has demonstrated that statehood emerged as a compromise between historic social movements and political parties (new and old) representing different socioeconomic interests in the regions of Chhattisgarh, Jharkhand and Uttarakhand. Statehood was granted quite some time after the most intense grassroots mobilisation (and without such mobilisation in Chhattisgarh). By the time statehood was granted, it had also become a vehicle for new actors who had ignored earlier calls for the reorganisation of state boundaries. Furthermore the borders of the new states themselves, with greatest consequences in Uttarakhand, were dictated by New Delhi and not by the regions concerned. The relative autonomy of the political timetable with regards to the occurrence, and certainly the timing, of territorial restructuring, has meant that the creation of these new states had something of an abstract quality. The achievement of statehood was not necessarily experienced on the ground as the direct or tangible outcome of a collective popular struggle. Yet, the new states were the repositories of multiple—and competing—imaginings of what a new state could be.

In the remainder of this brief concluding chapter, I will consider the experiences of Chhattisgarh, Jharkhand and Uttarakhand since having become states both from a political economy perspective, and from the point of view of trends in political representation, to ask what the effects of statehood have been since 2000. The results of state creation reflect some of the ambiguity involved in the process itself. The creation of new states has not necessarily produced federal sub-units with more homogenous preferences, more business-friendly environments or in which the rights of 'local' populations are protected over migrants. Pro-statehood campaigns as they slowly evolved had temporarily submerged some of the tensions between such divergent goals, but they have become apparent again since 2000. There is no uniform story to be told about the experiences of statehood across the new states.

The Political Economy of the New States

Those who argue that new or smaller states are good for economic development have focused on the increasing rates of economic growth seen in the new states, particularly in Chhattisgarh and Uttarakhand, as well as post-bifurcation Bihar,[3] since their formation. Between 2001–09, Uttarakhand's net state per capita domestic product grew at 9.1 per cent, Chhattisgarh's at 5.87 per cent and Bihar's at 5.86 per cent: above or at the average growth of all Indian states of 5.86 per cent. Uttarakhand had the fastest rate of per capita growth in the country. Jharkhand fared somewhat under the national average.[4] Yet, beyond headline growth figures, the experiences of all three new states raise questions about the structures and spatial geography of economic growth since liberalisation and its resulting exclusions.

Crude as headline data is, poverty statistics go some way to reveal this other story. While rural poverty across India has fallen by approximately 8 per cent, Chhattisgarh has seen a 1 per cent *increase* in poverty in rural areas, giving it the highest levels of rural poverty in all of India (see Table 8.1). Jharkhand, on the other hand, has seen an apparent decline in rates of rural poverty, though its urban poverty has risen by more than 7 per cent in the same period. Together Chhattisgarh and Jharkhand are home to an almost totemic combination of large *adivasi* populations, Maoist insurgency and repression by state and central armed forces, natural resource exploitation and large scale land acquisition, or land 'grabbing', for mining industries. I describe these factors as totemic in the sense that they have come to be seen as representing the negative repercussions of India's recent growth story, and are often conflated into a single narrative about its less salutary foundations.[5]

Yet the creation of new states is only part of this story. The extraction of minerals and coal has been increasing across India in the context of a commodity boom, not only in the new states. Chhattisgarh, in particular, has certainly pursued an aggressive, extractive industry-led growth strategy since its formation. This has intensified under the Raman Singh-led BJP administration (2003–8; 2008–) which replaced the Congress government led by Ajit Jogi in 2003. Jharkhand has attempted to pursue similar strategies, but in a context of considerably greater political instability. Analogous conflicts around land acquisition and natural resource exploitation have also been seen in older states like Orissa. Maoist-inspired activities had expanded in Chhattisgarh and Jharkhand since the 1980s, although it was partly the crackdown on Maoism in neighbouring Andhra Pradesh in the early 2000s—not the creation of new states per se—that pushed the insurgency into its adjacent regions.[6] One should resist the temptation to reason backwards from a position of hindsight to argue that the practice of federal reorganisation itself is connected to the straightforward capture of the political process by industrial elites seeking to expand into new territories with political support, or to politicians seeking to profit from the proceeds of natural resource exploitation, although such motivations among certain actors are not entirely absent. This book has demonstrated that such linear, mono-causal explanations do not capture the reality of a considerably more complex political process. Furthermore, there is a greater continuity, pre- and post-statehood, than such arguments would imply.

In Uttarakhand, the post-statehood experience has raised somewhat different questions about the spatial geography of India's economic growth story. Uttarakhand was originally intended to be a 'hill state' but its borders encompass the more densely populated plains areas of Haridwar, Udham Singh Nagar and Dehra Dun. It was designated a 'special category' status when it was created, along with other hilly states considered 'non-financially viable' on their own. This status gives the state access to special incentives for industry and to a higher ratio of central government grants to loans than other states. The new state of Uttarakhand has had success in attracting industry, particularly in high-skilled sectors, and this is reflected in its very high rates of economic growth. It has seen corresponding reductions in poverty according to Planning

Table 8.1: Rates of poverty in the new states.

State	Population Below Poverty Line (2009–10)			Population Below Poverty Line (2004–5)			% decrease 2004-5—2009–10		
	Rural	Urban	Total	Rural	Urban	Total	Rural	Urban	Total
Chhattisgarh	56.1	23.8	48.7	55.1	28.4	49.4	-1.0	4.6	0.7
Madhya Pradesh	42.0	22.9	36.7	53.6	35.1	48.6	11.6	12.2	11.9
Jharkhand	41.6	31.1	39.1	51.6	23.8	45.3	10	-7.3	6.2
Bihar	55.3	39.4	53.5	55.7	43.7	54.4	0.4	4.3	0.9
Uttarakhand	14.9	25.2	18.0	35.1	26.2	32.7	20.2	1.0	14.7
Uttar Pradesh	39.4	31.7	37.7	42.7	34.1	40.9	3.3	2.4	3.2
ALL INDIA	33.8	20.9	29.8	42.0	25.5	37.2	8.2	4.6	7.4

Source: Planning Commission estimates based on Tendulkar Committee Methodology, 2012.

Commission estimates, but much more in rural than urban areas, which probably also reflect patterns of migration from rural areas in the hills to towns. This has resulted in what Pant describes as 'unplanned, unregulated mini-urbanisation' and the emergence of new slum-like settlements. Furthermore new industrial investment has been overwhelmingly confined to the *terai* or plains districts of the state.[7] The state recognised this geographical bias by belatedly introducing a new Hill Policy in 2008 but its effects are uncertain as yet.

Statehood and Political Representation

As the empirical chapters of this book have shown, political regionalism has in part been associated with 'sons of the soil' tensions, whether in the claims for an *adivasi* state and allegations of internal colonialism in Jharkhand; the claim that 'local' communities had been sidelined from political power in Chhattisgarh; or the concern that new reservations policies in Uttar Pradesh would disadvantage the inhabitants of the Uttarakhand hills. One of the reasons for the emergence of political consensus around demands for statehood was an attempt by some politicians to unsettle the relationship between particular ethnic or 'local' communities and statehood claims, or to challenge attempts by social movements to associate regional political identities with redistributive claims by marginalised communities. Thus, rather than representing a moment at which political regimes with new, more inclusive social bases were constituted, processes of state formation rendered almost deliberately ambiguous the question of 'who' the new states were being created for.

Since the granting of statehood, Jharkhand has displayed greater political instability than possibly any other Indian state. At the time of writing, it has seen the formation of eight different short-lived governments with four different Chief Ministers, and two periods of President's Rule. Since state formation, the BJP's rising *adivasi* leader of the 1990s and Jharkhand's first Chief Minister Babulal Marandi left the BJP to form his own party, the Jharkhand Vikas Morcha. There is a strong impression that weakly organised political parties offer limited mobility for aspiring candidates, even as the promise to extract rents from mining and industrial ventures increases the lure of political careers. Jharkhand appears to exhibit something akin to what Yadav and Palshikar have described as a 'malady' of 'systemless competition'. This is a situation of extreme fluidity in which electoral competition is not bound by political party conventions, but in which individual entrepreneurship or loose, very short term groupings hold sway.[8] The absence of a stable political regime has reduced the ability of the state to pursue long-term developmental goals. The paralysis in governance in Jharkhand reflects, to an extent, the strength and spaces maintained by local resistance movements; it is also a mark of the absence of a political leadership that can effectively mediate between deeply divergent visions of development.

All political parties in Jharkhand appear to place a premium on tribal leadership—all four Chief Ministers have been *adivasis*—but substantive improvements in the material lives of *adivasis* or their political representation are harder to discern. Furthermore, there is no agreement among the state's political elite about whether the creation of the new state should entail positive discrimination for *adivasis*. This was exemplified by the so-called 'domicile controversy' which undermined Babulal Marandi's chief ministership after the state government sought to reserve all Class III and IV government jobs for people resident in the state since 1932.[9] Clashes ensued between supporters of the domicile policy and those who would have been considered 'outsiders' under such a policy. The delimimitation of Lok Sabha and Legislative Assembly constituencies has also been delayed because of a demand that the number of seats reserved for Scheduled Tribes should not be reduced. Furthermore, until late 2010, Jharkhand was the only state in India not to have held elections to *panchayats* since the seventy-third and seventy-fourth constitutional amendments were enacted. This delay followed a 2005 ruling by the Jharkhand High Court, challenging the reservation of the posts of *panchayat* chairperson for *adivasis* in scheduled areas where the tribal population has fallen below 50 per cent.[10] Thus whether, or how, Jharkhand is a 'tribal' state has been open to considerable contestation since its formation.

In Chhattisgarh, we see a pattern different to that in Jharkhand. As demonstrated in chapter four, the demand for statehood was associated particularly with OBC politicians the plains of Chhattisgarh. The new state has seen the consolidation, to an extent, of the presence of a somewhat larger number of OBCs in its governing elite although the chief minister since 2003, Raman Singh, is an upper caste Thakur. The political dominance of the plains areas, in addition to the fact that the two national parties—Congress and BJP—continue to dominate the new state's politics, has contributed to the absence of a strong tribal political voice in the state. Although the state is commonly bracketed along with Jharkhand in popular discourse as a 'tribal' state that was created to better represent *adivasis*, the demand for statehood in Chhattisgarh—as has been seen—was not made volubly by *adivasi* leaders and the question of tribal representation per se is not one that has defined Chhattisgarhi politics in a way that is comparable to Jharkhand.

The BJP has consolidated its electoral position in Chhattisgarh—as well as Madhya Pradesh—since 2000. It came to power in the first elections held in the state in 2003, and won a second term in 2008. As I argue elsewhere, Chhattisgarh's political class has over time neglected the issues facing its tribal majority regions, as well as the situation of small and marginal farmers. Serious issues that have not received adequate attention include displacement and the environmental externalities associated with extractive industries, Naxalism and state responses to it, and farmer suicides—a sizeable but unacknowledged problem, reflecting a situation of severe agrarian distress.[11] Chhattisgarh was home to one of the most controversial approaches to 'tackling' Naxalism—Salwa Judum. While this was described by the state government as a spontaneous people's uprising, the state had begun to arm tribal youth known as 'special police officers' to lead an anti-Maoist campaign from 2005. Salwa Judum was declared illegal by the Supreme Court of India in July 2011, which linked it to a scramble for the natural resources of the region and described it as a 'gross violation of human rights'.[12] On the other hand, the state government since 2003 has introduced innovative social policy reforms in the fields of health care, nutrition and subsidised food distribution, expanding the coverage of schemes sponsored by the central government in Delhi and strengthening their implementation.

When the new 'hill' state of Uttarakhand was created, substantial plains areas had been included on the grounds of making the state economically viable. Faster population growth in urban areas of these plains districts has meant that under the latest delimitation of constituencies for the state assembly, the number of plains seats will start to outnumber hill seats—thirty-six plains and thirty-four hill seats—within a decade of the state's formation.[13] There is no agreement among Uttarakhand's new political class about whether the new state should even be seen as a hill state. For instance, in 2005, State Congress President Harish Rawat criticised the proposed redrawing of assembly constituencies, saying: 'The delimitation process based on population is against tribals and hill people.' While then Health Minister, Tilak Raj Behad (also Congress) said: 'In democracy people are important and not stones and mountains.'[14] Politics and government formation since statehood was granted have also been unstable. This may reflect the fact that electoral politics has become considerably more local since 2000, as the region's nineteen assembly constituencies were increased to seventy. The BJP and Congress remain the major electoral players in the state but intra-party rivalry is endemic and there have been seven changes of Chief Minister since 2000.

Thus, in all three new states, the post-2000 scenarios raise questions about the political economy of development in India today, as well as the representative quality of democracy. This brief discussion of the new states since the granting of statehood demonstrates that debates about the potential consequences for further territorial reorganisation must be grounded in empirical realities and longer term histories, and not simply abstract reasoning about the numbers and sizes of states. The idea that creating more states is a simple panacea for reducing regional inequality is misleading. The wisdom of breaking up big states can seem self-evident in light of the developmental successes of older, smaller states such as Kerala or Himachal Pradesh which have developed a strong sense of regional community.[15] But these assumed virtues are not by themselves assured as a result of creating smaller states. The longer-term histories of regional political regimes and political economies remain important in shaping the conditions for economic growth and poverty reduction.

Broader Implications

The design of federal architecture matters. The remapping of the internal borders of federal systems is a much neglected issue in the study of comparative federalism, though it is very much a present day concern. Many federal systems in developing countries, with boundaries inherited from colonial administration or patterns of conquest, have created new federal sub-units. The process of state creation in India could profitably be compared with practices of federal design in other newer federations such as Nigeria, Brazil or neighbouring Pakistan. Another of India's South Asian neighbours, Nepal, is also currently restructuring its constitution along federal lines, and the design of its federal sub-units has been one of the thornier issues in this process. It would be instructive to ask what impact the processes of boundary change or state creation have had on developmental trajectories, structures of political competition and the management of ethnic conflict across these countries.

Literature on the political geography of federal systems is typically animated by concerns with the overall stability of federal political structures, the management of ethnic conflict in heterogeneous societies, the quality of representation and inter-regional redistribution. Despite the importance of federal reorganisation as an ongoing process in many countries, as well as considerable interest in the effects of borders for federal stability and the management of ethnic conflict, scholarship on comparative federalism has until now focused less closely on the question of the origins of internal borders. This book therefore makes an important contribution to the literature not only on Indian federalism, but on approaches to understanding institutional change in federal systems more generally.

Much of the literature on multi-ethnic or multicultural federalism could be said to be influenced by a normative stance that associates federalism with a 'politics of recognition'. This can lead to the assumption that territorial restructuring takes place to accommodate ethnic groups, rather than paying attention to the way in which different identities become salient at different times, and the processes by which these identities are mediated in the process of electoral politics. There is little research on the mechanisms, including the role of political parties and social movements, which link ethnicity, protest or everyday politics to the territorial design of federal institutions. By taking up these themes, this book adds to the literature on the design of federal institutions, and their influence on democracy and development in India. I hope that *Remapping India* demonstrates the utility of studying the lived experience of federal institutions and their embeddedness within the fabric of local politics and state-society relationships in order to understand when and why changes to territorial boundaries occur—and what the consequences of such changes might be.

APPENDIX

STATE REORGANISATION 1950–2000

1950   Part A: Assam, Bihar, Bombay, Madhya Pradesh, Madras, Orissa, Punjab, Uttar Pradesh, West Bengal
Part B: Hyderabad, Saurashtra, Mysore, Travancore-Cochin, Madhya Bharat, Vindhya Pradesh, Patiala and East Punjab States Union (PEPSU), Rajasthan
Part C: Delhi, Kutch, Himachal Pradesh, Bilaspur, Coorg, Bhopal, Manipur, Ajmer-Merwara, Tripura

1953   Andhra

1956   Andhra Pradesh (including Telugu speaking regions of Hyderabad state), Assam, Bihar, Bombay, Delhi (UT) Himachal Pradesh (UT), Jammu and Kashmir, Kerala, Madhya Pradesh, Madras, Manipur (UT), Mysore, Orissa, Punjab, Rajasthan, Uttar Pradesh, Tripura (UT), West Bengal

1960   Bombay divided into Gujarat and Maharashtra

1962   Goa, Daman and Diu (UT)

1963   Nagaland created from Assam

1966   Punjab divided into Punjab and Haryana

1971   Himachal Pradesh upgraded to full statehood

1972   Meghalaya created from Assam; Arunachal Pradesh (UT); Mizoram (UT)
Manipur, and Tripura upgraded to full statehood

1975   Sikkim integrated with India

1987   Arunachal Pradesh, Mizoram and Goa upgraded to full statehood

2000   Chhattisgarh created from Madhya Pradesh; Jharkhand from Bihar and Uttarakhand from Uttar Pradesh

NOTES

1. INTRODUCTION: THE COMPROMISE POLITICS OF STATEHOOD

1. The state was called Uttaranchal when originally formed, but in 2007 its name was changed to Uttarakhand, matching the name preferred by activists within the historical statehood movement. The name Uttarakhand is used throughout this book except where actors under discussion themselves use(d) the name Uttaranchal.
2. Discussion in Jamshedpur, 11 Oct. 2007.
3. Paul Pierson, *Politics in Time: History, Institutions and Social Analysis* (Princeton: Princeton University Press, 2004). See also James Mahoney and Kathleen Ann Thelen, 'A theory of gradual institutional change' in *Explaining Institutional Change: Ambiguity, Agency, and Power*, ed. James Mahoney and Kathleen Ann Thelen (Cambridge: Cambridge University Press, 2010).
4. Christophe Jaffrelot, *India's Silent Revolution: The Rise of the Lower Castes in North India* (London: Hurst & Company, 2003).
5. George Anderson, *Federalism: An Introduction* (Ontario: Oxford University Press, 1998), p. 19.
6. Ethiopia is an exception in this regard: its sub-units have a constitutionally mandated right to secede.
7. See Rotimi T. Suberu, *Federalism and Ethnic Conflict in Nigeria* (Washington, D.C.: United States Institute of Peace Press, 2001); D.C. Bach, 'Managing a Plural Society: The Boomerang Effects of Nigerian Federalism,' *Journal of Commonwealth and Comparative Politics* 27, no. 2 (1989).
8. Celina Souza, *Constitutional Engineering in Brazil: The Politics of Federalism and Decentralization* (Basingstoke: Palgrave Macmillan, 1997).
9. Alfred Stepan, 'Federalism and Democracy: Beyond the US Model,' *Journal of Democracy* 10, no. 4 (1999).

211

10. Government of India, *Report of the States Reorganisation Commission* (New Delhi: 1955), p. 165.

11. See Russell D. Murphy, *Strategic Calculations and the Admission of New States into the Union, 1789–1960: Congress and the Politics of Statehood* (Lewiston: Edwin Mellen Press, 2008); Charles Stewart and Barry R. Weingast, 'Stacking the Senate, Changing the Nation: Republican Rotten Boroughs, Statehood Politics, and American Political Development,' *Studies in American Political Development* 6 (1992).

12. On the origins of Canadian federalism see Ronald Watts, 'The American Constitution in Comparative Perspective: A Comparison of Federalism in the United States and Canada,' *The Journal of American History* 74, no. 3 (1987).

13. Katherine Adeney, *Federalism and Ethnic Conflict Regulation in India and Pakistan* (New York: Palgrave USA, 2007), p. 10.

14. See Valerie Bunce, *Subversive institutions: the Design and the Destruction of Socialism and the State* (Cambridge: Cambridge University Press, 1999); Philip G. Roeder, 'Soviet Federalism and Ethnic Mobilization,' *World Politics* 43, no. 2 (1991); Philip G. Roeder, 'Ethnofederalism and the Mismanagement of Conflicting Nationalisms,' *Regional & Federal Studies* 19, no. 2 (2009).

15. See, for instance, Adeney, *Federalism and Ethnic Conflict Regulation in India and Pakistan*; Alfred Stepan, Juan Linz, and Yogendra Yadav, *Crafting State-Nations: India and Other Multinational Democracies* (Baltimore: The Johns Hopkins University Press, 2011); Nancy Bermeo, 'Conclusion: The Merits of Federalism,' in *Federalism and Territorial Cleavages*, ed. Ugo M. Amoretti and Nancy Bermeo (London and Baltimore: The Johns Hopkins University Press, 2004); Nancy Bermeo, 'A New Look at Federalism: The Import of Institutions' *Journal of Democracy* 13, no. 2 (2002); Balveer Arora, 'Republic of India,' in *Diversity and Unity in Federal Countries*, ed. Luis Moreno and Cesar Colino (Montreal: McGill-Queens University Press, 2010).

16. See Balveer Arora, 'Adapting Federalism to India: Multilevel and Asymmetrical Innovations,' in *Multiple Identities in a Single State: Indian Federalism in Comparative Perspective*, ed. Balveer Arora and Douglas Verney (New Delhi: Konark Publishers Pvt Ltd, 1995 [1787–1788]).

17. James Madison, 'An extensive republic a remedy for mischiefs of faction' in Alexander Hamilton et al., *The Federalist papers* (New York: Palgrave Macmillan, 2010).

18. Pakistan (a not consistently democratic federation) has a slightly larger number of citizens per sub-unit.

19. Stepan, Linz, and Yadav, *Crafting State-Nations: India and Other Multinational Democracies*, p. 47.

20. Ramachandra Guha, *India after Gandhi: The History of the World's Largest Democracy* (London: Macmillian, 2007), p. 621.

21. On 'sons of the soil' see Myron Weiner, *Sons of the Soil: Migration and Ethnic*

Conflict in India (Princeton: Princeton University Press, 1978). Fearon and Laitin have more recently up such arguments, offering the following description of 'sons of the soil' conflict: 'First, it involves conflict between members of a minority ethnic group concentrated in some region of a country, and relatively recent, ethnically distinct migrants to this region from other parts of the same country. Second, the members of the minority group think of their group as indigenous, and as rightfully possessing the area as their group's ancestral (or at least very long-standing) home.' See James D. Fearon and David D. Laitin, 'Sons of the Soil, Migrants, and Civil War' *World Development* 39, no. 2 (2011), p. 200. Nativist or 'sons of the soil' politics are not only associated with statehood demands, but are also found in other political movements such as the Shiv Sena in Maharashtra.

22. Pradeep Kumar, *The Uttarakhand Movement: Construction of a Regional Identity* (New Delhi: Kanishka Publishers, Distributors, 2000).

23. Akhtar Majeed, 'The Changing Politics of States' Reorganization,' *Publius: The Journal of Federalism* 33, no. 4 (2003), p. 86.

24. MP Singh, 'A Borderless Internal Federal Space? Reorganization of States in India,' *India Review* 6, no. 4 (2007); Ranabir Samaddar, 'Rule, Governmental Rationality and the Reorganisation of States,' in *Interrogating Reorganisation of States: Culture, Identity and Politics in India*, ed. Sudha Pai and Asha Sarangi (New Delhi: Routledge, 2011), p. 60.

25. MP Singh, 'A Borderless Internal Federal Space?', p. 247.

26. Rasheeduddin Khan, ed. *Rethinking Indian Federalism* (Shimla: Inter-University Centre for Humanities and Social Sciences, Indian Institute of Advanced Study, 1997), p. 17.

27. Ramachandra Guha, 'Beyond Telangana: The Indian Republic is young enough to try out more states', *The Telegraph*, 15 Jan. 2011.

28. Yogendra Yadav and Suhas Palshikar, 'Ten Theses on State Politics in India,' *Seminar* 591 (2008).

29. See Maya Chadda, 'Integration through Internal Reorganization: Containing Ethnic Conflict in India,' *Ethnopolitics* 2, no. 1 (2002); Majeed, 'The Changing Politics of States' Reorganization'; Emma Mawdsley, 'Redrawing the Body Politic: Federalism, Regionalism and the Creation of New States in India,' *The Journal of Commonwealth and Comparative Politics* 40, no. 3 (2002).

30. Mawdsley, ibid., p. 48.

31. Gurharpal Singh, 'Resizing and Reshaping the State: India from Partition to the Present,' in *Right-Sizing the State: The Politics of Moving Borders*, ed. Brendan O'Leary, Ian S. Lustick, and Thomas Callaghy (Oxford: Oxford University Press, 2001). See also discussion in Adeney, *Federalism and Ethnic Conflict Regulation in India and Pakistan*, p. 14.

32. See Oliver Heath, 'Anatomy of BJP's Rise to Power: Social, Regional and Polit-

ical Expansion in 1990s,' in *Parties and Party Politics in India*, ed. Zoya Hasan (New Delhi: Oxford University Press, 2002); E. Sridharan, 'Coalition Strategies and the BJP's Expansion, 1989–2004,' *Commonwealth and Comparative Politics* 43, no. 2 (2005).

33. Samaddar, 'Rule, Governmental Rationality and the Reorganisation of States,' p. 58.

34. On 'market preserving federalism' in the Indian context see Sunita Parikh and Barry Weingast, 'A Comparative Theory of Federalism: India,' *Virginia Law Review* 83, no. 7 (1997), pp. 1593–1615; Jonathan Rodden and Susan Rose-Ackerman, 'Does Federalism Preserve Markets?,' *Virginia Law Review* 83, no. 7 (1997), pp. 1521–72.

35. For a summary of such arguments see Devesh Kapur, 'Does India need more States?,' *The Hindu*, 21 Aug. 2000.

36. On the significance of ethnic divisions of labour for ethnoregional movements more generally see Margaret Levi and Michael Hechter, 'A Rational Choice Approach to the Rise and Decline of Ethnoregional Political Parties,' in *New Nationalisms of the Developed West: Toward Explanation*, ed. Edward A. Tiryakian and Ronald Rogowski (Boston: Allen and Unwin, 1985).

37. Roy, A., 'Jharkhand: Internal Colonialism' reproduced in R.D. Munda and S. Bosu Mullick, eds., *The Jharkhand Movement: Indigenous Peoples' Struggle for Autonomy in India* (Copenhagen: International Work Group for Indigenous Affairs, 2003 [1982]), pp. 81–83. Others argues that Bihar as a whole experienced internal colonialism and exploitation at the hands of non-Biharis. See Sachchidanand Sinha, *The Internal Colony: A Study in Regional Exploitation* (New Delhi: Sindhu Publications, 1973).

38. Samaddar, 'Rule, Governmental Rationality and the Reorganisation of States,' p. 63.

39. Stuart Corbridge, 'The Contested Geographies of Federalism in Post-Reform India,' in *Understanding India's New Political Economy: A Great Transformation?*, ed. Sanjay Ruparelia, et al. (London: Routledge, 2011). Corbridge is drawing on notions of space outlined by Henri Lefebvre (1991).

40. Interview with Tata Steel spokesperson, Jamshedpur, 10 Oct. 2007.

41. Group interview, Ranchi, 17 Apr. 2007.

42. Ibid.

43. M.P. Singh, 'Political Parties and Political Economy of Federalism: A Paradigm Shift in Indian Politics,' *The Indian Journal of Social Science* 7, no. 2 (1994), p. 166. Singh mentions, in particular, the support for a presidential system by the late J.R.D. Tata.

44. K. Srinivasulu, 'Discourses on Telangana and Critique of the Linguistic Nationality Principle,' in *Interrogating Reorganisation of States: Culture, Identity and Politics in India*, ed. Sudha Pai and Asha Sarangi (New Delhi: Routledge, 2011), p. 180.

45. Atul Kohli, 'Politics of Economic Growth in India, 1980–2005. Part I: The 1980s,' *Economic and Political Weekly* XLI, no. 13 (2006); Atul Kohli, 'Politics of Economic Growth in India, 1980–2005. Part II: The 1990s and Beyond,' *Economic and Political Weekly* XLI, no. 14 (2006).

46. Home Minister LK Advani, speech to Lok Sabha, 25 July 2000.

47. Demographer Ashish Bose has argued in favour of reducing the size of states in order to improve access to public services, rather than trying to reduce overall population size. See Sreelatha Menon, 'Smaller State Size Key to Growth,' *Business Standard*, 17 Apr. 2011.

48. It is relevant to note that, counter-intuitively, decentralisation reforms do not always imply the devolution of greater power to sub-national governments. See, for instance, Tulia Gabriela Falleti, *Decentralization and Subnational Politics in Latin America* (Cambridge: Cambridge University Press, 2010). Furthermore the creation of new states does not in itself imply a change in the vertical division of powers and responsibilities between centre and states, simply a change in the size of administrative units at the intermediate level of government.

49. Ian Lustick, 'Thresholds of Opportunity and Barriers to Change in the Right-Sizing of States,' in *Right-Sizing the State*, ed. Brendan O'Leary, Ian Lustick, and Tom Callaghy (Oxford: Oxford University Press, 2001), pp. 79–80.

50. Kathleen Thelen and Sven Steinmo, 'Historical Institutionalism in Comparative Politics,' in *Structuring Politics*, ed. Sven Steinmo, Kathleen Thelen, and F. Longstreth (Cambridge: Cambridge University Press, 1992), p. 9.

51. Lustick, 'Thresholds of Opportunity and Barriers to Change in the Right-Sizing of States,' p. 84.

52. On the central government's cautious approach to earlier periods of reorganisation, see Paul Brass, *Language, Religion and Politics in North India* (Cambridge: Cambridge University Press, 1974).

53. See Kanchan Chandra, 'Ethnic Parties and Democratic Stability,' *Perspectives on Politics* 3, no. 2 (2005), pp. 235–252; James Manor, 'Making Federalism Work,' *Journal of Democracy* 9, no. 3 (1998), pp. 21–35.

54. Mahoney and Thelen, 'A Theory of Gradual Institutional Change,' p. 8.

55. On historical patterns of social dominance and their consequences in different regions of India, see the work of Francine Frankel and M.S.A. Rao, eds., *Dominance and State Power in Modern India: Decline of a Social Order*, vol. 1 (Delhi: Oxford University Press, 1989); Harriss, 'Poverty Reduction and Regime Differences Across India'; John Harriss, 'Borderlands of Economics': Institutions, Politics and Culture in the Explanation of Economic Change,' in *Power Matters: Essays on Institutions, Politics and Society in India*, ed. John Harriss (New Delhi: Oxford University Press, 2006).

2. HISTORY OF TERRITORIAL DESIGN AND FEDERAL THOUGHT IN INDIA

1. Jyotirindra Dasgupta, *Language Conflict and National Development: Group Politics and National Language Policy in India* (Berkeley: University of California Press, 1970), p. 117; Judith M. Brown, *Modern India: the origins of an Asian democracy* (Delhi; Oxford: Oxford University Press, 1985), p. 170.
2. Brown, ibid., p. 170.
3. See Robert D. King, *Nehru and the Language Politics of India* (New Delhi: Oxford University Press, 1997), p. 63. There was a simultaneous push by some nationalist leaders from north India, influenced by Hindu revivalism for Hindi to be embraced as the language of the nationalist movement in order to provide unity. In 1925, the compromise, to accept Hindustani as the official language for the conduct of its proceedings.
4. The classic account of this process is V.P. Menon, *The Story of the Integration of the Indian States* (Calcutta: Orient-Longmans, 1956).
5. See Judith Brown, *Nehru: A Political Life* (New Haven and London: Yale University Press, 2003), p. 216.
6. Sunil Khilnani, *The Idea of India* (London: Hamish Hamilton, 1997).
7. For the definitive history of India's constitutional design see Granville Austin, *Working a Democratic Constitution: the Indian Experience* (New Delhi; Oxford: Oxford University Press, 1999).
8. Given these centralised features, constitutional scholar K.C. Wheare famously described the Indian system as 'quasi-federal, not strictly federal' when judged against the 'federal principle' of a 'method of dividing powers so that the general and regional governments are each, within a sphere, co-ordinate and independent'. K.C. Wheare, *Federal Government* (London: Oxford University Press, 1963), p. 27.
9. Mohit Bhattacharya, 'The Mind of the Founding Fathers,' in *Federalism in India: Origins and Development*, ed. Nirmal Mukherji and Balveer Arora (New Delhi: Vikas Publishing House, 1992), p. 94.
10. A constitutional amendment in 1955 stated that a Bill for the purpose of changing the area, boundaries or name of any state must be referred by the President to the state legislature for 'expressing its views thereon' within a specified period. But Parliament is not obliged to accept or act upon the views of the state legislature, even if its views are received within the specified time. Furthermore, it is not obliged to refer the Bill back to the state legislature every time an amendment is passed to it.
11. Fali Nariman, 'Federalism in India—Emerging Trends and the Way Forward' (paper presented at the 4th International Conference on Federalism: Unity in Diversity, 'Learning from Each Other', New Delhi, 5–7 Nov. 2008).

12. The phrase comes from the 1869 *Texas vs White* case in the US Supreme Court which ruled that the attempted secession of the Confederate state government of Texas was illegal.

13. See, for example, Ivo Duka Duchacek, *Comparative Federalism: The Territorial Dimension of Politics* (New York, London: Holt, Rinehart & Winston, 1970).

14. Sumathi Ramaswamy, *Passions of the Tongue: Language Devotion in Tamil India, 1891–1970* (Berkeley; London: University of California Press, 1997); Lisa Mitchell, *Language, Emotion and Politics in South India: The Making of a Mother Tongue* (Bloomington: Indiana University Press, 2009).

15. Government of India, *Report of the States Reorganisation Commission*, p. 45.

16. Joseph E. Schwartzberg, 'Factors in the Linguistic Reorganisation of Indian States,' in *Region and Nation in India*, ed. Paul Wallace (New Delhi: American Institute of Indian Studies, 1985).

17. Paul Brass, *Language, Religion and Politics in North India* (Cambridge: Cambridge University Press, 1974); Paul Brass, 'Elite Interests, Popular Passions, and Social Power in the Language Politics of India,' in *Language and Politics in India*, ed. Asha Sarangi (New Delhi: Oxford University Press, 2009). Robert King makes a similar argument in *Nehru and the Language Politics of India*.

18. Brass, 'Elite Interests, Popular Passions, and Social Power in the Language Politics of India,' p. 187.

19. Brass, ibid.

20. For a discussion of dominant castes and linguistic reorganisation see Selig Harrison, *India: the Most Dangerous Decades* (Princeton: Princeton University Press, 1960); Christophe Jaffrelot, 'From Indian Territory to Hindu *Bhoomi*: The Ethnicisation of Nation-State Mapping in India,' in *The Politics of Cultural Mobilisation in India*, ed. John Zavos, Andrew Wyatt, and Vernon Hewitt (New Delhi: Oxford University Press, 2004), p. 201; Louise Tillin, 'Caste, Territory and Federalism,' *Seminar* 633 (2012).

21. Brass, *Language, Religion and Politics in North India*, pp. 17–18.

22. Cited in King, *Nehru and the Language Politics of India*, p. 110.

23. K. Mukerji, *Reorganisation of Indian States*, 1955, as quoted in King, ibid., p. 73.

24. King, ibid., p. 114.

25. On the Communist Party and the Andhra demand see Harrison, *India: the Most Dangerous Decades*, p. 222.

26. Adeney, *Federalism and Ethnic Conflict Regulation in India and Pakistan* (New York: Palgrave USA, 2007), p. 129.

27. Alfred Stepan, Juan Linz, and Yogendra Yadav, *Crafting State-Nations: India and Other Multinational Democracies* (Baltimore: The Johns Hopkins University Press, 2011), p. 126.

28. Guha, *India after Gandhi: The History of the World's Largest Democracy* (London: Macmillian, 2007), p. 191.

29. Nehru quoted in Baldev Raj Nayar, *Minority Politics in the Punjab* (Princeton: Princeton University Press, 1966), p. 52.
30. Paul Brass, *Ethnicity and Nationalism: theory and comparison* (New Delhi: Sage Publications, 1991), p. 291.
31. Brown, *Nehru*, p. 284.
32. 'Eradicate Communalism through "Indianisation"', Resolution 56.27 on Internal Affairs. 30 Dec. 1956, All-India Session of Bharatiya Jana Sangh. Bharatiya Jana Sangh, *Party Documents* (Delhi: Vithalbhai Patel Bhavan, 1973), p. 45.
33. Election manifestos of 1954 and 1957. Bharatiya Jana Sangh, *Party Documents*.
34. *Organiser*, 26 Jan. 1956 quoted in Christophe Jaffrelot, *The Hindu Nationalist Movement in India* (New York: Columbia University Press, 1996), p. 130. The call for administrative divisions based on *janapadas* was subsequently enshrined in the party's general policy manifesto agreed at the Vijayawada XII Plenary Session of the BJS in Jan. 1965. Bharatiya Jana Sangh, *Party Documents*. The *Puranas* identified a total of 165 territories, of which about 120 fall in present day India. They were classified according to geography and political status. See Rasheeduddin Khan, *Federal India: A Design for Change* (Delhi: Vikas Publishing House, 1992), p. 38.
35. Resolution 61.07, 'Growing Separatism', Lucknow IX All-India Session of the BJS, 1 Jan. 1961. Bharatiya Jana Sangh. Bharatiya Jana Sangh, *Party Documents*, p. 58.
36. Report of the Christian Missionary Activities Enquiry Committee, vol. 1 cited in Jaffrelot, *The Hindu Nationalist Movement in India*, p. 196.
37. Resolution 69.08 'Centre-State Relations', Bombay XV All-India Session of the BJS, Apr. 26 1969 Bharatiya Jana Sangh, *Party Documents*, p. 93. See also, Resolution 69.02: Proposed Malapuram District, Central Working Committee, Delhi, Feb. 16 1969. Bharatiya Jana Sangh, *Internal Affairs: Party Document* (New Delhi: BJP, 2005), p. 130.
38. Resolution 69.08. Bharatiya Jana Sangh, ibid.
39. For example Balraj Madhok, president of the Jana Sangh until 1967, who published a book on the subject in 1970. Balraj Madhok, *Indianisation? What, Why and How* (New Delhi: S. Chand, 1970). Madhok was expelled from the BJS in 1973.
40. Brown, *Nehru*, p. 214.
41. James Manor, '"Ethnicity" and Politics in India,' *International Affairs* 72, no. 3 (1996); James Manor, 'Making Federalism Work,' *Journal of Democracy* 9, no. 3 (1998), pp. 21–35.
42. The two other northeastern states, Manipur and Tripura, were formerly princely states and were upgraded from union territory status in 1972.
43. Sanjib Baruah, 'Nationalizing Space: Cosmetic Federalism and the Politics of Development in Northeast India,' *Development and Change* 34, no. 5 (2003), p. 923.

44. These measures include the reservation of the overwhelming majority of seats in the state assemblies of Arunachal Pradesh, Mizoram, Nagaland and Meghalaya for Scheduled Tribes; special rights accorded to Nagas and Mizos to manage cultural and legal practices; as well as provisions for autonomous district councils for 'tribal areas' of Assam, Meghalaya, Tripura and Mizoram with rights over land use, forest management and social customs under the Sixth Schedule. Such asymmetry in the provisions accorded to federal sub-units stands in contrast to the process of state creation elsewhere in the federation—with the exception of the disputed territory of Jammu and Kashmir. See Louise Tillin, 'United in Diversity? Asymmetry in Indian Federalism,' *Publius: The Journal of Federalism* 37, no. 1 (2007), pp. 45–67.
45. See Gyanesh Kudaisya, *Region, Nation, 'Heartland': Uttar Pradesh in India's Body-Politic* (New Delhi: Sage Publications, 2006), p. 381.
46. Government of India, *Report of the States Reorganisation Commission*, p. 133.
47. See Kudaisya, *Region, Nation, 'Heartland'*, p. 384. The SRC subsequently reported that about seventy of the MLA signatories disassociated themselves from this memorandum.
48. Government of India, *Report of the States Reorganisation Commission*, p. 163.
49. Ibid., p. 62.
50. Kudaisya, *Region, Nation, 'Heartland'*. See also Rasheeduddin Khan, 'Uttar Pradesh and Federal Balance in India,' in *Rethinking Indian Federalism*, ed. Rasheeduddin Khan (Shimla: Inter-University Centre for Humanities and Social Sciences, Indian Institute of Advanced Study, 1997).
51. Apr. 1954, cited in Kudaisya, *Region, Nation, 'Heartland'*, p. 391.
52. For a discussion of the role of this bodily metaphor in Hindu nationalist thought from the Hindu Mahasabha in the 1920s onwards see John Zavos, 'The Arya Samaj and the Antecedents of Hindu Nationalism,' *International Journal of Hindu Studies* 3, no. 1 (1999), pp. 74–5.
53. May 1954, cited in Kudaisya, *Region, Nation, 'Heartland'*, pp. 391–2.
54. Diana Eck, 'Ganga: The Goddess Ganges in Hindu Sacred Geography,' in *Devi: Goddesses of India*, ed. John Stratton Hawley and Donna M. Wulff (Berkeley: University of California Press, 1996), p. 142.
55. Cited in Kudaisya, *Region, Nation, 'Heartland'*, p. 394.
56. Ibid., p. 396.
57. Dissenting note to Government of India, *Report of the States Reorganisation Commission*.
58. B. R. Ambedkar, 'Thoughts on Linguistic States,' (Delhi: 1955), p. 14.
59. Ibid., p. 35.
60. In Bihar, according to the 1931 census, the upper castes (Brahmins, Vaishyas, Kshatriyas and Kayasths) made up 14 per cent of the population, in Madhya Pradesh 13 per cent and in Uttar Pradesh around 20 per cent compared with less than 5 per cent in states such as Tamil Nadu and Andhra Pradesh in south-

ern India. See Christophe Jaffrelot, *India's Silent Revolution: The Rise of the Lower Castes in North India* (London: Hurst & Company, 2003).

61. The four part *varna* system is more complete in north India than in south India where Brahmins are generally present only in small numbers, and kshatriyas and vaishyas are often not found. Moreover, the process which M.N. Srinivas described as 'Sanskritisation' (the emulation of upper caste lifestyles) was more prominent among lower castes in the north, whereas in the south, caste associations paved the way towards the earlier horizontal mobilisation of non Brahmin identities (see discussion in ibid., p. 149.)

62. Jaffrelot, ibid., p. 8.

63. On the incorporation of lower castes in South India see Myron Weiner, *Party Building in a New Nation: The Indian National Congress* (Chicago: University of Chicago Press, 1967); Jaffrelot, *India's Silent Revolution.*

64. Francine R. Frankel, *India's Political Economy 1947–2004: the Gradual Revolution*, 2nd ed. (New Delhi: Oxford University Press, 2005), p. 25.

65. We should be careful in drawing overly stark distinctions between north and south India in relation to the longer term effects of historic patterns of Congress party organisation on lower caste and Dalit empowerment. The middle castes that came to dominate the Congress (often called 'forward castes' in South India) have themselves perpetuated structures of dominance and exclusion in politics.

66. Government of India, *Report of the States Reorganisation Commission*, p. 169.

67. Ibid., p. 169.

68. Ibid., p. 170.

69. E. Sridharan, 'The Fragmentation of the Indian Party System, 1952–1999: Seven Competing Explanations,' in *Parties and Party Politics in India*, ed. Zoya Hasan (New Delhi: Oxford University Press, 2002), p. 482.

70. See Guha, *India after Gandhi*, p. 427.

71. See Frankel's discussion of the 'accommodative paradox' under Nehru. Congress' reliance on local landed elites as the bedrock of the party organisation had slowed the pace of land reform, in particular. See Frankel, *India's Political Economy 1947–2004.*

72. See Charles Robert Hankla, 'Party Linkages and Economic Policy: An Examination of Indira Gandhi's India,' *Business and Politics* 8, no. 3 (2006); James Manor, 'Party Decay and Political Crisis in India,' *Washington Quarterly* 4, no. 3 (1981).

73. Paul Brass, 'The Politicisation of the Peasantry in a North Indian State: Part I,' *Journal of Peasant Studies* 8, no. 4 (1980).

74. Lloyd Rudolph and Susanne Hoeber Rudolph, *In Pursuit of Lakshmi: The Political Economy of the Indian State* (Chicago and London: University of Chicago Press, 1987).

75. Harry Blair, 'Structural Change, the Agricultural Sector and Politics in Bihar,' in *State Politics in Contemporary India*, ed. J.R. Wood (Boulder and London: Westview Press, 1984), p. 67. Others, such as Francine Frankel, have questioned how much evidence there is to suggest that Yadavs and Kurmis provided the bulk of a new land-owning 'kulak' class in Bihar, suggesting that upper-caste bhumihars and rajputs cornered many of the gains of the limited land reforms in that state. See Francine Frankel, 'Caste, Land and Dominance in Bihar,' in *Dominance and State Power in Modern India*, ed. Francine Frankel and M.S.A. Rao (New Delhi: Oxford University Press, 1989), p. 98.

76. Yogendra Yadav, 'Electoral Politics in the Time of Change: India's Third Electoral System, 1989–99,' *Economic and Political Weekly* XXIV, no. 34/35 (1999).

77. Gail Omvedt, *Reinventing Revolution: New Social Movements and the Socialist Tradition in India* (New York: M.E. Sharpe, 1993), p. 47.

78. Rajni Kothari, 'The Non-Party Political Process,' *Praxis International* 3 (1985).

79. See analysis, for example, in Frankel, *India's Political Economy 1947–2004*, p. 547; Jyotirindra Dasgupta, 'A Season of Caesars: Emergency Regimes and Development Politics in Asia,' *Asian Survey* 18, no. 4 (1978).

80. Stuart Corbridge and John Harriss, *Reinventing India: Liberalization, Hindu Nationalism and Popular Democracy* (Cambridge: Cambridge University Press, 2000), p. 89.

81. Jaffrelot, *The Hindu Nationalist Movement in India*, p. 238.

82. Ibid., p. 283.

83. For more background on tensions between centralising and decentralising in this period see Austin, *Working a Democratic Constitution*.

84. For this view on India see Iqbal Narain, 'Cultural Pluralism, National Integration and Democracy in India,' *Asian Survey* 16, no. 10 (1976). See especially pp. 909–911.

85. Levi and Hechter, 'A Rational Choice Approach to the Rise and Decline of Ethnoregional Political Parties,' in *New Nationalisms of the Developed West: Toward Explanation*, ed. Edward A. Tiryakian and Ronald Rogowski (Boston: Allen and Unwin, 1985), p. 130.

86. The Jharkhand movement is often cited as a case in point, but see also Pradeep Kumar on Uttarakhand in Kumar, *The Uttarakhand Movement: Construction of a Regional Identity* (New Delhi: Kanishka Publishers, Distributors, 2000); Amit Prakash, *Jharkhand: Politics of Development and Identity* (New Delhi: Orient Longman, 2001).

87. Duncan Forrester, 'Subregionalism in India: the Case of Telangana,' *Pacific Affairs* 43, no. 1 (1970). See also the discussion of the Telangana demand in chapters six and seven of this book.

88. Ibid.; Weiner, *Sons of the Soil*.

89. Resolution 69.08, Bharatiya Jana Sangh, *Party Documents*.

90. Resolution 69.01, Telangana Agitation, Central Working Committee, Delhi, 16 Feb. 1969.

91. Resolution 73.01, Internal Situation, All-India Session of BJS, Kanpur, Feb. 10–11 1973; Bharatiya Jana Sangh, *Internal Affairs: Party Document*, p. 22.

92. Ibid.

93. Janata Party manifesto 1977: 'Bread and Liberty—a Gandhian Alternative' and 1980 Janata Party manifesto.

94. Balbir Dutt, *Kahani Jharkhand Andolan Ki (Story of the Jharkhand Movement)* (Ranchi: Crown Publications, 2005), p. 192.

95. Atul Kohli, *Democracy and Discontent: India's Growing Crisis of Governability* (Cambridge: Cambridge University Press, 1990); Manor, 'Party Decay and Political Crisis in India.'

96. James Manor, 'Parties and the Party System,' in *India's Democracy: An Analysis of Changing State-Society Relations*, ed. Atul Kohli (Princeton: Princeton University Press, 1988).

97. Jaffrelot, *The Hindu Nationalist Movement in India*, pp. 315–6.

98. Manor, 'Parties and the party system,' p. 78.

99. Atul Kohli, 'Can Democracies Accommodate Ethnic Nationalism? Rise and Decline of Self-Determination Movements in India,' *Journal of Asian Studies* 56, no. 2 (1997).

100. Paul R. Brass, *The Politics of India since Independence* (Cambridge: Cambridge University Press, 1990), p. 153.

101. Sumantra Bose, *Kashmir: Roots of Conflict, Paths to Peace* (Cambridge and London: Harvard University Press, 2003), p. 90; Jaffrelot, *The Hindu Nationalist Movement in India*, p. 331.

102. A Darjeeling Gorkha Hill Council came into being in West Bengal in 1988 following a peace accord between the central government, the government of West Bengal and the Gorkha National Liberation Front.

103. Brass, *The Politics of India since Independence*, p. 227.

104. Indeed, the Congress (I) rather than the BJP received some RSS support in 1983 and 1984 in north India, as well as in Kerala in the south. See Manor, 'Parties and the Party System,' p. 97.

105. Bharatiya Janata Party, 'Our Five Commitments,' (Delhi: 1984).

106. Ibid.

107. 'Centre-State Relations', resolution of the National Executive, Lucknow, Oct. 21–23 Oct. 1983. Bharatiya Janata Party, *BJP Party Documents 1980–2005. Volume I: Election Manifestoes* (New Delhi: Bharatiya Janata Party, 2005). In April 1984, a meeting was also organised by the BJP in Gorakhpur to discuss the division of big states. Balraj Madhok, a former opponent of linguistic reorganisation, explained here: 'I had the opportunity to visit Surguja district in Madhya Pradesh. Outside the circuit house in the district Headquarters of

Ambikapur, there was a sign on a pillar giving the distance to Bhopal. Between Ambikapur and Bhopal there are 854 kilometres. Travelling from Ambikapur to Raipur in jeep, I saw the backwardness of the area and the condition of the roads. This personal experience compelled me to believe in the need to divide big states. My now well-thought out view is that the political map of India needs to be redrawn… This has nothing to do with creating small states on the basis of self-determination. This is a question of the internal administration of the country. It would be better if responsible nationalist elements and party take this demand and the government gave it swift attention. In this way we can stop statehood movements falling into the wrong hands.' Quoted in Dutt, *Kahani Jharkhand Andolan Ki (Story of the Jharkhand Movement)*, p. 243.

108. 'Centre-State Relations', resolution of the BJP National Executive, Lucknow, 21–23 Oct. 1983.

109. The Sarkaria Commission finally reported in 1988 but little was done to implement its recommendations.

110. The 1984 manifesto recognised the 'unique, multi-hued synthesis of the cultural contributions made over centuries by different peoples and religions' See Jaffrelot, *The Hindu Nationalist Movement in India*, p. 317.

111. L.K. Advani, *My Country My Life* (Delhi: Rupa & Co, 2008), p. 322.

112. Bharatiya Janata Party, 'Report of the Working Group, Presented to the National Executive,' (Bhopal: 1985), p. 18.

113. Jaffrelot, *The Hindu Nationalist Movement in India.*; Brass, *Ethnicity and Nationalism.*

114. Corbridge and Harriss, *Reinventing India*, p. 123.

115. Thomas Blom Hansen, *The Saffron Wave: Democracy and Hindu Nationalism in Modern India*, p. 145.

116. L.K. Advani, Presidential speech to National Council, Vijayawada, 2–4 Jan. 1987 Bharatiya Janata Party, *BJP Party Documents 1980–2005. Volume I: Election Manifestoes*, p. 149. Italics in original.

117. The BJP's alliance strategy in the 1990s is discussed in Balveer Arora, 'Negotiating differences: federal coalitions and national cohesion,' in *Transforming India: Social and Political Dynamics of Democracy*, ed. Francine Frankel, et al. (New Delhi: Oxford University Press, 2000); Heath, 'Anatomy of BJP's Rise to Power: Social, Regional and Political Expansion in 1990s,'; Yogendra Yadav, Sanjay Kumar, and Oliver Heath, 'The BJP's New Social Bloc,' *Frontline* 16, No. 23.

118. Advani, *My Country My Life*, p. 323. The working group report stated: 'We are to have a mass following so as to become a cadre based mass party. Apparently cadre base and mass base seem to be contradictory in terms. However, there can be a happy marriage between these two. The cadre while widening their base should also see that they become capable enough to provide lead-

ership for the masses.' Bharatiya Janata Party, 'Report of the Working Group, Presented to the National Executive,' p. 25.

119. Sridharan, 'The Fragmentation of the Indian Party System, 1952–1999: Seven Competing Explanations,' p. 486.

120. Brass, *The Politics of India since Independence*, p. 201.

121. N. Mukarji and G. Mathew, 'Epilogue: Federal Issues 1988–90,' in *Federalism in India: Origins and Development*, ed. N. Mukarji and Balveer Arora (New Delhi: Vikas Publishing House, 1992), p. 284.

122. Yadav, 'Electoral Politics in the Time of Change.'

123. See Jaffrelot, *India's Silent Revolution*, chapter ten.

124. Yogendra Yadav, 'Understanding the Second Democratic Upsurge: Trends of Bahujan Participation in Electoral Politics in the 1990s,' in *Transforming India*, ed. Francine Frankel, et al. (New Delhi: Oxford University Press, 2000).

125. Yadav and Palshikar, 'Ten Theses on State Politics in India,' p. 14.

126. Lawrence Saez, *Federalism Without a Centre: the Impact of Political and Economic Reform on India's Federal System* (New Delhi: Sage Publications, 2002).

3. SOCIAL MOVEMENTS, POLITICAL PARTIES AND STATEHOOD: JHARKHAND AND UTTARAKHAND

1. Some material in this chapter was first published in Louise Tillin, 'Questioning Borders: Social Movements, Political Parties and the Creation of New States in India,' *Pacific Affairs* 84, no. 1 (2011)

2. Gail Omvedt, *Reinventing Revolution: New Social Movements and the Socialist Tradition in India* (New York: M.E. Sharpe, 1993); Smitu Kothari, 'Social Movements and the Redefinition of Democracy,' in *India Briefing, 1993*, ed. Philip Oldenburg (Boulder: Westview Press, 1993), pp. 139–140.

3. This argument is further examined in Tillin, 'Questioning Borders.' For an overview of such themes see Jack A. Goldstone, 'Introduction: Bridging Institutionalised and Noninstitutionalised Politics,' in *States, Parties and Social Movements*, ed. Jack A. Goldstone (Cambridge: Cambridge University Press, 2003); Doug McAdam and Sidney Tarrow, 'Ballots and Barricades: On the Reciprocal Relationship between Elections and Social Movements,' *Perspectives on Politics* 2 (2010); D. McAdam, S. Tarrow, and C. Tilly, *Dynamics of Contention* (Cambridge: Cambridge University Press, 2001).

4. Goldstone, 'Introduction,' pp. 2–3.

5. Mario Diani, 'Introduction: Social Movements, Contentious Actions and Social Networks: From Metaphor to Substance?,' in *Social Movements and Networks: Relational Approaches to Collective Action*, ed. Mario Diani and Doug McAdam (Oxford: Oxford University Press, 2003), p. 1.

6. Mario Diani, 'The Concept of Social Movement,' *Sociological Review* 40, no. 1 (1992), p. 2.

7. For an introduction see Stuart Corbridge, 'The Ideology of Tribal Economy and Society: Politics in Jharkhand, c.1950–1980,' *Modern Asian Studies* (1988); Arvind N. Das, *Agrarian Unrest and Socio-economic Change in Bihar, 1900–1980* (New Delhi: Manohar, 1983); Susana B. C. Devalle, *Discourses of Ethnicity: Culture and Protest in Jharkhand* (New Delhi and London: Sage, 1992); Nirmal Sengupta, 'Background of the Jharkhand Question,' in *Fourth World Dynamics: Jharkhand*, ed. Nirmal Sengupta (Delhi: Authors Guild Publications, 1982); Prakash, *Jharkhand: Politics of Development and Identity* (Hyderabad: Orient Longman, 2001); R.D. Munda and Bosu Mullick, *The Jharkhand Movement: Indigenous Peoples' Struggle for Autonomy in India* (Copenhagen: International Work Group for Indigenous Affairs, 2003); Alpa Shah, *In the Shadows of the State: Indigenous Politics, Environmentalism, and Insurgency in Jharkhand, India* (Durham: Duke University Press, 2010).

8. Vinita Damodaran, 'The Politics of Marginality and the Construction of Indigeneity in Chotanagpur,' *Postcolonial Studies* 9, no. 2 (2006), p. 184.

9. See Corbridge, 'The Ideology of Tribal Economy and Society: Politics in Jharkhand, c.1950–1980'; Damodaran, 'The Politics of Marginality,'; Devalle, *Discourses of Ethnicity*; Daniel J. Rycroft and Sangeeta Dasgupta eds, *The Politics of Belonging in India: Becoming Adivasi* (Abingdon: Routledge, 2011); Shah, *In the Shadows of the State*.

10. Damodaran, 'The Politics of Marginality,' pp. 183–184.

11. Corbridge, 'The Ideology of Tribal Economy and Society.'

12. By 2001, the official tribal population had been reduced to 26.3 per cent, compared to 31.15 per cent of Chotanagpur and 44.67 per cent of Santal Parganas who were classified as STs in 1951. See Stuart Corbridge, 'The Continuing Struggle for India's Jharkhand: Democracy, Decentralisation and the Politics of Names and Numbers,' *Commonwealth and Comparative Politics* 40, no. 3 (2002), p. 65.

13. From the late nineteenth century, *adivasis* migrated to work on tea plantations in Assam. In more recent decades, they have increasingly relied on seasonal migration for work in the construction sector. See Alpa Shah, 'The Labour of Love: Seasonal Migration from Jharkhand to the Brick Kilns of Other States in India,' *Contributions to Indian Sociology* 40, no. 1 (2006); Jonathan Demenge, *The Political Ecology of Road Construction in Ladakh.* (DPhil, Institute of Development Studies, University of Sussex, 2011).

14. See Omvedt, *Reinventing Revolution*, p. 128.

15. A.K. Roy, 'Jharkhand: Internal Colonialism,' in *The Jharkhand Movement: Indigenous Peoples' Struggle for Autonomy in India.*

16. See Stuart Corbridge, 'Tribal Politics, Finance and the State: the Jharkhand India, 1900–1980,' *Ethnic and Racial Studies* 12, no. 2 (1989), pp. 199–200.

17. Stuart Corbridge, 'Industrialisation, Internal Colonialism and Ethnoregional-

ism: the Jharkhand, India, 1880–1980,' *Journal of Historical Geography* 12, no. 2 (1987).

18. Omvedt, *Reinventing Revolution,* p. 127.

19. K.S. Singh and P.P. Mahato, 'The Mahato-Kurmi Mahasabha Movement in Chotanagpur,' in *Tribal Movements in India,* ed. K.S. Singh (New Delhi: Manohar, 1982); Damodaran, 'The Politics of Marginality.' Agrarian struggles were also taking place in north Bihar in this period but were different in nature, essentially pitting poor and landless peasantry against propertied groups. See Das, Arvind N. *Agrarian Unrest and Socio-Economic Change in Bihar* (New Delhi: Manohar, 1983).

20. R.N. Maharaj, 'Agrarian Movement in Dhanbad,' in *Fourth World Dynamics: Jharkhand,* ed. Nirmal Sengupta (Delhi: Authors Guild Publications, 1982), p. 172.

21. According to K.S. Singh there were 120 violent incidents in this period including the looting or forcible harvesting of crops on lands in 'illegal' possession of moneylenders, attacks on 'exploiters', arson and murder, with the largest number of incidents taking place in 1974. Singh, 'Tribal Autonomy Movements in Chotanagpur,' in *Tribal Movements in India,* ed. K.S. Singh, (New Delhi: Manohar, 1983), p. 12.

22. Soren has continued to face charges relating to cases from this period in recent years. He was acquitted by a sessions court in Jharkhand in this particular case in 2008.

23. Maharaj, 'Agrarian Movement in Dhanbad,' p. 194.

24. Roy, 'Jharkhand: Internal Colonialism.'

25. Economic and Political Weekly, From our Correspondents: 'Singhbhum: Exploitation, Protest and Repression,' *Economic and Political Weekly* XIV, no. 22 (1979).

26. Interviews with Shailendra Mahato who was a leader of the movement in Singhbhum (telephone, 17 Oct. 2007) and Sanjay Bosu Mullick—Ranchi, Oct. 16 2007.

27. People's Union for Civil Liberties, 'An Account of Police Firings on Adivasis in Singhbhum District, Bihar (1978–1983),' (1983).

28. Economic and Political Weekly, 'From our Correspondents, Bihar: Containing the Jharkhand Movement,' *Economic and Political Weekly* XIV, No, 14 (1979).

29. Interview with Shibu Soren, Ranchi, 20 Oct. 2007.

30. Interview with Stephen Marandi, Ranchi, 4 Oct. 2007 (former JMM politician; in 2007 he was an independent MLA and deputy chief minister).

31. See Harry Blair, 'Rising Kulaks and Backward Classes in Bihar: Social Change in the Late 1970s', *Economic and Political Weekly* XV, no. 2 (1980); Francine Frankel, 'Caste, Land and Dominance in Bihar,' in *Dominance and State Power in Modern India,* ed. Francine Frankel and M.S.A. Rao (New Delhi: Oxford University Press, 1989).

32. Blair, ibid., p. 69.

33. The agrarian and workers movement led by the JMM, and subsequent mobil-isations by AJSU etc. were less closely associated with the churches in Jharkhand.

34. Interview with Karia Munda, Khunti district, 2 Oct. 2007.

35. He was defeated by Congress in 1980 and did not return as an MP until 1989. He later went on to become Deputy Speaker in the Lok Sabha after the 2009 elections.

36. Interview with Devdas Apte, New Delhi, 12 Sept. 2007.

37. Weiner, *Sons of the Soil*, p. 189.

38. Interview with Subodh Kant Sahay (former Janata Party MLA, Congress MP (Ranchi) and Union Minister 2004–), New Delhi, 13 Sept. 2007.

39. Dutt, *Kahani Jharkhand Andolan Ki (Story of the Jharkhand Movement)* (Ranchi: Crown Publications, 2005), p. 225.

40. Ibid., p. 248.

41. McAdam, Tarrow, and Tilly, *Dynamics of Contention*, p. 67.

42. The murder also hastened the cooling of relations between leaders of the JMM and Congress, because of the naming of a man with reputed connections to Congress in relation with the murder. See Dutt, *Kahani Jharkhand Andolan Ki (Story of the Jharkhand Movement)*, p. 256.

43. Interview with Surya Singh Besra, Jamshedpur, 10 Oct. 2007.

44. Interview, 10 Oct. 2007.

45. This was set out, for instance, in a JCC Press Release on 13 Feb. 1989 and other JCC papers. In many rural areas of Jharkhand, the *sadans* were, however, descen-dants of historically dominant landlord communities and, as Alpa Shah has shown in more recent ethnographic research, continue to form a rural elite with a markedly different relationship to the state than *adivasis*, who are more often descendants of tenants. See Shah, *In the Shadows of the State*.

46. Prakash, *Jharkhand*.

47. JCC Press Release, 7 June 1989.

48. Interview, Ranchi, 16 Oct. 2007.

49. Shah, *In the Shadows of the State*, p. 10.

50. For critical views see ibid.; Kaushik Ghosh, 'Between Global Flows and Local Dams: Indigenousness, Locality, and the Transnational Sphere in Jharkhand, India,' *Cultural Anthropology* 21, no. 4 (2004).

51. The villages fall within assembly seats that are reserved for Scheduled Tribes so the reflections of Rajput respondents should be read in this context.

52. Focus group discussions held in Mandar and Torpa constituencies of Khunti district, Nov. 2007. Thanks to Anuj Kumar and Saurabh Suman for research assistance.

53. Interview with Inder Singh Namdhari, Ranchi, 13 Oct. 2007.

54. Interview, 13 Oct. 2007.

55. This was a view of Hinduism that was first popularised by nineteenth-century

Hindu reformers. See Gavin Flood, *An Introduction to Hinduism* (Cambridge: Cambridge University Press, 1996), p. 11.

56. 'Namdhari hits out at bosses, quits post', *Hindustan Times* (Patna edition), 10 Mar. 1990.

57. As the Committee on Jharkhand Matters, constituted in 1989, stated: 'Almost every memorandum and representation has complained of land alienation taking place in the tribal areas…Apart from private land-grab, state action for acquisition of land for large development projects also is responsible.' Committee on Jharkhand Matters, 'Report of Committee on Jharkhand Matters,' (1990), p. 45.

58. Interview, Jamshedpur, 10 Oct. 2007.

59. Interview, Ranchi, 11 Apr. 2007.

60. Interview with Surya Singh Besra, 10 Oct. 2007.

61. David Stuligross, *A Piece of Land to Call One's Own: Multicultural Federalism and Institutional Innovation in India* (PhD, University of California, 2001), p. 305.

62. Report of Committee on Jharkhand Matters, p. 1.

63. Ghosh, 'Between Global Flows.'

64. Report of Committee on Jharkhand Matters.

65. Ibid., p. 85.

66. Interview with Subodh Kant Sahay, Delhi, Sept. 13 2007. At this stage Sahay was a minister in the Janata Dal government but he subsequently joined Congress in 1995.

67. 'BJP-JMM meet at Ranchi on June 18', *Hindustan Times* (Patna edition), 6 June 1990.

68. 'BJP to oppose move for Development Council', *Hindustan Times* (Patna edition), 13 Feb. 1991.

69. Stuligross, *A Piece of Land to Call One's Own*, p. 318.

70. Interviews with Saryu Roy, Ranchi, 8 Oct. 2007; Sushil Kumar Modi (former leader of opposition in Bihar, and Deputy Chief Minister in Nitish Kumar government of Bihar 2005–), Patna, 29 Sept. 2007.

71. Interview with Babulal Marandi, Ranchi, 17 Oct. 2007.

72. Interview, Ranchi, 17 Oct. 2007.

73. He subsequently left the BJP in 2006 and formed a new party, the Jharkhand Vikas Manch—another sign of the extreme party fragmentation seen in Jharkhand.

74. Interview, 11 Oct. 2007.

75. Interview with Devdas Apte, Delhi, 12 Sept. 2007.

76. Phone interview with Shailendra Mahato, 17 Oct. 2007.

77. Interview, 11 Oct. 2007.

78. Focus group discussion in Torpa block, Oct. 2007.

79. Ramachandra Guha, *The Unquiet Woods: Ecological Change and Peasant Resis-*

tance in the Himalaya (expanded edition) (Oxford: Oxford University Press, 1999), pp. 10–11.

80. See Diana Eck, *India: A Sacred Geography* ((New York: Harmony, 2012). Kumar, *The Uttarakhand Movement: Construction of a Regional Identity* (New Delhi: Kanishka Publishers, Distributors, 2000), p. 36.

81. Eck, *India: A Sacred Geography*, p. 49.

82. Ibid.

83. Kumar, *The Uttarakhand Movement*, p. 38.

84. Guha, *The Unquiet Woods*, p. 57.

85. A good discussion of these accounts is provided by Emma Mawdsley, 'After Chipko: From Environment to Region in Uttaranchal,' *Journal of Peasant Studies* 25, no. 4 (1998).

86. Haripriya Rangan, *Of Myths and Movements: Rewriting Chipko into Himalayan History* (London; New York: Verso, 2000).

87. Guha, *The Unquiet Woods*.

88. Mawdsley, 'After Chipko'; See also Haripriya Rangan, 'From Chipko to Uttaranchal: The environment of protest and development in the Indian Himalaya,' in *Liberation Ecologies: Environment, Development, Social Movements*, ed. Richard Peet and Michael Watts (London and New York: Routledge, 2004).

89. Mawdsley, 'After Chipko,' p. 39.

90. Ibid; Rangan, 'From Chipko to Uttaranchal.'

91. See Guha, *The Unquiet Woods*, pp. 180–4.

92. Ibid., p. 155.

93. Much of this statehood related political activity in the 1970s was confined to the Garhwal side of the hills (formerly the princely state of Tehri Garhwal) where the former Raja, Manvendra Shah, also periodically raised the demand for statehood. See Indu Tewari, *Unity for Identity: Struggle for Uttarakhand State* (New Delhi: KK Publishers and Distributors, 2001), p. 55. The idea of statehood did not become salient in Kumaon (formerly part of the United Provinces) until much later.

94. 'Prthak Uttarakhand ka Adhar' (The Basis for a Separate Uttarakhand), *Nainital Samachar*, 12 Nov. 1977.

95. Rajiv Shah, 'Kaisa Hoga voh Parvatiya Rajya', *Nainital Samachar*, 1–14 May 1979.

96. Narendra Rautela, 'Andhere Me Duba Unka Parvatiya Rajya' (Their hill state gets lost in darkness), *Nainital Samachar*, 1 Apr. 1981.

97. Some interviewees reported that Congress also reached out repeatedly to the UKD for a potential merger in this period.

98. See Emma Mawdsley, 'The Abuse of Religion and Ecology: The Vishva Hindu Parishad and Tehri Dam,' *Worldviews* 9, no. 1 (2005).

99. Interview with Narayan Singh Jantawal, Nainital, 3 Nov. 2007 (acting president of UKD in 2007).

100. This summary of pro-statehood activities draws from information in Emma Mawdsley, *Non-Secessionist Regionalism in India: The Demand for a Separate State of Uttarakhand* (DPhil, University of Cambridge, 1997).
101. 'Naye Bharat ke liye Naye Uttarakhand' (New Uttarakhand for a New India), *Nainital Samachar*, 12 July 1988.
102. Joshi had been elected MP for Almora in the 1977–80 Janata government.
103. D. Nityanand, 'Uttaranchal: Itihasik Paridrshya evam Vikas Ke Aayam (Uttaranchal: Historical Perspective and extent of Development),' (Dehra Dun: Chavi Prakashan, 2004).
104. Interview with Bachi Singh Rawat, BJP MP for Nainital (and, at time of interview, state party president), 24 Oct. 2007.
105. Interview with Rishiraj Debral, son of Devendra Shastri (first RSS full timer in Uttarakhand, Janata Party MLA 1977–80 and later BJP Member of the Legislative Council). Dehra Dun, 15 Nov. 2007.
106. Mukul Sharma, 'Passages from Nature to Nationalism: Sunderlal Bahugana and Tehri Dam Opposition in Garhwal,' *Economic and Political Weekly* XLIV, no. 8 (2009), p. 37.
107. Kumar, *The Uttarakhand Movement*, p. 6.
108. Nityanand, 'Uttaranchal: Itihasik Paridrshya evam Vikas Ke Aayam (Uttaranchal: Historical Perspective and Extent of Development).'
109. Ibid.
110. The party's official reasoning for the decision to name the new state Uttaranchal, as opposed to Uttarakhand, was the its desire for a combination of the words Uttarakhand and Kumaon (which came from the word Kurmanchal). In 1960, the state government had divided the region into the Uttarakhand Mandal (commissionary) and Kumaon Mandal, passing the Kumaon and Uttarakhand Zamindari Abolition Act 1960 in the same year, 'Uttaranch Rajya ko 'Uttaranchal' Nam Dene Tatha Rajya Gatan ki Prshtbhumi' (Background to the giving of the name Uttaranchal to Uttaranch State and the creation of the state, by Bachi Singh Rawat (BJP MP, Nainital), written in 2006. The BJP wanted a name which encompassed both parts of the region, but it also seems likely that the desire to differentiate the BJP's demand from other demands for statehood, made since 1979 by the UKD, was also a motivation.
111. Conversations during fieldwork in 2007. Although it should be noted that such memories did not necessarily resonate with the whole population—the extent of dalit participation in the protests, for example, is hard to gauge.
112. Emma Mawdsley, 'Uttarakhand agitation and Other Backward Classes,' *Economic and Political Weekly* XXXI, no. 4 (1996).
113. Mawdsley, 'After Chipko,' p. 49.
114. Interview with Dr S.P. Sati, Srinigar (Garhwal), 3 May 2007. See also 'Leaderless, rudderless', *Times of India*, 6 Oct. 1994.

115. Interview with Sushila Balooni, Uttarakhand movement activist, former Janata Party regional president and UKD MLA candidate, who subsequently joined the BJP. Dehra Dun, 2 May 2007.
116. Kumar, *The Uttarakhand Movement*, p. 92.
117. Interview with P.C. Thapliyal, Dehra Dun, 30 Apr. 2007.
118. See, for instance, 'PM holds talks on Uttarakhand', 4 Sept. 1994 and 'Mulayam told to resolve agitation', 5 Sept. 1994, *Times of India (front page)*.
119. This paragraph draws especially on a conversation with Jitendra Anthwal, a local journalist who covered the regional movement in 1994–5. Dehra Dun, 16 Nov. 2007.
120. Sharma, 'Passages from Nature to Nationalism.'; Mawdsley, 'The Abuse of Religion and Ecology.'

4. STATEHOOD WITHOUT A MOVEMENT: CHHATTISGARH

1. Lawrence Babb, *The Divine Hierarchy: Popular Hinduism in Central India* (New York and London: Columbia University Press, 1975); Samuel Berthet, 'Tribals, OBCs, Reformist Movements and Mainstream Politics in Chhattisgarh,' in *Rise of the Plebeians? The Changing Face of the Indian Legislative Assemblies*, ed. Christophe Jaffrelot and Sanjay Kumar (New Delhi: Routledge, 2009).
2. Indian Bureau of Mines Annual Year Book 2010.
3. Nandini Sundar, *Subalterns and Sovereigns: an Anthropological History of Bastar, 1854–2006*, 2nd edition (Delhi and Oxford: Oxford University Press, 2009), pp. 7–8.
4. Ibid.
5. See Archana Prasad, 'The Political Economy of 'Maoist Violence' in Chhattisgarh,' *Social Scientist* 38, no. 3/4 (2010).
6. See Sundar, *Subalterns and Sovereigns*, afterword; Jason Miklian, 'The Purification Hunt: the Salwa Judum Counterinsurgency in Chhattisgarh, India,' *Dialectical Anthropology* 33, no. 3 (2009).
7. Census of India 2001: Data Highlights: The Scheduled Tribes, Chhattisgarh.
8. J Parry, 'Two Cheers for Reservation: the Satnamis and the Steel Plant,' in *Institutions and Inequalities: Essays in honour of Andre Beteille*, ed. J Parry (New Delhi: Oxford University Press, 1999).
9. Saurabh Dube, *Untouchable Pasts: Religion, Identity and Power in a Central Indian Community, 1780–1950* (Albany: SUNY Press, 1998), p. 149. According to Pawan Diwan, a poet-activist, former MP (and leader of the some-time Prthak Chhattisgarh Party—separate Chhattisgarh party), Sunderlal Sharma was the first person to write about a 'Chhattisgarh *pranth*' (region) in 1870. Interview with Pawan Diwan, 29 Nov. 2007.
10. D.E.U. Baker, 'The Changing Leadership of the Congress in the Central Prov-

inces and Berar, 1919–39,' in *Congress and the Raj*, ed. D.A. Low (London: Heinemann, 1977), p. 230.

11. Interview with V.C. Shukla, Raipur, Nov. 29 2007.

12. Baker, 'The Changing Leadership of the Congress in the Central Provinces and Berar, 1919–39,' p. 253.

13. H.L. Shukla, *Social History of Chhattisgarh* (Delhi: Agam Kala Prakashan, 1985), p. 129.

14. After the States Reorganisation Commission report in 1956, the demand was partially fulfilled by the merger of Vidarbha and neighbouring Marathi-speaking provinces into the province of Bombay, and the eventual creation of Maharashtra in 1960. The demand for a stand-alone Vidarbha state, however, continues to be raised periodically.

15. Interview in Brahminpara, Raipur, 7 Dec. 2007.

16. In 1959, Madhya Pradesh passed a Land Ceiling Act restricting a single family's holdings to twenty-eight acres. This affected 270,000 proprietors across Madhya Pradesh compared to the 4.6 million with less than 30 acres. Jaffrelot, *The Hindu Nationalist Movement in India* (New York: Columbia University Press, 1996), p. 173.

17. Focus group discussion in Brahminpara, Raipur on 7 Dec. 2007.

18. According to the 1931 census, Kurmis constituted 2.9 per cent of the population of Chhattisgarh. See figures in Jaffrelot, *The Hindu Nationalist Movement in India*, p. 133.

19. Discussion with Dr K. Chandraker, who became additional secretary of this group in 1953. 5 Dec. 2007, Kurud, Chhattisgarh.

20. Hari Thakur, 'Chhattisgarh ke Mahan Saput (Chhattisgarh's Great Sons),' (Raipur, 2000).

21. Ibid.

22. Interview with Purushottam Kaushik, Socialist MP (1977–80; 1989–91), Mahasamund district, 6 Dec. 2007.

23. Interview with Keyur Bhushan, joint secretary of Chhattisgarh Mahasabha who went on a fourteen day hunger strike during the *dhan satyagraha*. Bhushan later became a Congress MP in 1980. 3 Dec. 2007, Raipur.

24. Interview with Keyur Bhushan.

25. Other Socialist politicians saw the statehood question as marginal, a view expressed for instance by Pradeep Choubey, a Socialist/Janata Party MLA from 1977–80. Interview, Durg, 1 Dec. 2007.

26. Information in this paragraph is drawn from an interview with Purushottam Kaushik, Mahasamund district, 6 Dec. 2007.

27. Boundary changes make it difficult to establish precise Chhattisgarh constituencies before this.

28. Interview with Purushottam Kaushik, 6 Dec. 2007.

29. Discussion in Raipur, 30 Nov. 2007.

30. Government of India, 'All India Report on Agricultural Census 1970–71,' (1971), p. 60. Unfortunately the All India Report on Agricultural Census 1970–71 does not break down figures to the district level. Therefore it has only been possible to develop an approximate profile for Chhattisgarh based on the figures for the rice-growing region of Madhya Pradesh (which includes some districts outside Chhattisgarh).

31. NB. These figures are approximate due to data limitations and included for indicative purposes only.

32. Brass, 'The Politicisation of the Peasantry in a North Indian State: Part I,' *Journal of Peasant Studies* 8, no. 4 (1980), pp. 395–426.

33. Francine Frankel, 'Caste, Land and Dominance in Bihar,' in *Dominance and State Power in Modern India*, ed. Francine Frankel and M.S.A. Rao (New Delhi: Oxford University Press, 1989), p. 93.

34. Government of India, 'All India Report on Agricultural Census 1970–71.'

35. National Sample Survey Organisation, 'Cultivation Practices in India, NSS 54th Round (January-June 1998),' (Delhi: 1999), pp. 31–5.

36. Figures calculated from Districtwise Number, Area and Average Size of Operational Holdings in Madhya Pradesh, Agricultural Census 1995–96, Department of Agriculture, Government of Madhya Pradesh. Accessed via indiastat.com.

37. This is in line with a deterioration in the size of landholdings across India since 1960. The NSS Landholding Survey records that in 2002–3 marginal holdings (1 hectare or less) constituted 70 per cent of all operational holdings across India (up from 39 per cent in 1960–61), while holdings over 4 hectares comprised less than 5 per cent. National Sample Survey Organisation, 'Some Aspects of Operational Land Holdings in India, 2002–3: NSS 59th Round (January-December 2003),' (Delhi: 2006), p. i and 18.

38. Interview with Keyur Bhushan, 3 Dec. 2007.

38. Rajni Kothari, 'The Congress 'System' in India '*Asian Survey* 4, no. 12 (1964).

40. Interview with Purushottam Kaushik, Dec. 6 2007. Translated from Hindi.

41. A Singh, 'The Land Question in Chhattisgarh,' in *Land Reforms in India: Issues of Equity in Rural Madhya Pradesh*, ed. P.K. Jha (Delhi: Sage Publications, 2002); B. Dogra, 'Tribal Miners: The Search for Salvation,' in *On a Rainbow in the Sky…the Chhattisgarh Mukti Morcha*, ed. Centre for Education and Communication (New Delhi: Centre for Education and Communication, 1998), p. 46.

42. 'NSA to crush Dalli-Rajhara Mine Workers,' *EPW* XVI, no. 13 (1981).

43. 'NSA to crush Dalli-Rajhara Mine Workers.'

44. See V. Venkatesan, "A Verdict and Some Questions," *Frontline*, 26 Feb.–11 Mar.

45. S.G. Niyogi, 'Chhattisgarh and National Question (no date),' in Centre for Education and Communication, in *On a Rainbow in the Sky…The Chhattis-*

garh Mukti Morcha, ed. Centre for Education and Communication (New Delhi: Centre for Education and Communication, 1998). Originally published in Janata, May Day 1981.

46. Parry, 'Two Cheers for Reservation,' p. 133.
47. Archana Prasad, 'Unravelling the forms of 'Adivasi' Organisation and Resistance in Colonial India,' *Indian Historical Review* 33, no. 1 (2006). p. 227.
48. This description draws on Sundar's account in *Subalterns and Sovereigns*, pp. 194–221.
49. Ibid., p. 202.
50. Ibid., p. 223. Pravir Chandra had discussed the formation of a Chamber of Princes to demand the restoration of princely states—this was interpreted by the government as reflecting potentially secessionist ambitions. See ibid., p. 210.
51. Ibid., p. 223.
52. Sundar, *Subalterns and Sovereigns*, p. 258.
53. Ibid., p. 13.
54. There was a lesser church presence in the Bastar region to the south of Chhattisgarh.
55. The role of Arjun Singh in boosting Chhattisgarhi *asmita* or sentiment is also highlighted by Samuel Berthet. See Berthet, 'Tribals, OBCs, Reformist Movements,' p. 329.
56. A. Sadgopal and S.B. Namra, 'Sangarsh aur Nirman, Shankar Guha Niyogi aur unke Naye Bharat ka Sapna (Struggle and Construction, Shankar Guha Niyogi and his dream of a new India),' (Delhi: Rajkamal Prakashan, 1993).
57. People's Union for Democratic Rights, 'Shankar Guha Niyogi and the Chhattisgarh People's Movement,' (Delhi: 1991).
58. Interview with Pawan Diwan, near Rajim, 29 Nov. 2007.
59. This was something that even V.C. Shukla acknowledged. Interview, Raipur, 29 Nov. 2007.
60. 'NSA to crush Dalli-Rajhara Mine Workers,' p. 564.
61. Berthet, 'Tribals, OBCs, Reformist Movements,' p. 353.
62. First elected in 1977.
63. First became an MLA in 1972.
64. Interviews with Bhupesh Baghel, deputy leader of opposition (Congress MLA, a Kurmi), Purana Bhilai, 1 Dec. 2007; Digvijay Singh, former Chief Minister of Madhya Pradesh 1993–2003, 3 Apr. 2007.
65. Berthet, 'Tribals, OBCs, Reformist Movements,' p. 333.
66. Indicative data on the caste composition of MLAs from Chhattisgarh over time was compiled during fieldwork.
67. See for example, the letter written by Chandulal Chandrakar to PM Narasimha Rao after the 1993 state assembly resolution. *Pradhanmantri ko Sansad Chandulal Chandrakar ka Patr: Congress Ghoshana part ke anurup Chhattisgarh Rajya*

Banaye (Chandrakar's letter to PM: create Chhattisgarh in line with Congress manifesto), *Deshbandhu*, 8 Oct. 1994.

68. Chandulal Chandraker, a veteran journalist, entered politics at a by-election in 1972.
69. Interview with Digvijay Singh, New Delhi, 3 Apr. 2007.
70. Interview with Charandas Mahant, Chhattisgarh PCC President, Raipur, 15 Mar. 2007.
71. Interview with Pawan Diwan, 4 Dec 2007.
72. Interview with V.C. Shukla, Raipur, 29 Nov. 2007.
73. Interview with Bhupesh Baghel, Deputy leader of Congress in Chhattisgarh Legislative Assembly. Bhilai, 1 Dec. 2007.
74. Interview with Dr M.L. Yadu, Raipur, 5 Dec. 2007.
75. '*Chhattisgarh ka Rajnitik Shunya Bharne Arjun Singh ka Sankalp: Kharsiya se Chunav Larna Nischit*' (Arjun Singh's resolution to fill Chhattisgarh's political vacuum: decision to fight election from Kharsiya), 3 Mar. 1988, *Deshbandhu*.
76. '*Prthak Chhattisgarh ki Mang Prajatantrik Adhikar hai use roka nahi jana chahiye*' (The demand for a separate Chhattisgarh is a democratic right, it should not be stopped—Arjun Singh), 1 Apr. 1993, *Deshbandhu* (Rajnandgaon edition).
77. 'BJP faces an Uphill Task in MP', *The Hindu*, 2 Nov. 1993.
78. Interview with Pawan Diwan, 29 Nov. 2007.
79. Interview with Keshav Singh Thakur, Raipur, 7 Dec. 2007.
80. Jaffrelot, *India's Silent Revolution*, p. 438.
81. Sundar, *Subalterns and Sovereigns*, p. 2.
82. 'Tendu policy, key issue in Chhattisgarh', *The Hindu*, 10 Nov. 1993.
83. Interview with Ramesh Bais, New Delhi, 9 May 2007.
84. Interview with Chandrashekhar Sahu, Raipur, 22 Nov. 2007.
85. Jaffrelot, *India's Silent Revolution*, p. 478.
86. Gaur quoted in ibid., p. 497.
87. Interview with Chandrashekhar Sahu (Raipur, 22 Nov. 2007). See also, '*Congress-Bhajapaykaran ke Chakkar me Chhattisgarh Rajya ka Muddha Jan Andolan Nahi Ban Saka*' (In the orbit of Congress-BJP, Chhattisgarh statehood issue cannot be made a people's movement), *Deshbandhu*, 25 Oct 1995, Bhilainagar by Chatursingh Thakur.
88. Interview with Ramesh Bais, Delhi, 9 May 2007.
89. Discussion at the Raipur Development Authority, 3 Dec. 2007.
90. Interview with Lakhiram Agrawal, Raipur, 8 Nov. 2007.
91. Jaffrelot, *India's Silent Revolution*, p. 449.
92. Interview with V.C. Shukla.
93. Focus group discussions in a number of villages in Chhattisgarh, Nov. 2007.

5. THE VIEW FROM THE STATE CAPITALS

1. Andrew Wyatt, *Party System Change in South India: Political Entrepreneurs, Patterns and Processes* (Abingdon: Routledge, 2009), p. 17.

2. See discussion in chapter two, and in Paul Brass, *Language, Religion and Politics in North India* (Cambridge: Cambridge University Press, 1974).

3. Louise Tillin, 'Statehood and the Politics of Intent,' *Economic and Political Weekly* XLVI, no. 20 (2011).

4. Will Kymlicka, *Politics in the Vernacular: Nationalism, Multiculturalism and Citizenship* (Oxford: Oxford University Press, 2001), p. 102.

5. Brendan O'Leary, 'An iron law of nationalism and federation: A (neo-Diceyian) theory of the necessity of a federal Staatsvolk, and of consociational rescue,' *Nations and Nationalism* 7, no. 3 (2001).

6. See Mitchell, *Language, Emotion and Politics in South India: The Making of a Mother Tongue* (Bloomington: Indiana University Press, 2009).

7. For a discussion of the Hindi language movement in Uttar Pradesh, see Gyanesh Kudaisya, *Region, Nation, 'Heartland': Uttar Pradesh in India's Body-Politic* (New Delhi: Sage Publications, 2006), p. 381.

8. Adeney, *Federalism and Ethnic Conflict Regulation in India and Pakistan*, p. 217.

9. My thanks to an anonymous reviewer for this observation.

10. See discussion in J.R. Wood, ed. *State Politics in Contemporary India* (London; Boulder: Westview Press, 1984); John Harriss, 'Poverty Reduction and Regime Differences Across India,' in *Changing Paths: International Development and the New Politics of Inclusion*, ed. Peter Houtzager and Mick Moore (Ann Arbor: University of Michigan Press, 2003); Frankel and Rao, *Dominance and State Power in Modern India* (New Delhi: Oxford University Press, 1989).

11. Jaffrelot, *India's Silent Revolution*, p. 311.

12. DL Sheth, 'Ram Manohar Lohia on Caste in Indian Politics,' in *Caste and Democratic Politics in India*, ed. G. Shah (London: Anthem Press, 2004), p. 79.

13. Jaffrelot, *India's Silent Revolution*, p. 253.

14. See discussion in Christopher Fuller, 'Introduction: Caste Today,' in *Caste Today*, ed. Christopher Fuller (New Delhi: Oxford University Press, 1996).

15. See Lucia Michelutti, 'The Vernacularization of Democracy: Political Participation and Popular Politics in North India,' *Journal of the Royal Anthropological Institute* 13, no. 3 (2007); Jeffrey Witsoe, 'Corruption as Power: Caste and the Political Imagination of the Postcolonial State,' *American Ethnologist* 38, no. 1 (2011).

16. A summary of the date of different state commissions can be found in Frankel and Rao, *Dominance and State Power in Modern India*.

17. Yadav, 'Understanding the Second Democratic Upsurge: Trends of Bahujan Participation in Electoral Politics in the 1990s,' p. 132.

18. See chapter nine of Jaffrelot, *India's Silent Revolution*.

19. The BJP formed a government in 1990 for the first time. Since then Congress ruled from 1993–1998; and 1998–2003. The BJP has been in power from 2003–08; 2008–in both Chhattisgarh and Madhya Pradesh.

20. Lloyd Rudolph and Susanne Hoeber Rudolph, *In Pursuit of Lakshmi: The Political Economy of the Indian State*, (Chicago and London: University of Chicago Press, 1987), p. 183.

21. Rudolph and Rudolph, 'Transformation of Congress Party: Why 1980 was not a Restoration,' *Economic and Political Weekly* XVI (1981).

22. Zoya Hasan, *Quest for Power: Oppositional Movements and Post-Congress Politics in Uttar Pradesh* (Delhi: Oxford University Press, 1998).

23. For a detailed discussion of the regional variation in caste systems in the north Indian plain see Joseph E. Schwartzberg, 'The Distribution of Selected Castes in the North Indian Plain,' *Geographical Review* 55, no. 4 (1965).

24. Brass, 'The Politicisation of the Peasantry in a North Indian State: Part I,' *Journal of Peasant Studies* 8, no. 4 (1980), pp. 395–426.

25. Jaffrelot, *India's Silent Revolution*, p. 354.

26. See Sudha Pai, 'Making of a Political Community: the Congress Party and the Integration of Madhya Pradesh,' in *Interrogating Reorganisation of States: Culture, Identity and Politics in India*, ed. Asha Sarangi and Sudha Pai (New Delhi: Routledge, 2011).

27. Christophe Jaffrelot, 'The Rise of the Other Backward Classes in the Hindi Belt,' *Journal of Asian Studies* 59, no. 1 (2000), p. 107.

28. Frankel and Rao, *Dominance and State Power*, p. 422.

29. Wayne Wilcox, 'Madhya Pradesh,' in *State Politics in India*, ed. Myron Weiner (Princeton: Princeton University Press, 1968); S. Mitra, 'Political Integration and Party Competition in Madhya Pradesh: Congress and the opposition in Parliamentary Elections 1977–1984,' in *Diversity and Dominance in Indian Politics*, ed. R. Sisson and R. Roy (New Delhi: Sage Publications, 1990); Pai, 'Making of a Political Community.'

30. Shaibal Gupta, 'Socio-Economic Base of Political Dynamics in Madhya Pradesh,' *Economic and Political Weekly* XL, no. 48 (2005), p. 5093.

31. Ibid.

32. Interview with Digvijay Singh, New Delhi, 3 Apr. 2007.

33. Jaffrelot, *India's Silent Revolution*, p. 436. The major recommendations of the Commission included 35 per cent reservations for OBCs in all government, semi-governmental and public sector services, as well as in government run or government-aided education institutions. See ibid., pp. 435–6.

34. 'Prthak Chhattisgarh ke Nam Par Rajniti Nahi Chalegi: Mukhyamantri ki Phatkar' (Politics will not run in the name of a separate Chhattisgarh: Chief Minister's bombshell), *Deshbandhu*, 18 May 1981.

35. 'Prospects remote for Chhattisgarh state', *The Hindu*, 22 Mar. 1994; 'Chhat-

tisgarh Rajya ke Liye Sarvsammat Sankalp' (Unanimous resolution for Chhat-tisgarh state), *Deshbandhu*, 18 Mar. 1994.

36. *The Hindu*, 19 Mar. 1994.

37. Interview with Digvijay Singh, New Delhi, 3 Apr. 2007.

38. See James Manor, 'Digvijay Singh in Madhya Pradesh, India: Supplementing Political Institutions to Promote Inclusion,' in *Against the Odds: Politicians, Institutions and the Struggle against Poverty*, ed. Marcus Melo, Njuguna Ng'ethe, and James Manor (2012); Sudha Pai, *Developmental State and the Dalit Question in Madhya Pradesh: Congress Response* (New Delhi: Routledge, 2011).

39. Tewari, *Unity for Identity: Struggle for Uttarakhand State* (New Delhi: KK Publishers and Distributors, 2001), p. 58.

40. Jaffrelot, *India's Silent Revolution*, p. 368

41. Hasan, *Quest for Power*, p. 121.

42. Ibid., p. 161.

43. Ibid., p. 159; Jaffrelot, *India's Silent Revolution*, p. 484.

44. Ian Duncan, 'Dalits and Politics in Rural North India: The Bahujan Samaj Party in Uttar Pradesh,' *Journal of Peasant Studies* 27, no. 1 (1999), p. 38.

45. See Ian Duncan, 'New Political Equations in North India: Mayawati, Mulayam, and Government Instability in Uttar Pradesh,' *Asian Survey* 37, no. 10 (1997). In 1995, the BSP withdrew support to the government, forcing Mulayam Singh Yadav to resign. President's Rule was introduced. In this period, the Governor Motilal Vora declared the whole of Uttarakhand to be a backward region and thus eligible for the 27 per cent reservations. This prompted Mulayam Singh to launch an 'aarakshan bachao' (save reservations) campaign in Jan. 1996, after he had left office as Chief Minister in 1995. See Jaffrelot, *India's Silent Revolution*, p. 374.

46. Interview with a former Chief Secretary, Government of Uttar Pradesh. Delhi, 17 Sept. 2007.

47. 'Anti-reservations stir in UP gathers momentum,' *Times of India*, 5 Aug. 1994.

48. 'Mulayam flayed over 'Uttaranchal',' *Times of India*, 20 Aug. 1994.

49. '3 killed as violence marks UP Bandh', *Times of India*, 14 Sept. 1994.

50. 'Quota row will be resolved: Mulayam,' *Times of India*, 29 Aug. 1994.

51. 'Tiwari has task cut out for him in UP', *Times of India*, 27 Aug. 1994.

52. M. Joshi, 'The Uttarakhand Question: Is Separation Necessary,' *Times of India*, 20 Sept. 1994.

53. Congress MP Harikesh Bahadur, quoted in 'Parties make Capital of Uttarakhand Stir', *Times of India*, 9 Sept. 1994.

54. Subhash C. Kashyap, 'Uttarakhand: Case for a Separate State,' *Times of India*, 19 Sept. 1994.

55. See Manor's discussion of the difference between Karpoori Thakur and Devaraj Urs in Karnataka as Chief Ministers in the 1970s who attempted to prise apart

the power of dominant classes. James Manor, 'Pragmatic Progressives in Regional Politics: The Case of Devaraj Urs,' *Economic and Political Weekly* XV, no. 5/7 (1980).

56. Frankel, 'Caste, Land and Dominance in Bihar,' p. 123.
57. Jaffrelot, *India's Silent Revolution*, p. 378.
58. See, for example, Jeffrey Witsoe, 'Social Justice and Stalled Development: Caste Empowerment and the Breakdown of Governance in Bihar,' in *India in Transition: Economics and Politics of Change*, ed. Francine Frankel (Philadelphia: Center for the Advanced Study of India, 2006); Stuart Corbridge, *Seeing the State: Governance and Governmentality in India* (Cambridge: Cambridge University Press, 2005); Santhosh Mathew and Mick Moore, 'State Incapacity by Design: Understanding the Bihar Story,' *IDS Working Paper* 2011, no. 366 (2011).
59. Witsoe, 'Corruption as Power,' p. 78.
60. This subsequently merged with a section of the Janata Dal to become the JD (U).
61. S. Thakur, *Subaltern Saheb: Bihar and the Making of Laloo Yadav* (New Delhi: Picador India, 2006), p. 35.
62. Interview with Brishim Patel, JD(U), Patna, 27 Sept. 2007.
63. 'Vananchal over my Dead Body, says Laloo', *The Statesman*, 14 Sept. 1998.
64. 'Bihar Govt. Withdraws Resolution on Jharkhand', *The Hindu*, 16 Sept. 1998.
65. 'Bihar Assembly Rejects Vananchal Bill', *The Statesman*, 21 Sept. 1998; 'Union Cabinet Recommends Rabri Dismissal', *The Statesman*, 22 Sept. 1998.
66. Interview with Sushil Kumar Modi, Patna, 29 Sept. 2007.
67. Interview with Saryu Roy, Ranchi, 8 Oct. 2007.

6. FEDERAL POLITICS AND THE CREATION OF NEW STATES

1. Interview in Delhi, 18 Sept. 2007.
2. Paul Pierson, 'Big, Slow-Moving, and … Invisible,' in *Comparative Historical Analysis in the Social Sciences*, ed. James Mahoney and Dietrich Rueschemeyer (Cambridge: Cambridge University Press, 2003), p. 178.
3. Oliver Heath, 'Anatomy of BJP's Rise to Power: Social, Regional and Political Expansion in 1990s,' in *Parties and Party Politics in India*, ed. Zoya Hasan (New Delhi: Oxford University Press, 2002).
4. 'Full Statehood for Delhi, Vananchal may be next', *The Statesman*, 29 June 1998.
5. L.K. Advani responding to introduction of the Madhya Pradesh Reorganisation Bill in the Lok Sabha (in Hindi), 25 July 2000.
6. 'Statehood Bills introduced to Lok Sabha', *The Statesman*, 25 July 2000.
7. Mawdsley, 'Redrawing the Body Politic: Federalism, Regionalism and the Creation of New States in India,' *The Journal of Commonwealth and Comparative Politics* 40, no. 3 (2002).

8. Jharkhand = 14; Chhattisgarh = 11 and Uttarakhand = 5 (this is with the inclusion of Haridwar constituency).

9. They did this by trying to persuade non-BJP MLAs in Jharkhand not to support Nitish Kumar. Interview, 17 Oct. 2007, Ranchi.

10. Interview, New Delhi, 6 Nov. 2007.

11. Rob Jenkins, 'Rajput Hindutva, Caste Politics, Regional Identity and Hindu Nationalism in Contemporary Rajasthan,' in *The BJP and the Compulsions of Politics in India*, ed. Thomas Blom Hansen and Christophe Jaffrelot (Delhi: Oxford University Press, 1998).

12. See Suhas Palshikar and Rajeshwari Deshpande, 'Electoral Competition and Structures of Domination in Maharashtra,' *Economic and Political Weekly* XXXIV, no. 34/35 (1999).

13. For a good overview of the Vidarbha movement over time see Ajit Kumar, 'Statehood for Vidarbha,' *Economic and Political Weekly* XXXVI, no. 50 (2001), pp. 4614–17.

14. Bharatiya Janata Party, *BJP Party Documents 1980–2005. Volume I: Election Manifestoes* (New Delhi: Bharatiya Janata Party, 2005).

15. Suhas Palshikar, 'Shiv Sena: A Tiger with Many Faces?,' in *India's Political Parties*, ed. Peter De Souza and E. Sridharan (New Delhi: Sage Publications, 2006); Thomas Blom Hansen, 'BJP and the Politics of Hindutva in Maharashtra,' in *The BJP and the Compulsions of Politics in India*.

16. Discussion during interviews in Vidarbha, Nov. 2008.

17. Hansen, 'BJP and the Politics of Hindutva in Maharashtra,' p. 158.

18. 'Pawar adds punch to Vidarbha plan', *The Economic Times Mumbai*, 15 Sept. 2003; 'Pawar ready to back Vidarbha statehood', *Times of India*, 15 Sept. 2003.

19. In the ensuing 1996 Lok Sabha elections, the BJP and Shiv Sena won nine of eleven seats in Vidarbha. However, in the 1998 elections Congress and the RPI between them won all seats in Vidarbha, defeating all BJP and Shiv Sena candidates.

20. This is in line with Donald Horowitz's theory of secession in which 'advanced' groups in 'backward' regions of a state are the most reluctant secessionists because of their involvement in the economies of the advanced region. Donald Horowitz, *Ethnic Groups in Conflict* (Berkeley: University of California Press, 1985).

21. Lisa Mitchell, *Language, Emotion and Politics in South India: The Making of a Mother Tongue* (Bloomington: Indiana University Press, 2009).

22. Such fears were noted in the report of the States Reorganisation Commission, which actually recommended that Telangana remain a separate state until elections in or around 1961, at which point its merger might be considered if two thirds of the legislature of the Telugu-speaking region of Hyderabad state vote in favour. These findings were set aside by the government.

23. The description in this paragraph draws on Duncan Forrester, 'Subregionalism in India: the Case of Telangana,' *Pacific Affairs* 43, no. 1 (1970).

24. K.C. Suri, 'Telugu Desam Party,' in *India's Political Parties*, ed. Peter De Souza and E. Sridharan (Delhi: Sage Publications, 2006).

25. K. Srinivasulu, 'Caste, Class and Social Articulation in Andhra Pradesh: Mapping Differential Regional Trajectories,' *ODI Working Paper* 179 (2002), p. 4.

26. Richard Snyder and D.J. Samuels, 'Legislative Malapportionment in Latin America: Historical and Comparative Perspectives,' in *Federalism and Democracy in Latin America*, ed. E.L. Gibson (Baltimore and London: Johns Hopkins University Press, 2004), p. 137.

27. The Constitution (Eighty Fourth Amendment) Act 2002. Last Accessed: 1 June 2009, at: http://india.gov.in/govt/documents/amendment/amend84.htm. The statement of objects and reasons was written by Arun Jaitley (Minister of Law, Justice and Company Affairs) and dated 8 Nov. 2000, the very day that the state of Uttaranchal came into being (Chhattisgarh was born a week earlier and Jharkhand a week later).

28. See Yogendra Yadav, 'The Paradox of Political Representation,' *Seminar* 586 (2008); A. McMillan, 'Population Change and the Democratic Structure,' *Seminar* 506 (2001).

29. Incidentally, it is not clear either that the freeze on seat distribution was in the electoral interests of the BJP. Parties with a stronger showing in the south than the north (including the BJP) would have benefited more. See A. McMillan, 'Delimitation, Democracy, and End of Constitutional Freeze,' *Economic and Political Weekly* XXXV, no. 15 (2000).

30. See A. McMillan, 'Constitution 91st Amendment Bill: A Constitutional Fraud?,' *Economic and Political Weekly* XXXVI, no. 14–15 (2001).

7. AFTER 2000: FURTHER REORGANISATION

1. Khan, *Federal India: A Design for Change* (Delhi: Vikas Publishing House, 1992), p. 108.

2. See, for instance, K.C. Suri, 'Andhra Pradesh: Fall of the CEO in Arena of Democracy,' *Economic and Political Weekly* XXXIX, no. 51 (2004); Anant Maringanti, 'Telangana: Righting Historical Wrongs or Getting the Future Right?,' *Economic and Political Weekly* XLV, no. 4 (2010).

3. See Tillin, 'Statehood and the Politics of Intent,' *Economic and Political Weekly* XLVI, no. 20 (2011)

4. Committee for Consultations on the Situation in Andhra Pradesh, 'Report [of the Srikrishna Committee],' (New Delhi: 2010), p. 43.

5. Discussion with Congress MP, Hyderabad, 16 Jan. 2011.

6. K. Srinivasulu and D. Satyanarayana, 'By-elections and Telangana Agitation,' *Economic and Political Weekly* XLV, no. 33 (2010).

7. As Sudipta Kaviraj asserts, 'People having the same language do not have it in the same way. Socially, linguistic competence confers on people capacities, and its absence correspondingly takes them away.' See Sudipta Kaviraj, 'Writing, Speaking, Being: Language and the Historical Formation of Identities in India,' in *Language and Politics in India*, ed. Asha Sarangi (New Delhi: Oxford University Press, 2009), p. 313. The present reincarnation of the Telangana demand in part involves a response to a perception that the Telangana dialect of Telugu is held to be inferior by other Telugu-speakers, and a sense that this perception has implications for the social and economic advancement of Telangana Telugu speakers. This sense has led to a willingness to challenge a language-based political unit.

8. See Committee for Consultations on the Situation in Andhra Pradesh, 'Report [of the Srikrishna Committee],' p. 319.

9. This is according to provisional data of the 2011 census. No other state is home to more than 10 per cent of the population.

10. BSP Chief Minister Mayawati first indicated her support for the 'trifurcation' of Uttar Pradesh on 9 Oct. 2007 (see 'Unsure Maya takes a step back as trifurcation debate hots up', *Indian Express*, 7 Nov. 2007).

11. 'Mayawati for trifurcation of Uttar Pradesh', *Times of India*, 11 Dec. 2009. The Samajwadi Party responded with the riposte that if the Chief Minister was finding it difficult to govern, then she should quit. See 'Mayawati's demand for trifurcation draws flak', *The Hindu*, 13 Dec. 2009.

12. Interview with Swami Prasad Maurya, Lucknow, 20 Jan. 2011.

13. See also Nicholas Jaoul, 'Learning the Use of Symbolic Means: Dalits, Ambedkar Statues and the State in Uttar Pradesh,' *Contributions to Indian Sociology* 40, no. 2 (2006).

14. Jagpal Singh, 'Region, Caste and Politics of 'Reverse Discrimination': The Case of Harit Pradesh,' in *Rethinking State Politics in India: Regions within Regions*, ed. Ashutosh Kumar (New Delhi: Routledge, 2011).

15. Ibid., p. 226.

16. Government of Uttar Pradesh, 'Uttar Pradesh Human Development Report,' (2007).

17. Jagpal Singh, 'Politics of Harit Pradesh: The Case of Western UP as a Separate State,' *Economic and Political Weekly* XXXVI, no. 31 (2001).

18. There is some evidence of faster rates of poverty reduction and economic growth in the region compared to other parts of the state from the later 1990s, particularly as a result of diversification in agriculture into horticulture and spread of irrigation. Government of Uttar Pradesh, 'Uttar Pradesh Human Development Report.'

19. See, for instance, Perspectives, 'Drought by Design: The Man-made Calamity in Bundelkhand,' *Economic and Political Weekly* XLV, no. 5 (2010).

20. Virendra Nath Bhatt, 'It's raining politics over parched Bundelkhand', *Indian Express*, 4 Aug. 2009.
21. 'UP Congress seeks Bundelkhand state', *The Hindu*, 12 Jan. 2008.
22. 'Lalu support for Mayawati on separate Poorvanchal', *Indian Express*, 13 Oct. 2007; 'Nitish supports Mayawati's stand on four new states,' *Indian Express*, 16 Nov. 2011.
23. 'Split Uttar Pradesh, Jairam Ramesh says', *Times of India*, 17 July 2012.

8. CONCLUSION

1. On path dependency see James Mahoney, 'Path Dependence in Historical Sociology,' *Theory and Society* 29, no. 4 (2000). On critical junctures, see Ruth Berins Collier and David Collier, *Shaping the Political Arena: Critical Junctures, the Labor Movement, and Regime Dynamics in Latin America* (Princeton: Princeton University Press, 1991).
2. Their definition of an order is of a constellation of rules, practices, institutions and ideas that hold together over time. Karen Orren and Stephen Skowronek, *The Search for American Political Development* (Cambridge: Cambridge University Press, 2004), p. 16.
3. The experience of Bihar will not be considered here in detail, but for an insightful discussion of the shift in Bihari politics during the 2000s see Santhosh Mathew and Mick Moore, 'State Incapacity by Design: Understanding the Bihar Story,' *IDS Working Paper* 2011, no. 366 (2011).
4. Utsav Kumar and Arvind Subramanian, 'Growth in India's States in the First Decade of the 21st Century: Four Facts,' *Economic and Political Weekly* XLVII, no. 3 (2012).
5. Alpa Shah discusses this representation and reality in Alpa Shah, 'India Burning: The Maoist Revolution,' in *A Companion to the Anthropology of India*, ed. Isabella Clark-Decès (Oxford: Wiley-Blackwell, 2011).
6. Shortly before this book went to press, a large-scale Maoist attack targeted a convoy of senior Congress Party politicians in Chhattisgarh. The attack, in Bastar on 25 May 2013, killed more than twenty-five people including Mahendra Karma, state Congress president Nand Kumar Patel and VC Shukla, who died of his injuries soon afterwards.
7. Pushpesh Pant, 'Dream Turning into a Nightmare in Uttarakhand,' *Economic and Political Weekly* XLVII, no. 14 (2012), p. 20.
8. Yadav, Yogendra, and Suhas Palshikar, 'Party System and Electoral Politics in the Indian States, 1952–2002: From Hegemony to Convergence,' in *India's Political Parties*, ed. Peter Ronald de Souza and E. Sridharan (New Delhi: Sage, 2006), pp. 74–115.
9. The policy was later ruled illegal by the Jharkhand High Court which labelled it

'hostile discrimination of the public at large.' Subsequent BJP leaders sought to distance themselves from the policy for fear that the policy had become a liability for the party among non-tribal and migrant populations. As the subsequent BJP Chief Minister Arjun Munda said, 'Jharkhand is very much within the constitutional framework of the country…There is only one domicile in the country and that is one's identity as an Indian.' See Kalyan Chaudhuri, 'Discord over Domicile,' *Frontline*, 7–20 June 2003.

10. The 2005 Jharkhand High Court verdict which challenged the reservation of seats was overturned by the Supreme Court in Jan. 2010 paving the way for panchayat elections to be held.

11. Louise Tillin, 'Politics in a New State: Chhattisgarh,' *Seminar* 591(2008).

12. *Nandini Sundar and Others versus State of Chhattisgarh*, Supreme Court of India (2011).

13. Delimitation Commission of India, 'Delimitation of Parliamentary and Assembly Constituencies in the State of Uttaranchal' (2006). Following protests from the hill districts, the Delimitation Commission revised its original proposals for an even starker redistribution in favour of the plains districts based on population alone by creating above-average size constituencies in the hill districts and below-average constituencies in the plains districts.

14. 'Plain Tales from the Hills,' *Indian Express*, 13 Mar. 2005.

15. See, for instance, Prerna Singh, 'We-ness and Welfare: A Longitudinal Analysis of Social Development in Kerala, India,' *World Development* 39, no. 2 (2011); Jean Dreze, 'Primary priorities—Learning lessons from Himachal,' *Times of India*, 23 July 1997.

BIBLIOGRAPHY

Adeney, Katherine, *Federalism and Ethnic Conflict Regulation in India and Pakistan*, New York: Palgrave USA, 2007.

Advani, L.K., *My Country My Life*, Delhi: Rupa & Co, 2008.

Ambedkar, B.R., 'Thoughts on Linguistic States,' Delhi: 1955.

Anderson, George, *Federalism: An Introduction*, Oxford: Oxford University Press, 2008.

Arora, Balveer, 'Adapting Federalism to India: Multilevel and Asymmetrical Innovations,' In Balveer Arora and Douglas Verney (eds), *Multiple Identities in a Single State: Indian Federalism in Comparative Perspective*. New Delhi: Konark Publishers Pvt Ltd, 1995, pp. 71–104.

————, 'Negotiating Differences: Federal Coalitions and National Cohesion,' In Francine Frankel, Zoya Hasan, Rajeev Bhargava and Balveer Arora (eds) *Transforming India: Social and Political Dymanics of Democracy*. New Delhi: Oxford University Press, 2000, pp. 176–206.

————, 'Republic of India.' In Luis Moreno and Cesar Colino (eds) *Diversity and Unity in Federal Countries*. Montreal: McGill-Queens University Press, 2010, pp. 200–26.

Austin, Granville, *Working a Democratic Constitution: The Indian Experience*, New Delhi and Oxford: Oxford University Press, 1999.

Babb, Lawrence, *The Divine Hierarchy: Popular Hinduism in Central India*, New York and London: Columbia University Press, 1975.

Bach, D.C., 'Managing a Plural Society: The Boomerang Effects of Nigerian Federalism,' *Journal of Commonwealth and Comparative Politics* 27, no. 2 (1989), pp. 218–45.

Baker, D.E.U., 'The Changing Leadership of the Congress in the Central Provinces and Berar, 1919–39,' In D.A. Low (ed.) *Congress and the Raj*. London: Heinemann, 1977, pp. 225–58.

Baruah, Sanjib, 'Nationalizing Space: Cosmetic Federalism and the Politics of

Development in Northeast India,' *Development and Change* 34, no. 5 (2003). pp. 915–39.

Bermeo, Nancy, 'Conclusion: The Merits of Federalism,' In Ugo M. Amoretti and Nancy Bermeo (eds) *Federalism and Territorial Cleavages*. London and Baltimore: The Johns Hopkins University Press, 2004, pp. 457–82.

———, 'A New Look at Federalism: The Import of Institutions,' *Journal of Democracy* 13, no. 2 (2002), pp. 96–110.

Berthet, Samuel, 'Tribals, OBCs, Reformist Movements and Mainstream Politics in Chhattisgarh.' In Christophe Jaffrelot and Sanjay Kumar (eds) *Rise of the Plebeians The Changing Face of the Indian Legislative Assemblies*. New Delhi: Routledge, 2009, pp. 326–359.

Bharatiya Jana Sangh, *Party Documents*. Delhi: Vithalbhai Patel Bhavan, 1973.

———, *Internal Affairs: Party Document*, New Delhi: BJP, 2005.

Bharatiya Janata Party, *BJP Party Documents 1980–2005. Volume I: Election Manifestoes*, New Delhi: Bharatiya Janata Party, 2005.

———, 'Our Five Commitments,' Delhi: 1984.

———, 'Report of the Working Group, Presented to the National Executive,' Bhopal, 1985.

Bhattacharya, Mohit, 'The Mind of the Founding Fathers,' In Nirmal Mukherji and Balveer Arora (eds) *Federalism in India: Origins and Development*. New Delhi: Vikas Publishing House, 1992.

Blair, Harry, 'Rising Kulaks and Backward Classes in Bihar: Social Change in the Late 1970s,' *Economic and Political Weekly* XV, no. 2 (1980), pp. 64–74.

———, 'Structural Change, the Agricultural Sector and Politics in Bihar,' In J.R. Wood (ed.) *State Politics in Contemporary India*. Boulder and London: Westview Press, 1984, pp. 53–81.

Bose, Sumantra, *Kashmir: Roots of Conflict, Paths to Peace*, Cambridge, London: Harvard University Press, 2003.

Brass, Paul, 'Elite Interests, Popular Passions, and Social Power in the Language Politics of India,' In Asha Sarangi (ed.) *Language and Politics in India*. New Delhi: Oxford University Press, 2009, pp. 183–217.

———, *Ethnicity and Nationalism: Theory and Comparison*, New Delhi: Sage Publications, 1991.

———, *Language, Religion and Politics in North India*, Cambridge: Cambridge University Press, 1974.

———, 'The Politicisation of the Peasantry in a North Indian State: Part I,' *Journal of Peasant Studies* 8, no. 4 (1980), pp. 395–426.

———, *The Politics of India since Independence*, Cambridge: Cambridge University Press, 1990.

Brown, Judith, *Modern India: The Origins of an Asian Democracy*, Delhi; Oxford: Oxford University Press, 1985.

BIBLIOGRAPHY

————, *Nehru: A Political Life*, New Haven and London: Yale University Press, 2003.

Bunce, Valerie, *Subversive Institutions: The Design and the Destruction of Socialism and the State*, Cambridge: Cambridge University Press, 1999.

Chadda, Maya, 'Integration through Internal Reorganization: Containing Ethnic Conflict in India,' *Ethnopolitics* 2, no. 1 (2002), pp. 44–61.

Chandra, Kanchan, 'Ethnic Parties and Democratic Stability,' *Perspectives on Politics* 3, no. 2 (2005), pp. 235–52.

Chaudhuri, Kalyan, 'Discord over Domicile,' *Frontline*, 7–20 June 2003.

Collier, Ruth Berins, and David Collier, *Shaping the Political Arena: Critical Junctures, the Labor Movement, and Regime Dynamics in Latin America*, Princeton: Princeton University Press, 1991.

Committee for Consultations on the Situation in Andhra Pradesh, 'Report [of the Srikrishna Committee],' New Delhi, 2010.

Committee on Jharkhand Matters, 'Report of Committee on Jharkhand Matters,' 1990.

Corbridge, Stuart, 'The Contested Geographies of Federalism in Post-Reform India,' In Sanjay Ruparelia, Sanjay Reddy, John Harriss and Stuart Corbridge (eds) *Understanding India's New Political Economy: A Great Transformation?* London: Routledge, 2011, pp. 66–80.

————, 'The Continuing Struggle for India's Jharkhand: Democracy, Decentralisation and the Politics of Names and Numbers,' *Commonwealth and Comparative Politics* 40, no. 3 (2002), pp. 55–71.

————, 'The Ideology of Tribal Economy and Society: Politics in Jharkhand, c.1950–1980,' *Modern Asian Studies* (1988), pp. 1–42.

————, 'Industrialisation, Internal Colonialism and Ethnoregionalism: The Jharkhand, India, 1880–1980,' *Journal of Historical Geography* 12, no. 2 (1987), pp. 249–66.

————, *Seeing the State: Governance and Governmentality in India*. Cambridge: Cambridge University Press, 2005.

————, 'Tribal Politics, Finance and the State: The Jharkhand India, 1900–1980,' *Ethnic and Racial Studies* 12, no. 2 (1989), pp. 175–208.

Corbridge, Stuart, and John Harriss, *Reinventing India: Liberalization, Hindu Nationalism and Popular Democracy*, Cambridge: Cambridge University Press, 2000.

Damodaran, Vinita, 'The Politics of Marginality and the Construction of Indigeneity in Chotanagpur,' *Postcolonial Studies* 9, no. 2 (2006), pp. 179–96.

Das, Arvind N., *Agrarian Unrest and Socio-Economic Change in Bihar, 1900–1980*, New Delhi: Manohar, 1983.

Dasgupta, Jyotirindra, *Language Conflict and National Development: Group Politics and National Language Policy in India*, Berkeley: University of California Press, 1970.

————, 'A Season of Caesars: Emergency Regimes and Development Politics in Asia,' *Asian Survey* 18, no. 4 (1978), pp. 315–49.

Delimitation Commission of India, 'Delimitation of Parliamentary and Assembly Constituencies in the State of Uttaranchal,' 2006.

Demenge, Jonathan, *The Political Ecology of Road Construction in Ladakh*, Unpublished DPhil thesis, Institute of Development Studies, University of Sussex: 2011.

Devalle, Susana B.C., *Discourses of Ethnicity: Culture and Protest in Jharkhand*, New Delhi and London: Sage, 1992.

Dhar, H., 'Split in Jharkhand Mukti Morcha,' *Economic and Political Weekly* XV, no. 31 (1980).

Diani, M., 'The Concept of Social Movement,' *Sociological Review* 40, no. 1 (1992),pp. 1–25.

————, 'Introduction: Social Movements, Contentious Actions and Social Networks: From Metaphor to Substance?' In M. Diani and Doug McAdam (eds) *Social Movements and Networks: Relational Approaches to Collective Action*. Oxford: Oxford University Press, 2003, pp. 1–20.

Dogra, B., 'Tribal Miners: The Search for Salvation,' In *On a Rainbow in the Sky… The Chhattisgarh Mukti Morcha*, ed. by Centre for Education and Communication. New Delhi: Centre for Education and Communication, 1998.

Dube, Saurabh, *Untouchable Pasts: Religion, Identity and Power in a Central Indian Community, 1780–1950*, Albany: SUNY Press, 1998.

Duchacek, Ivo Duka, *Comparative Federalism: The Territorial Dimension of Politics*, New York and London: Holt, Rinehart & Winston, 1970.

Duncan, Ian, 'Dalits and Politics in Rural North India: The Bahujan Samaj Party in Uttar Pradesh,' *Journal of Peasant Studies* 27, no. 1 (1999), pp. 35–60.

————, 'New Political Equations in North India: Mayawati, Mulayam, and Government Instability in Uttar Pradesh,' *Asian Survey* 37, no. 10 (1997), pp. 979–96.

Dutt, Balbir, *Kahani Jharkhand Andolan Ki (Story of the Jharkhand Movement)*, Ranchi: Crown Publications, 2005.

Eck, Diana, 'Ganga: The Goddess Ganges in Hindu Sacred Geography,' In John Stratton Hawley and Donna M. Wulff (eds) *Devi: Goddesses of India*. Berkeley: University of California Press, 1996, p. 137–53.

————, *India: A Sacred Geography*, New York: Harmony, 2012.

Economic and Political Weekly, 'From Our Correspondents, Bihar: Containing the Jharkhand Movement,' *Economic and Political Weekly* 14 (1979), pp. 648–50.

————, 'NSA to Crush Dalli-Rajhara Mine Workers,' *Economic and Political Weekly* XVI, no. 13 (1981), pp. 559–65.

BIBLIOGRAPHY

————, 'Singhbhum: Exploitation, Protest and Repression,' *Economic and Political Weekly* (1979), pp. 940–43.

Falleti, Tulia Gabriela, *Decentralization and Subnational Politics in Latin America*. Cambridge: Cambridge University Press, 2010.

Fearon, James D., and David D. Laitin, 'Sons of the Soil, Migrants, and Civil War,' *World Development* 39, no. 2 (2011), pp. 199–211.

Flood, Gavin, *An Introduction to Hinduism*, Cambridge: Cambridge University Press, 1996.

Forrester, Duncan, 'Subregionalism in India: The Case of Telangana,' *Pacific Affairs* 43, no. 1 (1970), pp. 5–21.

Frankel, Francine, 'Caste, Land and Dominance in Bihar,' In Francine Frankel and M.S.A. Rao (eds) *Dominance and State Power in Modern India: Decline of a Social Order*. New Delhi: Oxford University Press, 1989.

————, *India's Political Economy 1947–2004: The Gradual Revolution*, 2nd ed. Delhi; Oxford: Oxford University Press, 2005.

Frankel, Francine, and M.S.A. Rao (eds). *Dominance and State Power in Modern India: Decline of a Social Order*, Vol. 1, New Delhi: Oxford University Press, 1989.

Fuller, Chris, 'Introduction: Caste Today,' In Chris Fuller (ed.) *Caste Today*. New Delhi: Oxford University Press, 1996.

Ghosh, Kaushik, 'Between Global Flows and Local Dams: Indigenousness, Locality, and the Transnational Sphere in Jharkhand, India,' *Cultural Anthropology* 21, no. 4 (2004), pp. 501–34.

Goldstone, J., 'Introduction: Bridging Institutionalised and Noninstitutionalised Politics.' In J. Goldstone (ed.) *States, Parties and Social Movements*. Cambridge: Cambridge University Press, 2003.

————, ed. *States, Parties and Social Movements*, Cambridge: Cambridge University Press, 2003.

Government of India, 'All India Report on Agricultural Census 1970–71,' 1971.

————, *Report of the States Reorganisation Commission*. New Delhi: 1955.

Government of Uttar Pradesh, 'Uttar Pradesh Human Development Report,' 2007.

Guha, Ramachandra' *India after Gandhi: The History of the World's Largest Democracy*, London: Macmillian, 2007.

————, *The Unquiet Woods: Ecological Change and Peasant Resistance in the Himalaya* (Expanded Edition). Oxford: Oxford University Press, 1999.

Gupta, Shaibal, 'Socio-Economic Base of Political Dynamics in Madhya Pradesh,' *Economic and Political Weekly* XL, no. 48 (2005), pp. 5093–100.

Hamilton, Alexander, James Madison, John Jay, and Michael A. Genovese, *The Federalist Papers*, New York: Palgrave Macmillan, 2010 [1787–1788].

BIBLIOGRAPHY

Hankla, Charles Robert, 'Party Linkages and Economic Policy: An Examination of Indira Gandhi's India,' *Business and Politics* 8, no. 3 (2006), pp. 1–29.

Hansen, Thomas Blom, 'BJP and the Politics of Hindutva in Maharashtra,' In Thomas Blom Hansen and Christophe Jaffrelot (eds), *The BJP and the Compulsions of Politics in India*. New Delhi: Oxford University Press, 1998.

———, *The Saffron Wave: Democracy and Hindu Nationalism in Modern India*, Princeton: Princeton University Press, 1999.

Harrison, Selig, *India: The Most Dangerous Decades*, Princeton University Press, 1960.

Harriss, John, 'Borderlands of Economics': Institutions, Politics and Culture in the Explanation of Economic Change,' In John Harriss (ed.) *Power Matters: Essays on Institutions, Politics and Society in India*. New Delhi: Oxford University Press, 2006., pp. 13–28.

———, 'Poverty Reduction and Regime Differences across India.' In Peter Houtzager and Mick Moore (eds) *Changing Paths: International Development and the New Politics of Inclusion*. Ann Arbor: University of Michigan Press, 2003.

Hasan, Zoya, *Quest for Power: Oppositional Movements and Post-Congress Politics in Uttar Pradesh*, Delhi: Oxford University Press, 1998.

Heath, Oliver, 'Anatomy of BJP's Rise to Power: Social, Regional and Political Expansion in 1990s,' In Zoya Hasan (ed.) *Parties and Party Politics in India*. New Delhi: Oxford University Press, 2002, pp. 232–57.

Horowitz, Donald, *Ethnic Groups in Conflict*, Berkeley: University of California Press, 1985.

Jaffrelot, Christophe, 'From Indian Territory to Hindu *Bhoomi*: The Ethnicisation of Nation-State Mapping in India,' In John Zavos, Andrew Wyatt and Vernon Hewitt (eds) *The Politics of Cultural Mobilisation in India*. New Delhi: Oxford University Press, 2004.

———, *The Hindu Nationalist Movement in India*, New York: Columbia University Press, 1996.

———, *India's Silent Revolution: The Rise of the Lower Castes in North India*, London: Hurst & Company, 2003.

———'The Rise of the Other Backward Classes in the Hindi Belt,' *Journal of Asian Studies* 59, no. 1 (2000), pp. 86–108.

Jaoul, Nicholas, 'Learning the Use of Symbolic Means: Dalits, Ambedkar Statues and the State in Uttar Pradesh,' *Contributions to Indian Sociology* 40, no. 2 (2006), pp. 175–207.

Jenkins, Rob, 'Rajput Hindutva, Caste Politics, Regional Identity and Hindu Nationalism in Contemporary Rajasthan,' In Thomas Blom Hansen and Christophe Jaffrelot (eds) *The BJP and the Compulsions of Politics in India*. Delhi: Oxford University Press, 1998, pp. 101–20.

BIBLIOGRAPHY

Kailash, K.K., 'Varieties of Comparative State Politics Research in India,' *Seminar* 620 (2011).

Kaviraj, Sudipta. 'Writing, Speaking, Being: Language and the Historical Formation of Identities in India.' In Asha Sarangi (ed.) *Language and Politics in India.* New Delhi: Oxford University Press, 2009.

Khan, Rasheeduddin, *Federal India: A Design for Change*, Delhi: Vikas Publishing House, 1992.

———, ed. *Rethinking Indian Federalism*, Shimla: Inter-University Centre for Humanities and Social Sciences, Indian Institute of Advanced Study, 1997.

———, 'Uttar Pradesh and Federal Balance in India,' In Rasheeduddin Khan (ed.) *Rethinking Indian Federalism.* Shimla: Inter-University Centre for Humanities and Social Sciences, Indian Institute of Advanced Study, 1997.

Khilnani, Sunil, *The Idea of India*, London: Hamish Hamilton, 1997.

King, Robert D., *Nehru and the Language Politics of India*, New Delhi: Oxford University Press, 1997.

Kohli, Atul, 'Can Democracies Accommodate Ethnic Nationalism? Rise and Decline of Self-Determination Movements in India.' *Journal of Asian Studies* 56, no. 2 (1997), pp. 325–44.

———, *Democracy and Discontent: India's Growing Crisis of Governability*, Cambridge: Cambridge University Press, 1990.

———, 'Politics of Economic Growth in India, 1980–2005. Part I: The 1980s,' *Economic and Political Weekly* 41, no. 13 (2006).

———'Politics of Economic Growth in India, 1980–2005. Part II: The 1990s and Beyond,' *Economic and Political Weekly* 41, no. 14 (2006).

———, *Poverty Amid Plenty in the New India*, Cambridge: Cambridge University Press, 2012.

Kothari, Rajni, 'The Congress 'System' in India,' *Asian Survey* 4, no. 12 (1964), pp. 1161–73.

———, 'The Non-Party Political Process,' *Praxis International* 3 (1985), pp. 333–49.

Kothari, Smitu, 'Social Movements and the Redefinition of Democracy,' In Philip Oldenburg (ed.) *India Briefing, 1993.* Boulder: Westview Press, 1993.

Kothari, Smitu, and Neerja Chowdhury, 'Trade Union for Social Change,' In Centre for Education and Communication (ed.) *On a Rainbow in the Sky… The Chhattisgarh Mukti Morcha.* New Delhi: Centre for Education and Communication, 1998, pp. 29–39.

Kudaisya, Gyanesh, *Region, Nation, 'Heartland': Uttar Pradesh in India's Body-Politic.* New Delhi: Sage Publications, 2006.

Kumar, Ajit, 'Statehood for Vidarbha,' *Economic and Political Weekly* 36, no. 50 (2001), pp. 4614–17.

Kumar, Pradeep, *The Uttarakhand Movement: Construction of a Regional Identity*, New Delhi: Kanishka Publishers, Distributors, 2000.

BIBLIOGRAPHY

Kumar, Utsav, and Arvind Subramanian, 'Growth in India's States in the First Decade of the 21st Century: Four Facts,' *Economic and Political Weekly* XLVII, no. 3 (2012), pp. 48–57.

Kymlicka, Will, *Politics in the Vernacular: Nationalism, Multiculturalism and Citizenship*, Oxford: Oxford University Press, 2001.

Levi, Margaret, and Michael Hechter, 'A Rational Choice Approach to the Rise and Decline of Ethnoregional Political Parties,' In Edward A. Tiryakian and Ronald Rogowski (eds) *New Nationalisms of the Developed West: Toward Explanation*. Boston: Allen and Unwin, 1985, pp. 128–47.

Lustick, Ian, 'Thresholds of Opportunity and Barriers to Change in the Right-Sizing of States,' In Brendan O'Leary, Ian Lustick and Tom Callaghy (eds) *Right-Sizing the State*. Oxford: Oxford University Press, 2001.

Madhok, Balraj, *Indianisation? What, Why and How*, New Delhi: S. Chand, 1970.

Maharaj, R.N., 'Agrarian Movement in Dhanbad,' In Nirmal Sengupta (ed.) *Fourth World Dynamics: Jharkhand*. Delhi: Authors Guild Publications, 1982.

Mahoney, James, 'Path Dependence in Historical Sociology,' *Theory and Society* 29, no. 4 (2000), pp. 507–48.

Mahoney, James, and Kathleen Ann Thelen, 'A Theory of Gradual Institutional Change,' In James Mahoney and Kathleen Ann Thelen (eds), *Explaining Institutional Change: Ambiguity, Agency, and Power*. Cambridge: Cambridge University Press, 2010.

Majeed, Akhtar, 'The Changing Politics of States' Reorganization,' *Publius: The Journal of Federalism* 33, no. 4 (2003), pp. 83–98.

Manor, James, 'Digvijay Singh in Madhya Pradesh, India: Supplementing Political Institutions to Promote Inclusion,' In Marcus Melo, Njuguna Ng'ethe and James Manor (eds), *Against the Odds: Politicians, Institutions and the Struggle against Poverty*. London: Hurst and Co, 2012.

———''Ethnicity' and Politics in India,' *International Affairs* 72, no. 3 (1996), pp. 459–75.

———, 'Making Federalism Work,' *Journal of Democracy* 9, no. 3 (1998),pp. 21–35.

———, 'Parties and the Party System,' In Atul Kohli (ed.), *India's Democracy: An Analysis of Changing State-Society Relations*. Princeton: Princeton University Press, 1988.

———, 'Party Decay and Political Crisis in India,' *Washington Quarterly* 4, no. 3 (1981), pp. 25–40.

———, 'Pragmatic Progressives in Regional Politics: The Case of Devaraj Urs,' *Economic and Political Weekly* XV, no. 5/7 (1980).

Maringanti, Anant, 'Telangana: Righting Historical Wrongs or Getting the Future Right?,' *Economic and Political Weekly* XLV, no. 4 (2010),pp. 33–38.

Mathew, Santhosh, and Mick Moore, 'State Incapacity by Design: Understanding the Bihar Story,' *IDS Working Paper* 2011, no. 366 (2011).

Mawdsley, Emma, 'The Abuse of Religion and Ecology: The Vishva Hindu Parishad and Tehri Dam,' *Worldviews* 9, no. 1 (2005), pp. 1–24.

———, 'After Chipko: From Environment to Region in Uttaranchal,' *Journal of Peasant Studies* 25, no. 4 (1998), pp. 36–54.

———, 'Non-Secessionist Regionalism in India: The Demand for a Separate State of Uttarakhand,' DPhil, University of Cambridge, 1997.

———, 'Nonsecessionist Regionalism in India: The Uttarakhand Separate State Movement,' *Environment and Planning A* 29, no. 12 (1997), pp. 2217–35.

———, 'Redrawing the Body Politic: Federalism, Regionalism and the Creation of New States in India,' *The Journal of Commonwealth and Comparative Politics* 40, no. 3 (2002), pp. 34–54.

———, 'Uttarakhand Agitation and Other Backward Classes,' *Economic and Political Weekly* 31, no. 4 (1996), pp. 205–10.

McAdam, D., S. Tarrow, and C. Tilly, *Dynamics of Contention*. Cambridge: Cambridge University Press, 2001.

McAdam, Doug, and Sidney Tarrow, 'Ballots and Barricades: On the Reciprocal Relationship between Elections and Social Movements,' *Perspectives on Politics* 2 (2010), pp. 529–42.

McMillan, A., 'Constitution 91st Amendment Bill: A Constitutional Fraud?' *Economic and Political Weekly* (2001), pp. 1171–4.

———, 'Delimitation, Democracy, and End of Constitutional Freeze,' *Economic and Political Weekly* (2000), pp. 1271–6.

———'Population Change and the Democratic Structure,' *Seminar* 506 (2001).

Menon, V.P., *The Story of the Integration of the Indian States*, Calcutta: Orient-Longmans, 1956.

Michelutti, Lucia, 'The Vernacularization of Democracy: Political Participation and Popular Politics in North India,' *Journal of the Royal Anthropological Institute* 13, no. 3 (2007), pp. 639–56.

Miklian, Jason, 'The Purification Hunt: The Salwa Judum Counterinsurgency in Chhattisgarh, India,' *Dialectical Anthropology* 33, no. 3 (2009), pp. 441–59.

Mitchell, Lisa, *Language, Emotion and Politics in South India: The Making of a Mother Tongue*, Bloomington: Indiana University Press, 2009.

Mitra, S., 'Political Integration and Party Competition in Madhya Pradesh: Congress and the Opposition in Parliamentary Elections 1977–1984,' In R. Sisson and R. Roy (eds), *Diversity and Dominance in Indian Politics*. New Delhi: Sage Publications, 1990.

Mukarji, N., and G. Mathew, 'Epilogue: Federal Issues 1988–90,' In N. Mukarji and Balveer Arora (eds), *Federalism in India: Origins and Development*. New Delhi: Vikas Publishing House, 1992.

Mullick, S.B., 'Introduction,' In R.D. Munda and S.B. Mullick (eds), *The Jharkhand Movement: Indigenous Peoples' Struggle for Autonomy in India*. Copenhagen: International Work Group for Indigenous Affairs, 2003, pp. ix-xvii.

Munda, R.D., and S. Bosu Mullick, eds, *The Jharkhand Movement: Indigenous Peoples' Struggle for Autonomy in India*, Copenhagen: International Work Group for Indigenous Affairs, 2003.

Murphy, Russell D., *Strategic Calculations and the Admission of New States into the Union, 1789–1960: Congress and the Politics of Statehood*, Lewiston: Edwin Mellen Press, 2008.

Nandini Sundar and Others Versus State of Chhattisgarh, Supreme Court of India (2011).

Narain, Iqbal, 'Cultural Pluralism, National Integration and Democracy in India,' *Asian Survey* 16, no. 10 (1976).

Nariman, Fali, 'Federalism in India—Emerging Trends and the Way Forward,' Paper presented at the 4th International Conference on Federalism: Unity in Diversity, "Learning from Each Other", New Delhi, November 5–7 2008.

National Sample Survey Organisation, 'Cultivation Practices in India, NSS 54th Round (January-June 1998),' Delhi: 1999.

———, 'Some Aspects of Operational Land Holdings in India, 2002–3: NSS 59th Round (January-December 2003),' Delhi: 2006.

Nayar, Baldev Raj, *Minority Politics in the Punjab*, Princeton: Princeton University Press, 1966.

Nityanand, D., 'Uttaranchal: Itihasik Paridrshya Evam Vikas Ke Aayam (Uttaranchal: Historical Perspective and Extent of Development),' Dehra Dun: Chavi Prakashan, 2004.

Niyogi, S.G., 'Chhattisgarh and National Question (no date),' In Centre for Education and Communication (ed.), *On a Rainbow in the Sky...The Chhattisgarh Mukti Morcha*. Delhi: Centre for Education and Communication, 1998.

O'Leary, Brendan, 'An Iron Law of Nationalism and Federation: A (Neo-Diceyian) Theory of the Necessity of a Federal Staatsvolk, and of Consociational Rescue,' *Nations and Nationalism* 7, no. 3 (2001), pp. 273–96.

Omvedt, Gail, *Reinventing Revolution: New Social Movements and the Socialist Tradition in India*, New York: M.E. Sharpe, 1993.

Orren, Karen, and Stephen Skowronek, *The Search for American Political Development*, Cambridge: Cambridge University Press, 2004.

Pai, Sudha, *Developmental State and the Dalit Question in Madhya Pradesh: Congress Response*, New Delhi: Routledge, 2011.

BIBLIOGRAPHY

———, 'Making of a Political Community: The Congress Party and the Integration of Madhya Pradesh,' In Asha Sarangi and Sudha Pai (eds), *Interrogating Reorganisation of States: Culture, Identity and Politics in India*. New Delhi: Routledge, 2011, pp. 69–106.

Palshikar, Suhas, 'Shiv Sena: A Tiger with Many Faces?,' In Peter De Souza and E. Sridharan (eds), *India's Political Parties*. New Delhi: Sage Publications, 2006.

Palshikar, Suhas, and Rajeshwari Deshpande, 'Electoral Competition and Structures of Domination in Maharashtra,' *Economic and Political Weekly* XXXIV, no. 34/35 (1999), pp. 2409–22.

Pant, Pushpesh, 'Dream Turning into a Nightmare in Uttarakhand,' *Economic and Political Weekly* XLVII, no. 14 (2012), pp. 18–21.

Parikh, Sunita, and Barry Weingast, 'A Comparative Theory of Federalism: India,' *Virginia Law Review* 83, no. 7 (1997), pp. 1593–615.

Parry, J., 'Two Cheers for Reservation: The Satnamis and the Steel Plant,' In J. Parry (ed.) *Institutions and Inequalities: Essays in Honour of Andre Beteille*. New Delhi: Oxford University Press, 1999.

Pierson, Paul, 'Big, Slow-Moving, And … Invisible,' In James Mahoney and Dietrich Rueschemeyer (eds), *Comparative Historical Analysis in the Social Sciences*. Cambridge: Cambridge University Press, 2003.

———, *Politics in Time: History, Institutions and Social Analysis*, Princeton: Princeton University Press, 2004.

Prakash, Amit, *Jharkhand: Politics of Development and Identity*, New Delhi: Orient Longman, 2001.

Prasad, Archana, 'The Political Economy of 'Maoist Violence' in Chhattisgarh,' *Social Scientist* 38, no. 3/4 (2010), pp. 3–24.

———, 'Unravelling the Forms of 'Adivasi' Organisation and Resistance in Colonial India,' *Indian Historical Review* 33, no. 1 (2006), pp. 225–44.

Ramaswamy, Sumathi, *Passions of the Tongue: Language Devotion in Tamil India, 1891–1970*, Berkeley: University of California Press, 1997.

Rangan, Haripriya, 'From Chipko to Uttaranchal: The Environment of Protest and Development in the Indian Himalaya,' In Richard Peet and Michael Watts (eds), *Liberation Ecologies: Environment, Development, Social Movements*. London: Routledge, 2004.

———, *Of Myths and Movements: Rewriting Chipko into Himalayan History*, London; New York: Verso, 2000.

Rodden, Jonathan, and Susan Rose-Ackerman, 'Does Federalism Preserve Markets?' *Virginia Law Review* 83, no. 7 (1997), pp. 1521–72.

Roeder, Philip G., 'Ethnofederalism and the Mismanagement of Conflicting Nationalisms,' *Regional & Federal Studies* 19, no. 2 (2009), pp. 203–19.

———, 'Soviet Federalism and Ethnic Mobilization,' *World Politics* 43, no. 2 (1991), pp. 196–232.

Rokkan, S., and S.M. Lipset, *Party Systems and Voter Alignments: Cross-National Perspectives*, New York: Free Press, 1967.

Roy, A.K., 'Jharkhand: Internal Colonialism,' In R.D. Munda and S.B. Mullick (eds), *The Jharkhand Movement: Indigenous Peoples' Struggle for Autonomy in India*. Copenhagen: International Work Group for Indigenous Affairs, 2003.

Rudolph, Lloyd, and Susanne Hoeber Rudolph, *In Pursuit of Lakshmi: The Political Economy of the Indian State*, Chicago and London: University of Chicago Press, 1987.

————, 'Transformation of Congress Party: Why 1980 Was Not a Restoration,' *Economic and Political Weekly* XVI (1981).

Rycroft, Daniel J. and Sangeeta Dasgupta eds, *The Politics of Belonging in India: Becoming Adivasi*, Abingdon: Routledge, 2011.

Sadgopal, A., and S.B. Namra, 'Sangarsh Aur Nirman, Shankar Guha Niyogi Aur Unke Naye Bharat Ka Sapna (Struggle and Construction, Shankar Guha Niyogi and His Dream of a New India),' Delhi: Rajkamal Prakashan, 1993.

Saez, Lawrence, *Federalism without a Centre: The Impact of Political and Economic Reform on India's Federal System*, New Delhi: Sage Publications, 2002.

Samaddar, Ranabir, 'Rule, Governmental Rationality and the Reorganisation of States,' In Sudha Pai and Asha Sarangi (eds), *Interrogating Reorganisation of States: Culture, Identity and Politics in India*. New Delhi: Routledge, 2011, pp. 48–68.

Schwartzberg, Joseph E, 'The Distribution of Selected Castes in the North Indian Plain,' *Geographical Review* 55, no. 4 (1965), pp. 477–95.

————, 'Factors in the Linguistic Reorganisation of Indian States,' In Paul Wallace (ed.), *Region and Nation in India*. New Delhi: American Institute of Indian Studies, 1985, pp. 155–82.

Sengupta, Nirmal, 'Background of the Jharkhand Question,' In Nirmal Sengupta (ed.), *Fourth World Dynamics: Jharkhand*. Delhi: Authors Guild Publications, 1982.

Shah, Alpa, *In the Shadows of the State: Indigenous Politics, Environmentalism, and Insurgency in Jharkhand, India*, Durham, N.C.: Duke University Press, 2010.

————, 'India Burning: The Maoist Revolution,' In Isabella Clark-Decès (ed.), *A Companion to the Anthropology of India*. Oxford: Wiley-Blackwell, 2011.

————, 'The Labour of Love: Seasonal Migration from Jharkhand to the Brick Kilns of Other States in India,' *Contributions to Indian Sociology* 40, no. 1 (2006), pp. 91–118.

Sharma, Mukul, 'Passages from Nature to Nationalism: Sunderlal Bahugana and Tehri Dam Opposition in Garhwal,' *Economic and Political Weekly* XLIV, no. 8 (2009), pp. 35–42.

Sheth, D.L., 'Ram Manohar Lohia on Caste in Indian Politics,' In G. Shah (ed.), *Caste and Democratic Politics in India*. London: Anthem Press, 2004.

BIBLIOGRAPHY

Shukla, H.L., *Social History of Chhattisgarh*, Delhi: Agam Kala Prakashan, 1985.

Singh, A., 'The Land Question in Chhattisgarh,' In P.K. Jha (ed.) *Land Reforms in India: Issues of Equity in Rural Madhya Pradesh*. Delhi: Sage Publications, 2002.

Singh, Gurharpal, 'Resizing and Reshaping the State: India from Partition to the Present,' In Brendan O'Leary, Ian S. Lustick and Thomas Callaghy (eds), *Right-Sizing the State: The Politics of Moving Borders*. Oxford: Oxford University Press, 2001, pp. 138–68.

Singh, Jagpal, 'Politics of Harit Pradesh: The Case of Western UP as a Separate State,' *Economic and Political Weekly* XXXVI, no. 31 (2001).

———, 'Region, Caste and Politics of 'Reverse Discrimination': The Case of Harit Pradesh,' In Ashutosh Kumar (ed.), *Rethinking State Politics in India: Regions within Regions*, New Delhi: Routledge, 2011, pp. 220–45.

Singh, K.S., 'Tribal Autonomy Movements in Chotanagpur,' In K.S. Singh (ed.), *Tribal Movements in India*. New Delhi: Manohar, 1983.

Singh, K.S., and P.P. Mahato, 'The Mahato-Kurmi Mahasabha Movement in Chotanagpur,' In K.S. Singh (ed.), *Tribal Movements in India*. New Delhi: Manohar, 1982, pp. 109–19.

Singh, M.P., 'Political Parties and Political Economy of Federalism: A Paradigm Shift in Indian Politics,' *The Indian Journal of Social Science* 7, no. 2 (1994), pp. 155–77.

———, 'A Borderless Internal Federal Space? Reorganization of States in India,' *India Review* 6, no. 4 (2007), pp. 233–50.

Singh, Prerna, 'We-Ness and Welfare: A Longitudinal Analysis of Social Development in Kerala, India,' *World Development* 39, no. 2 (2011), pp. 282–93.

Sinha, Sachchidanand, *The Internal Colony: A Study in Regional Exploitation*, New Delhi: Sindhu Publications, 1973.

Snyder, Richard, and D.J. Samuels, 'Legislative Malapportionment in Latin America: Historical and Comparative Perspectives,' In E.L. Gibson (ed.), *Federalism and Democracy in Latin America*. Baltimore and London: Johns Hopkins University Press, 2004., pp. 131–72.

Souza, Celina, *Constitutional Engineering in Brazil: The Politics of Federalism and Decentralization*, Basingstoke: Palgrave Macmillan, 1997.

Sridharan, E., 'Coalition Strategies and the BJP's Expansion, 1989–2004,' *Commonwealth and Comparative Politics* 43, no. 2 (2005), pp. 194–221.

———., 'The Fragmentation of the Indian Party System, 1952–1999: Seven Competing Explanations,' In Zoya Hasan (ed.), *Parties and Party Politics in India*. New Delhi: Oxford University Press, 2002.

Srinivasulu, K., 'Caste, Class and Social Articulation in Andhra Pradesh: Mapping Differential Regional Trajectories,' *ODI Working Paper* 179 (2002).

BIBLIOGRAPHY

————, 'Discourses on Telangana and Critique of the Linguistic Nationality Principle,' In Sudha Pai and Asha Sarangi (eds), *Interrogating Reorganisation of States: Culture, Identity and Politics in India*. New Delhi: Routledge, 2011, pp. 164–89.

Srinivasulu, K., and D. Satyanarayana, 'By-Elections and Telangana Agitation,' *Economic and Political Weekly* XLV, no. 33 (2010), pp. 12–14.

Stepan, Alfred, 'Federalism and Democracy: Beyond the US Model,' *Journal of Democracy* 10, no. 4 (1999), pp. 19–34.

Stepan, Alfred, Juan Linz, and Yogendra Yadav, *Crafting State-Nations: India and Other Multinational Democracies*, Baltimore: The Johns Hopkins University Press, 2011.

Stewart, Charles, and Barry R. Weingast, 'Stacking the Senate, Changing the Nation: Republican Rotten Boroughs, Statehood Politics, and American Political Development,' *Studies in American Political Development* 6 (1992), pp. 232–71.

Stuligross, David, *A Piece of Land to Call One's Own: Multicultural Federalism and Institutional Innovation in India*, PhD, University of California, 2001.

Suberu, Rotimi T., *Federalism and Ethnic Conflict in Nigeria*, Washington, D.C.: United States Institute of Peace Press, 2001.

Sundar, Nandini, *Subalterns and Sovereigns: An Anthropological History of Bastar, 1854–2006*, 2nd edition, New Delhi: Oxford University Press, 2009.

Suri, K.C., 'Andhra Pradesh: Fall of the CEO in Arena of Democracy,' *Economic and Political Weekly* XXXIX, no. 51 (2004), pp. 5493–97.

————, 'Telugu Desam Party.' In Peter De Souza and E. Sridharan (eds), *India's Political Parties*. Delhi: Sage Publications, 2006.

Tewari, I., *Unity for Identity: Struggle for Uttarakhand State*, New Delhi: KK Publishers and Distributors, 2001.

Thakur, S., *Subaltern Saheb: Bihar and the Making of Laloo Yadav*, New Delhi: Picador India, 2006.

Thelen, Kathleen, and Sven Steinmo, 'Historical Institutionalism in Comparative Politics,' In Sven Steinmo, Kathleen Thelen and F. Longstreth (eds), *Structuring Politics*. Cambridge: Cambridge University Press, 1992.

Tillin, Louise, 'Caste, Territory and Federalism,' *Seminar* 633 (2012).

————, 'Politics in a New State: Chhattisgarh,' *Seminar* 591 (2008), pp. 23–27.

————, 'Questioning Borders: Social Movements, Political Parties and the Creation of New States in India,' *Pacific Affairs* 84, no. 1 (2011), pp. 67–87.

————'Statehood and the Politics of Intent,' *Economic and Political Weekly* XLVI, no. 20 (2011).

————, 'United in Diversity? Asymmetry in Indian Federalism,' *Publius: The Journal of Federalism* 37, no. 1 (2007), pp. 45–67.

Watts, Ronald, 'The American Constitution in Comparative Perspective: A

Comparison of Federalism in the United States and Canada,' *The Journal of American History* 74, no. 3 (1987), pp. 769–92.

Weiner, Myron, *Party Building in a New Nation: The Indian National Congress*, Chicago: University of Chicago Press, 1967.

———, *Sons of the Soil: Migration and Ethnic Conflict in India*, Princeton: Princeton University Press, 1978.

Wheare, K.C., *Federal Government*, London: Oxford University Press, 1963.

Wilcox, Wayne, 'Madhya Pradesh,' In Myron Weiner (ed.), *State Politics in India*. Princeton: Princeton University Press, 1968, pp. 127–76.

Witsoe, Jeffrey, 'Corruption as Power: Caste and the Political Imagination of the Postcolonial State,' *American Ethnologist* 38, no. 1 (2011), pp. 73–85.

———, 'Social Justice and Stalled Development: Caste Empowerment and the Breakdown of Governance in Bihar,' In Francine Frankel (ed.), *India in Transition: Economics and Politics of Change*. Philadelphia: Center for the Advanced Study of India, 2006.

Wood, J.R., ed., *State Politics in Contemporary India*, London; Boulder: Westview Press, 1984.

Wyatt, Andrew, *Party System Change in South India: Political Entrepreneurs, Patterns and Processes*, Abingdon: Routledge, 2009.

Yadav, Yogendra, 'Electoral Politics in the Time of Change: India's Third Electoral System, 1989–99.' *Economic and Political Weekly* XXXIV, no. 34/35 (1999), pp. 2393–99.

———, 'The Paradox of Political Representation,' *Seminar* 586 (2008).

———, 'Understanding the Second Democratic Upsurge: Trends of Bahujan Participation in Electoral Politics in the 1990s.' In Francine Frankel, Zoya Hasan, Rajeev Bhargava and Balveer Arora (eds), *Transforming India: Social and Political Dynamics of Democracy*. New Delhi: Oxford University Press, 2000.

Yadav, Yogendra, Sanjay Kumar, and Oliver Heath, 'The BJP's New Social Bloc,' *Frontline* (1999).

Yadav, Yogendra, and Suhas Palshikar, 'Party System and Electoral Politics in the Indian States, 1952–2002: From Hegemony to Convergence,' In Peter Ronald de Souza and E. Sridharan (eds), *India's Political Parties*. New Delhi: Sage, 2006, pp. 74–115.

———,'Ten Theses on State Politics in India,' *Seminar* 591 (2008).

———, 'Transitions, Stagnations and Transformations,' *Seminar* 620 (2011), pp. 14–20.

INDEX

INDEX

INDEX

INDEX

INDEX